# COOKING
# FROM AN
# ITALIAN
# GARDEN

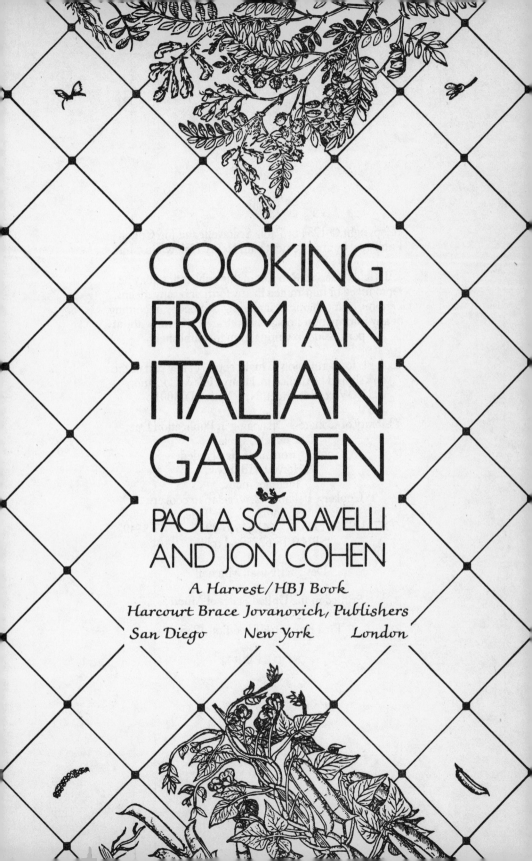

# COOKING FROM AN ITALIAN GARDEN

## PAOLA SCARAVELLI AND JON COHEN

A Harvest/HBJ Book

Harcourt Brace Jovanovich, Publishers

San Diego    New York    London

Library of Congress Cataloging in Publication Data
Scaravelli, Paola.
Cooking from an Italian garden.
"A Harvest/HBJ book."
Includes index.
1. Cookery, Italian.   2. Vegetarian cookery.
I. Cohen, Jon S.     II. Title.
TX723.S355 1985     641.5'636'0945     85-5549
ISBN 0-15-622592-1 (pbk.)

Designer: Susan Mitchell

Printed in the United States of America

First Harvest/HBJ edition 1985

B C D E F G H I J

To Alberto, whose enthusiasm for our project,
deep knowledge of Italian cuisine, and great love of good
food inspired us more than he can imagine.

# Acknowledgments

We would like to thank Elizabeth and Gerald Donaldson, who inspired the book and whose constant support helped bring it to completion; our sons David and Lorenzo, who beyond the call of family duty participated in the making of the book; and finally those family cooks who supplied us with much of the substance that makes up *Cooking from an Italian Garden*.

# Contents

# Preface

I came to North America for the first time many years ago. To be precise, I was a student in a small preparatory school located in a glorious valley just outside of Santa Barbara, California. My family in Italy were vegetarians, and although I did eat meat occasionally, I never really missed it, since the vegetarian fare at home was so varied, tasty, and nutritious. Imagine my surprise, then, to discover that even in California, with magnificent vegetables at their disposal, Americans were simply unable to cook them properly. Out of desperation, I became a confirmed carnivore on this side of the Atlantic.

That was many years ago, and much has changed. Although I still return to the farm outside Florence every summer and have lived in Italy off and on over the past twenty-five years, I now make my home in Toronto, a city with the sixth-largest population of Italians in the world. Vegetable cooking has certainly improved in the New World, but I am still struck each time I return to Florence by how much more flavorful and varied the vegetable dishes are there. At Casa Scaravelli (there and here), a vegetarian diet does not mean the nutritious but boring "beans and rice" that seems to be the *sine qua non* of vegetarianism in North America. Our meals are wholesome, of course, but they are also tasty, inventive, and joyous.

We have attempted to incorporate these same features (taste, invention, and pleasure) into this cookbook. Beans figure in it—who can imagine a cookbook written by a Florentine that did not include Fagioli all'Ucceletto?—and so does rice: one of the great Italian dishes is Risotto alla Milanese. But there is more, much more, as you will find out when you explore the recipes in our book.

This book includes recipes from all over Italy, such as Caponata Siciliana from the deep south and Fonduta Val d'Aosta from the far north, and captures the full range of Italian vegetable cooking. For the most part, the recipes are traditional ones that we have collected from friends, relatives, and family cooks. They have all been adapted for North American kitchens and are easy to prepare—so easy, indeed, that when our sons began cooking at the ages of ten and twelve, they had no difficulty preparing them. And, rest assured, they satisfy the North American palate. In fact, the real inspiration behind this book was the pressure of friends in Canada and the United States who, having visited us here and at the farm in Italy, wanted to know how to reproduce in their own kitchens what they ate and enjoyed.

Do not be put off by the absence of meat dishes in this book. We have no intention of making a pitch for vegetarianism—that is a personal matter with which we are not really concerned. However, the recipes cover the full range of courses, from antipasti to desserts. Furthermore, they are so nourishing and satisfying that it is unlikely that you will even notice, much less object to, the absence of meat.

A couple of words of advice: First, food is only as good as the ingredients. Make an effort to obtain the best-quality raw materials available; it will pay off in terms of flavor and, in the long run, cost. Second, the recipes are foolproof. That is, if you follow them to the letter, good results are guaranteed. As my aunt once observed, anyone who can read and follow instructions can cook. However, Italian cooking, like Italian life in general, does not follow hard-and-fast rules. Use the recipes as Dante used Virgil, as a guide, not as a master. Be creative, take chances, become an Italian cook. And now, as they say in Italy, *Buon appetito!*

Paola Scaravelli
Toronto, February 1984

# COOKING
# FROM AN
# ITALIAN
# GARDEN

# Introduction

It is always a pleasure to travel around Italy, and we do it as often as we can. The country, unified only since 1861, is from a cultural and gastronomical point of view still a group of independent regions or municipalities and it is impossible to appreciate this diversity, much less savor it, unless you travel. For example, each small hill town around Florence makes its own pecorino cheese, and each is different. The Parmesan cheese one buys in Parma or the mozzarella one eats in Battipaglia is incomparably better than the same cheese found in other regions. And then there are regional specialties—Risotto alla Milanese, Pane Toscano, Gnocchi alla Romano—that one simply does not find in other areas.

Geography as well as history has contributed to this diversity. Olive trees do not grow in the north, so butter, not olive oil, is used in cooking. Rice is not grown in the south and does not figure in southern cuisine. The best eggplant dishes come from the south, where eggplants flourish, while the best asparagus is grown in the more temperate north.

There are, however, some features of Italian cuisine that seem to be national in character. All Italians eat seasonally. There is no market for peaches in midwinter, nor does anyone seek artichokes in midsummer. Italians also demand high-quality produce and they usually get it. There is much to be said for these practices.

The Italian meal is also structured the same in most parts of the country. It begins with an antipasto or first course and ends with fruit, or occasionally a sweet dessert. It is the ensemble, not any particular part, that provides nourishment and pleasure. For this reason, the parts must complement one another in terms of nutrition, flavor, and appearance. The sample menus at the end of the book illustrate some successful combinations of both elaborate five-course meals and simple suppers and luncheons. In using the recipes in this book, do think of them as a whole and not as a series of individual meals.

The recipes are arranged for the most part in the order in which they would be served at an Italian dinner. You can, of course, mix them together as you wish, but there is a lot to be said for beginning a meal with an antipasto, a soup, or a steaming plate of pasta before digging into the main course. And there is nothing quite as refreshing at the end of a meal as a fresh crisp salad followed by fruit or a light dessert. It is worth noting that Italians eat small portions of the main course, whether meat or not, and balance it with pasta, vegetables, salad, and fruit.

There is nothing complicated or recondite about Italian cooking or about the recipes in this book. We do, however, have some tips on the ingredients, on cheeses, on wines, and on cooking techniques that you might find useful or informative.

# HERBS AND SEASONINGS

Herbs play an integral part in Italian cuisine, and, like all other aspects of Italian cooking, tend to be regional in their use. Many, such as rosemary, mint, and sage grow wild, while others, such as basil and parsley, are carefully cultivated. Some can be used fresh or dried, while others, in particular basil, must be used fresh or properly preserved, but not dried.

## *Parsley*

Parsley has been used in Italian cuisine since Roman times and is perhaps even more a part of Italian cooking than tomatoes. There are two kinds available in American markets, the regular curly-leafed variety and the more aromatic Italian parsley with large pinnate leaves. Although the former is adequate for most dishes, the latter is superior and should be used if possible. You can grow your own parsley year round in a window box or find it fresh in markets, so there is no need to preserve it.

## *Basil*

An absolute must for many Italian dishes, so grow your own basil or find a reliable source. It is a sweet, strongly aromatic herb, to many the most precious of all. There are many varieties of basil, but the most common and easiest to handle is the Italian variety with large, smooth dark green leaves. We have tried without success to keep plants indoors over the cold, dark Toronto winters, but it can be done on warm, sunny windowsills. If you are as unsuccessful as we have been, here are two ways to preserve basil.

*Freezing:* At the height of summer when the plants are large and full of leaves, pick the leaves and tender tops, rinse them only to remove dust, and set them aside to dry for a few minutes on paper towels. Pack in small, airtight plastic bags and place in the freezer.

*Salted:* Pick the leaves, rinse off the dust, and set aside to dry for a few minutes on paper towels. Place the leaves between layers of coarse salt in a Mason jar, cover, and store in the refrigerator. When ready to use, remove the salt from the leaves and use as directed. Remember to adjust for salt in the recipe, since basil preserved in this way is a little salty.

In all the recipes in the book, use fresh, frozen, or salted basil unless otherwise directed. Do not use dried or powdered basil. It has no flavor.

## Rosemary

Rosemary is a perennial herb that grows wild all over Italy. It has a strong, slightly bitter taste that, if used with discretion, can enliven the flavor of many vegetables. Rosemary, unlike basil and parsley, must be cooked. If handled with care (rosemary plants like sun and moisture on their leaves), the plants can be kept for years, indoors in the winter in cold areas, outdoors in the summer. If you are unable to find fresh rosemary, use it dried but adjust quantities since the dried is stronger than the fresh.

## Sage

Sage is a delightful herb with a mild, pungent flavor. It is a perennial that grows wild in Italy, but is hardy enough to be cultivated in gardens throughout North America. If you cannot grow your own or find a source of fresh sage, use it dried, but try to obtain whole dried leaves, not the powder.

## Oregano

Another herb that grows wild in Italy and is used extensively in Italian cooking, especially in the south, is oregano. It is a perennial that is very easy to cultivate in a home garden. The fresh variety is quite mild and fragrant, but it is most commonly used dried. It is then quite strong, so employ it with care.

## Mint

Mint is a hardy perennial that, once established in a damp, shady part of your garden, will make a positive nuisance of itself. If you cannot grow it, use dried mint or, if you can, obtain it fresh. There are many varieties of mint, and all are suitable for the recipes in this book. The Italians tend to use whatever wild mint they can find—in Rome, they use *mentuccia*, in Florence, *nepitella*. Some wild varieties are quite strong, so use it with caution.

## Saffron

If you've ever wondered why saffron is so expensive, just calculate how many worker hours it takes to collect enough stamens from crocuses, each of which has only three, to make one teaspoon of the wonderful golden spice and you have your answer. Saffron has been prized since ancient times, making its way into southern Europe from the East with the Arabs and to the rest of Europe with the returning Crusaders. Fortunately, a little saffron goes a long way—a pinch is enough to make Risotto alla Milanese for six. Always buy high-quality saffron; you will pay more per ounce, but it is cheaper in the long run.

## Pine Nuts

Pine nuts are the seeds of the stone pine that grows all through Italy and other areas bordering the Mediterranean. They are packed inside the pine cones and must first be dislodged from the cone and then removed from their shell. Their mild, slightly piny flavor has great appeal, especially, it seems, for children. You can see them in the summer at seaside resorts crouched over pine cones intent on dislodging the treasures within.

Pine nuts may not be available in your local supermarket, but you will have no difficulty finding them in Greek or Italian markets, and they will last for a long time if stored in a closed jar in the refrigerator.

## Capers

Capers are the unopened floral buds of the caper plant that grows wild, clinging to walls and cliffs, throughout the Mediterranean. Capers are most commonly pickled in vinegar, although they are also available preserved in salt. Either type is suitable for the recipes in this book but, if using salted ones, remember to rinse them well. They have a strong, pungent flavor, perfect for enlivening many dishes; however, because of their strength, they must be used with discretion. If they are unavailable in your local supermarket, try an Italian grocery.

## Garlic

What would Italian food be without the flavor of garlic? Although it is incorrect to presume that every dish is laced with garlic, it is true that garlic is used extensively in Italian cooking. It is, however, used with great discretion, to flavor a dish, not to overwhelm it.

The way in which garlic is prepared and added to a dish has a dramatic impact on its flavor and the flavor it will impart to the other ingredients. For example, when garlic is chopped or sliced and sautéed in oil or butter, it will lose much of its sharp bite but it will retain and impart to the dish a rich, mellow taste. If cloves are slightly crushed, sautéed in oil or butter, and discarded before the other ingredients are added, the garlic flavor will be very mild. If garlic is chopped and added to liquid ingredients, it will be much milder than if it were first sautéed. Sautéing seals in the volatile oils while boiling evaporates them. Garlic cut into large pieces will be stronger than garlic that is finely chopped or minced. Since squeezing garlic through a press separates the pulp from the juice, we prefer to mince our garlic. Finally, the flavor of garlic intensifies over time, so if you plan to prepare a dish a long time in advance, adjust the quantity of garlic accordingly.

When choosing garlic, select large firm heads with firm, full cloves. Although garlic is available all year round, the best garlic is available in summer. We usually buy large quantities at that time and store the heads in a paper bag in the refrigerator. They keep for months and are usually superior to those you find in midwinter.

## *Italian Vegetable Pickles (Sott'aceti)*

Available in most Italian groceries, Sott'aceti are fresh vegetables pickled in vinegar and spices. They can be made quite easily at home. Many vegetables are suitable for pickling, but the best and most common are carrots, string beans, cauliflower, and miniature cucumbers. In the following recipe, we recommend equal amounts of the four vegetables. The recipe makes 1 quart of pickled vegetables.

> 1 cup peeled carrots cut into 1½-inch strips
> 1 cup string beans cut into 1½-inch segments
> 1 cup cauliflower cut into small flowerets
> 1 cup miniature pickling cucumbers
> 3 cups water
> 6 cups white wine vinegar
> 1 teaspoon coarse salt
> 6 peppercorns
> 1 bay leaf
> 1 garlic clove, peeled (optional)
> 1 dried hot pepper (optional)

Prepare the vegetables and set aside.

Combine in a saucepan water, 2 cups vinegar, and salt, and bring to a boil. Add the vegetables and continue boiling for 3 minutes. Drain, discard the liquid, and set the vegetables aside.

Place the peppercorns, bay leaf, and, if desired, the garlic and hot pepper in a 1-quart Mason jar. Add the vegetables. Bring the remaining vinegar to a boil in a saucepan and boil for 5 minutes. Pour over the vegetables, making sure that they are completely covered by the vinegar. When cool, seal and set aside for 1 week before using.

## Olive Oil

The best and most expensive commercial olive oil is *olio extra vergine* from Lucca in Tuscany. We strongly recommend that you use it for salads. You can use less expensive olive oil from southern Italy for general cooking, but keep in mind that the olive oil you use will have a definite impact on the flavor of the dish.

## Salt

Salt is very much a matter of taste. We have indicated the amount we usually use for these recipes, but adjust to suit your preferences.

# CHEESES

Italy has a large variety of cheeses, many of them highly localized and many soft or semisoft that must be eaten fresh. We describe here only those cheeses that are featured in recipes in the book.

## Gorgonzola

Gorgonzola ranks with Roquefort and Stilton as one of the world's great blue cheeses. It is creamy, mild, and magnificent. Gorgonzola comes from Lombardy and was once made in damp caves, an ideal climate for the growth of the bacteria that gives Gorgonzola its distinctive flavor and aroma. The cheese must be eaten fresh. It discolors quickly when exposed to air and rapidly loses its delicate flavor. In fact, most Gorgonzola sold in North America is flown in.

## Mozzarella

The best mozzarella in Italy comes from an area between Naples and the river Sele, a flat, marshy plain, perfect for the European buffaloes whose milk is used to make the cheese. Whenever we journey to Paestum, the ancient site of a prosperous town of Magna Grecia, we always visit the small cheese factories in the area where authentic mozzarella is made. The cheese is prepared in large tubs by skilled workmen who use their hands and wooden paddles to shape and wrap the cheese as it solidifies. The result is a fresh, wonderfully textured, and mild cheese.

Since fresh mozzarella does not keep, the one from this area is rarely found north of Rome and, even then, it does not compare with its very fresh counterpart. Cow's milk mozzarella is, of course, available all over Italy and serves as a reasonable substitute for the genuine article. It is now possible to find this kind of mozzarella in some areas in North America, and if you have a source, do use it. The typical hard North American mozzarella is so far removed from the original that it is best regarded as a different cheese. It is, however, perfectly adequate for many dishes that call for mozzarella, and where it is not, we indicate the appropriate substitute. The flavor and texture of the hard mozzarella can be improved if it is soaked in milk to cover for an hour before using.

## Bel Paese

Bel Paese, a cheese from Lombardy, is a relatively recent arrival on the Italian scene. It is a strictly commercial cheese, made on a large scale in factories, and is sold all over Italy, Europe, and in many other parts of the world. The Bel Paese available in North America is similar but not identical to the Italian version. It is less creamy and more strongly flavored. It is, nevertheless, an excellent mild semisoft cheese with the additional virtue of having a relatively low butterfat content. We use it in some recipes as a substitute for mozzarella.

## Pecorino

All pecorino cheese is made from ewe's milk. The name "pecorino" derives from *pecora*, Italian for sheep. In Tuscany, as in other parts of Italy, every village makes its own pecorino. Each one is distinctive; all are mild when fresh and very pleasant. These cheeses are, however, difficult to find outside of their locality, much less outside of Italy. The pecorino cheese we call for in this book is Pecorino Sardo, a strong, aged pecorino from Sardinia, or Romano (Pecorino Romano), a similar cheese from the area around Rome. Both should be purchased in large pieces and freshly grated when required. Pecorino or Romano is often used together with Parmesan but can also be employed as a substitute when more bite and sharpness are desired. It is also saltier, so adjust seasoning accordingly. These cheeses keep well if sealed and stored in the refrigerator.

## Parmesan

Parmesan is probably the best known of all Italian cheeses and certainly one of Italy's greatest gifts to lovers of good food. Grana is the generic name for all similar cheeses made in the Po valley, but only those made in and around Parma can be called Parmigiano Reggiano, the best by far of all the grana. It is very expensive, in part because demand outstrips supply, in part because production costs are high. Parmesan is made with high-quality milk and must age at least two years before it is ready. But it is worth the expense. There is, quite simply, no cheese that compares with the flavor and versatility of Parmesan.

Parmesan should be purchased in pieces and freshly grated when needed. A good Parmesan is straw colored, has a nutty, slightly salty flavor, and melts in your mouth. It should be hard without being dry. It is a delightful table cheese and, of course, perfect for cooking and for grating over pasta. Parmesan can be kept for a few weeks well sealed in the refrigerator and can also be stored in airtight plastic bags in the freezer. Do not allow it to dry out. It is always sold with the rind which, while unsuitable for eating or grating, can be added to soups to flavor them. Do not substitute already-grated Parmesan for the real thing. There is simply no relation between it and freshly grated Parmesan.

## Ricotta

Three or four times a week when we are on our farm, someone in the family rushes into Fiesole early in the morning to buy ewe's milk ricotta from the one vendor who still sells it. It is the best ricotta we've ever had, but the supply is small and shrinking every year. Ricotta made from cow's milk, the more conventional kind and the only type available in North America, is, however, perfectly adequate and, in many cases, excellent.

Ricotta is Italy's version of cottage cheese, somewhat milder and usually more moist. It must be used fresh. It will not last more than three days even if kept in the refrigerator. In southern Italy, ricotta is salted, drained, and sold as a hard cheese, something like feta. This, however, is not the ricotta used in recipes in this book. If your ricotta is very moist you can drain it by placing the ricotta in cheesecloth, suspending it over the kitchen sink, and leaving it for an hour. The weight of the cheese will force the water out.

## Fontina

Fontina is a delicious, semisoft, creamy cheese with a slightly nutty flavor that is produced in the Aosta valley in the Piedmont. It is an excellent table cheese, and we use it extensively for cooking, as many recipes in this book indicate. It is, unfortunately, not always easy to find in North America, and after much experimentation we settled on a good Swiss Gruyère as the best substitute. Although Sweden and Denmark also make a cheese called fontina, it is very different from the Italian variety. Of course, if the Italian fontina is available, use it.

# WINES

Wine production in Italy has expanded enormously since the Second World War and is today not only impressively large but in many areas very modern. Modernization, as we all know, is a mixed blessing. In this case, it is reshaping the ancient landscape, replacing the Renaissance tapestry of intermingled crops with the hard edges of monocropping. For example, in Tuscany, the traditional field pattern, which mixed vines, olive trees, and arable fields, has given way to vineyards with row upon row of vines marching over the hills between concrete pillars, all carefully spaced for tractor cultivation. For wine lovers, at least, this has been a boon. The wine has never been so good, nor so plentiful. Today Italy is the largest wine producer in the world and one of the largest exporters.

Every region of the country produces wine, some of it outstanding, almost all of it drinkable. The largest output comes from the south, the area with the least distinguished wines. Much of this wine is mixed in with other wines, especially wines from the north, to raise the sugar content and in consequence the alcoholic strength of these wines.

We cannot possibly review all the wines of Italy here. We will instead list those that we know are available in North America, that have a certain distinction, and that we happen to like. We break them down into reds and whites and give some indication of their body and dryness. They are a suitable accompaniment for the recipes in this book, although, of course, so are wines from many other countries.

The most full-bodied Italian red wines include Barolo, Barbaresco, Barbera, Spanna, Valtellina, and Amarone Classico. These wines must be well aged, especially the Barolo and Amarone, which are practically undrinkable if they are less than five years old. Somewhat less robust reds include Merlot, Brunello di Montalcino, Dolcetto d'Alba, and Torgiano. Valpolicella, Chianti Classico, and the more distinguished Chianti Classico Riserva, Carmignano, Vino Nobile di Montepulciano, Lambrusco, Cirò—a rosé—and Corvo are some of the very fine light red wines.

Italian white wines on the whole tend to be light, somewhat fruity, and very flavorful. We prefer, among the whites, Pinot Grigio—especially from the Colli Orientali of Friuli—the Grave del Friuli, Tokai, Soave—especially Soave Classico—Lacrima Christi, the whites from the Colli Benci, Vernaccia of San Gimignano, Verdicchio dei Castelli di Jesi, and the Roman whites, which include Colli Albani, Frascati, and Velletri. Orvieto tends to be sweeter than most of these wines but still quite pleasant.

# COOKING TECHNIQUES

## *Deep Frying*

When deep frying, the oil should be hot enough to seal whatever is being cooked but not so hot as to scorch it. Adjust the temperature to the length of time it will take to cook the ingredients. Deep-fried raw vegetables, for example, take longer to cook than croquettes in which all the ingredients are already cooked.

We use a light seed oil, such as safflower, sunflower, or corn oil, for deep frying. The oil can be reused a few times if filtered through cheesecloth or a fine strainer and stored in a glass jar. We use a wok for deep frying. It is a most un-Italian implement but useful nonetheless.

## Sautéing

In sautéing, the oil or butter is not the cooking medium, it is instead the heat of the flame on the pan that does the trick. The oil or butter coats and flavors the ingredients and protects them from direct heat. Vegetables should be sautéed at a heat high enough to cook them quickly but, of course, not so high that they burn.

## Boiling

There is nothing easier than boiling vegetables, but if done incorrectly, the technique can ruin perfectly good food. When cooking tender greens such as spinach, do not add water to the pan, since enough water clings to the leaves after washing to cook the vegetables. Simply place the spinach in a covered pan over medium heat and when the water begins to boil, simmer the spinach until tender. For tougher greens such as collards, place about ½ inch of water in a saucepan, bring it to a rapid boil, add the greens, and simmer them, covered, until tender. This technique seals in the color and flavor of the greens. Boil artichokes and other similar vegetables in the same way but with water to cover.

## Steaming

For most vegetables, we prefer steaming to boiling. In steaming, the vegetables are suspended above boiling water and are cooked by the steam. It takes longer than boiling, but fewer nutrients are lost and the flavor of the vegetables is more intense. You can improvise a steamer with a wire rack in a saucepan or a wok or you can purchase an inexpensive vegetable steamer that fits most saucepans.

## Water Bath (Bagno Maria)

This technique is attributed to Maria de Cleofa, an Italian alchemist and cook who apparently developed it for both of her arts. A modern version is, of course, the double boiler. If you do not have one of these handy devices, simply add water to a large, low-sided saucepan and place it over the heat. Place a smaller saucepan in the water and do your cooking in the smaller pan. A water bath reduces the intensity of the heat and slows the cooking process. A water bath can also be employed for baking, a useful technique for savory and sweet puddings.

## Blanching

This is a technique used most often for peeling such foods as tomatoes and almonds. Bring to a boil enough water to cover the ingredients, plunge them into the boiling water for a minute, drain, and peel. This is also the way to parboil vegetables. Just leave them in the water a little longer.

# SAUCES

Italian cooking does not rely heavily on sauces and the sauces Italians do use are not, for the most part, heavy. They are employed primarily for pasta, boiled meats and vegetables, and some egg dishes.

We have tried to include in this section all the traditional sauces used in Italian cooking such as béchamel, three tomato sauces, hollandaise, mayonnaise, pesto, and green sauce. We have also included some less common sauces for pasta, vegetables, vegetable puddings, savory soufflés, and eggs. All the sauces are easy to prepare and serve the purpose of enhancing simply cooked foods without overwhelming them. As you will discover, with the correct sauce, a plate of steamed vegetables can be transformed into a special and impressive dish.

♦ ♦ ♦ ♦ ♦

## *Besciamella*

BÉCHAMEL
SAUCE

MAKES 1⅔ CUPS MEDIUM-
THICK SAUCE

Although the Marquis Louis de Béchameil, the *maître de chef* for Louis XIV, is usually given credit for the invention of béchamel sauce (thus the name), it is more probable that the French merely assumed as their own a sauce invented a few centuries earlier in Italy. Whoever deserves the credit, it is a culinary masterpiece and absolutely essential in Italian cooking.

To make a heavier sauce, add less milk; to make a lighter sauce, add more.

1¾ *cups milk*
4 *tablespoons unsalted butter*
4 *tablespoons unbleached all-purpose flour*
¼ *teaspoon salt*

Heat the milk over a low flame in a small saucepan, being careful not to let it boil or scorch.

In a heavy 2-quart saucepan, melt the butter over a medium heat. Add the flour to the butter and cook, stirring constantly with a wooden spoon or wire whisk, for 1 minute. Reduce the heat to low, stir in the salt, and add the milk, a little at a time, stirring constantly across the entire bottom of the pan, until all the milk is added. Continue to cook the sauce, stirring constantly, until it thickens.

Béchamel sauce is best if used immediately, since it will otherwise form a skin. If not used immediately, coat the surface with melted butter to prevent a skin from forming.

### VARIATIONS

A half cup of heavy cream can be substituted for a half cup of the milk to make a richer béchamel sauce. If you would like an even more substantial sauce, stir in 1 or 2 egg yolks just after you remove the sauce from the heat.

♦ ♦ ♦ ♦ ♦

## *Maionese*

### MAYONNAISE

Homemade mayonnaise is so far superior to even the best commercial product that they are, for all practical purposes, different foods. Fortunately, with a food processor, it is almost as easy to make your own mayonnaise as it is to open a jar of the commercial type. And it is not much more difficult to make it with a whisk or hand-held electric mixer.

Mayonnaise is essentially an emulsion in which oil is held suspended in eggs or egg yolks. The trick in making mayonnaise, then, is to make sure that the suspension holds. The oil must be added to the eggs or yolks very slowly in the beginning so that they can incorporate the oil without difficulty. Eggs can hold only so much oil in suspension—if the limit is exceeded, the bonds break and the ingredients separate. Thus the proportion of eggs to oil is critical.

We give two basic recipes for mayonnaise, one made by hand, the other with a food processor. Use olive oil or a mixture of olive oil and seed oil. We always use lemon juice instead of vinegar, but this is a matter of taste.

Egg yolks and olive oil should be at room temperature when used to make mayonnaise.

## *Hand-made Mayonnaise*

MAKES 1¾ CUPS SAUCE

2 extra-large egg yolks
*juice of 1 lemon*
*1½ cups olive oil or a mixture of olive oil and seed oil*
*salt and freshly ground pepper*

Wash a large, heavy mixing bowl with hot water and dry well. Place the egg yolks in the bowl and beat with a whisk or hand-held electric mixer until the yolks begin to thicken slightly, about 2 minutes. Add 1 tablespoon of lemon juice and a pinch of salt and pepper, and incorporate.

Begin adding the oil in the center of the yolks, a few drops at a time, beating constantly. Continue, adding the oil very slowly until ¼ cup of oil has been incorporated. From this point, you can add the oil at a slightly faster pace, but you must beat constantly to maintain the emulsion. If your arm tires, rest. When all the oil has been incorporated, add salt, pepper, and lemon juice to taste.

If the emulsion does not hold and the ingredients separate, transfer the oil-and-egg mixture to a small bowl, add another egg yolk to the large bowl and repeat the process, beginning with the egg-and-oil mixture and then adding any remaining oil.

### Machine-made Mayonnaise

*1 extra-large egg*
*1½ cups olive oil, or a mixture of seed oil and olive oil*
*juice of 1 lemon*
*salt and freshly ground pepper to taste*

If using a food processor, insert the metal chopping blade. Add the whole egg, run for 15 seconds, and pour in the oil through the feed tube slowly in a thin stream until it is all used. Add half the lemon juice, salt, and pepper, process for a few seconds, taste, adjust for seasoning, process, and set aside.

If the emulsion breaks, remove the egg-and-oil mixture, place another whole egg in the processor and add first the egg-and-oil mixture to it then any remaining oil.

#### VARIATIONS

*Mayonnaise with Pesto Sauce:* Add 3 tablespoons of Pesto (see recipe) to the mayonnaise once it's made, combine well, and use as directed.

*Mayonnaise with Capers:* Add 1 tablespoon of finely chopped capers and 2 tablespoons of chopped parsley to the mayonnaise. Chopped Italian Vegetable Pickles (see recipe) can also be added in addition to or instead of the capers.

*Mayonnaise with Herbs:* Add ¼ cup of one or more chopped fresh herbs such as basil, parsley, chives, oregano, or tarragon to the mayonnaise.

♦ ♦ ♦ ♦ ♦

### Salsa Olandese

HOLLANDAISE SAUCE

Hollandaise, like mayonnaise, is an emulsion sauce, also made with eggs, but in this case the yolks hold butter, not oil, in suspension. The trick in making hollandaise is to keep the egg yolks at a low, even heat as the melted butter is added and to add the butter slowly enough to permit the yolks to absorb it. And, of course, the proportions have to be correct. Three extra-large egg yolks can hold in suspension about one cup of butter.

Hollandaise sauce transforms any simple steamed or boiled vegetable into an elegant dish. It is also delicious with hard-boiled or poached eggs.

We give two ways of making the sauce, the first by hand, the second in a blender or food processor.

### Hollandaise Made by Hand

MAKES 1 CUP SAUCE

3 extra-large egg yolks
6 to 8 ounces unsalted butter
2 tablespoons lemon juice
salt and freshly ground pepper to taste

Place the egg yolks in the top half of a double boiler, bring the water to a simmer (do not allow it to boil), beat the egg yolks with a wooden spoon for 1 minute, add 1 tablespoon of butter, and beat constantly with the wooden spoon until the butter is melted and incorporated. Continue the process, beating constantly and adding small pieces of butter until all the butter is incorporated into the sauce. Remove from the heat, add the lemon juice, salt, and pepper, beat to incorporate, and keep warm until ready to use. If at any time during the cooking the egg yolks begin to solidify at the bottom of the pan, remove from the heat to cool. You can even add a teaspoon of cold water, if necessary, to cool the mixture.

### Hollandaise Made by Machine

Note the change in proportions. Hollandaise made by machine requires more egg yolks and less butter.

4 extra-large egg yolks
2 tablespoons lemon juice
pinch of salt
½ cup unsalted butter
freshly ground pepper to taste

Place the egg yolks, lemon juice, and salt in the bowl of the blender or in the food processor equipped with the metal chopping blade. Bring the butter to a boil in a small saucepan. Process the egg yolks for a few seconds, then, with the machine still running at a high speed, pour in the boiling butter very slowly in a trickle. Taste the sauce and adjust for seasoning.

Hollandaise sauce should be served warm, but cannot be reheated over direct heat. It can, however, be placed near a source of heat and kept warm in this way until served.

If the sauce is allowed to cool completely—for example, if it is made a day ahead of time and stored in the refrigerator—it must, in effect, be remade. Place 2 tablespoons of the sauce in the top half of a double boiler, bring the water to a simmer and, while beating, add the remaining sauce, 1 teaspoon at a time.

♦ ♦ ♦ ♦ ♦

*Pomarola*

TOMATO
SAUCE
I

MAKES 1½ TO 2 CUPS SAUCE

This is our standard, everyday tomato sauce made with tomatoes, onion, and basil. It serves a wide range of uses in this book and is one of the fundamentals of Italian cooking. It is also, not insignificantly, the number one pasta sauce. In the late summer and early fall, when the plum tomatoes mature, we usually set aside a weekend and can or freeze enough sauce to get us through the year. Although this may seem like more work than it's worth, we find it very convenient and satisfying to have good tomato sauce available whenever we need it.

When tomatoes are out of season, use canned Italian plum tomatoes, not the fresh, tasteless variety, to make the sauce. As there are differences in the quality of canned plum tomatoes, use Italian ones that contain tomatoes and tomato juice, perhaps some basil, and nothing else.

The whole object in making tomato sauce is to evaporate the water in the tomatoes to obtain a dense, richly flavored essence of tomatoes. In Italy, even today, people who are able to still make their tomato sauce in large cast-iron pots over an open fire out-of-doors. It is not done for romance or to save money on gas or electricity, but because the liquid evaporates much more rapidly outside and considerably speeds up the process. When making sauce at home, use a saucepan with as large a surface area as possible to hasten evaporation. The myth that it takes hours to make tomato sauce is just that, a myth. The length of time will, of course, depend on the water content of the tomatoes, but if you use ripe, fleshy plum tomatoes, you will be surprised how quickly the tomatoes will reduce to a thick, tasty sauce.

Tomato sauce can be kept covered in the refrigerator for about 1 week. It can also be stored for months in the freezer.

> ⅓ *cup olive oil*
> 1 *large onion, finely chopped*
> 3 *pounds fresh, ripe plum tomatoes, cut in half, and*
> *seeded, or 3 cups canned Italian plum tomatoes,*
> *drained*
> ½ *teaspoon sugar, if using fresh tomatoes*
> 1 *teaspoon salt*
> 4 *large basil leaves, roughly torn*
> *freshly ground pepper to taste*

Heat 2 tablespoons of olive oil in a heavy, large, low-sided saucepan or frying pan, add the onion, and sauté over a medium heat until transparent. Add the tomatoes, sugar if necessary, and salt, and cook over a medium heat, stirring occasionally with a wooden spoon, until the sauce thickens, about 20 minutes.

Pass the tomatoes through a food mill to eliminate the skins (if using fresh tomatoes) and to purée the vegetables. Do not use a blender or food processor for this operation. The seeds of tomatoes contain a bitter oil, and if any seeds remain in the sauce they will release their bitterness when ground.

Return the sauce to the heat and continue cooking until the desired consistency is achieved. Tomato sauce can be thinned by adding water and thickened by longer cooking.

When cooked, remove from the heat and add the basil, pepper, and remaining olive oil. Serve hot over pasta or use as directed.

NOTE: If you decide to make large batches of tomato sauce in the fall and can or freeze it, try to obtain a machine called a tomato squeezer, available in well-stocked housewares stores, which separates the skins and seeds from the tomato pulp. They come in many sizes and price ranges, from very simple hand-cranked affairs (the one we use) to large, complex electric appliances.

◆ ◆ ◆ ◆ ◆

## *Sugo Finto*

TOMATO
SAUCE
II

MAKES 1½ TO 2 CUPS SAUCE

In this version of tomato sauce, parsley, carrots, and celery are cooked with the tomatoes, thus creating a richer, more full-bodied sauce. Use as an alternative to the preceding light tomato sauce.

⅓ cup olive oil

1 large onion, finely chopped

1 medium carrot, finely chopped

1 celery stalk, finely chopped

pinch of dried oregano

1 tablespoon finely chopped parsley

3 pounds fresh, ripe tomatoes, cut in half lengthwise
    and seeded, or 3 cups canned Italian plum
    tomatoes, with their juice

¼ teaspoon sugar

1 teaspoon salt

¼ cup dry white wine (optional)

freshly ground pepper to taste

Heat 3 tablespoons of olive oil in a large, heavy, low-sided saucepan or frying pan, add the onion, and sauté over a medium heat until transparent. Stir in the carrot, celery, oregano, and parsley, and continue cooking, stirring frequently, until lightly browned. Blend in the tomatoes, sugar, salt, white wine, if desired, and pepper, and cook over medium heat, stirring occasionally, for 30 minutes, until the sauce begins to thicken.

Pass the tomato sauce through a food mill to eliminate the skins and purée it. Return it to the pan and cook until the desired consistency is obtained. Add the remaining oil before serving or storing.

◆ ◆ ◆ ◆ ◆

## *Pomarola con Peperoni*

TOMATO
SAUCE
WITH
PEPPERS

MAKES 1½ TO 2 CUPS SAUCE

Peppers and tomatoes are both in the nightshade family and have, as this sauce demonstrates, a natural affinity for each other. We like to serve it with short, stout pasta such as penne or rigatoni.

*3 pounds fresh, ripe Italian plum tomatoes, cut in half lengthwise and seeded, or 3 cups canned Italian plum tomatoes, with their juice*
*½ teaspoon sugar*
*2 cloves*
*½ teaspoon salt*
*2 tablespoons butter*
*2 tablespoons olive oil*
*1 large onion, finely sliced*
*1 garlic clove, finely chopped*
*2 green, red, or yellow bell peppers, seeded and thinly sliced lengthwise*
*freshly ground pepper to taste*
*¼ teaspoon cayenne pepper (optional)*

Place the tomatoes, sugar, cloves, and salt in a large sauté pan, bring to a boil, and cook, covered, over a medium heat, stirring occasionally, for 5 minutes. Remove the cover and continue cooking, stirring occasionally for 20 minutes.

Heat the butter and oil in a frying pan, add the onion, and sauté over medium heat until transparent. Add the garlic, sauté another minute, add the peppers, and sauté for 5 minutes. Set aside.

Remove and discard the cloves from the tomatoes. Pass the tomato sauce through a food mill to eliminate the skins and purée. Stir the purée into the pepper mixture and simmer over a low heat for 5 minutes. Add black pepper and, if you wish, cayenne pepper.

◆ ◆ ◆ ◆ ◆

## *Pesto*

FRESH
BASIL
AND
GARLIC
SAUCE

MAKES 1½ CUPS SAUCE

Pesto is a pungent, aromatic sauce, redolent of its Mediterranean origin. There are few dishes in any cuisine that compare with the exquisite flavor and mouth-watering aroma of a steaming plate of pasta with pesto sauce. It also does wonders when combined with mayonnaise or served as a sauce for steamed vegetables and boiled potatoes. It has a strong flavor, so be temperate in its use—a little goes a long way. If you grow your own basil or are able to obtain fresh basil in the summer and fall, make extra pesto sauce and freeze it. It freezes well and can, in this way, be enjoyed all winter.

We find it best to freeze the sauce in small jars, such as those used for baby food. One such jar provides enough pesto sauce for 6 people. When freezing pesto, reduce the amount of oil and add it when the sauce is thawed.

There are at least as many recipes for pesto as there are municipalities in Liguria. Some include no pine nuts, some include milk or butter or both, some use only Parmesan while others combine Parmesan with Sardinian Pecorino. The recipe below represents the one we prefer. It is given in two parts. The first is the old-fashioned way to make pesto, in a mortar; the second is the way we and almost everyone else make it today, in a blender or food processor. Those in the know agree that the traditional way produces a smoother, more flavorful sauce. They contend that grinding the leaves in a mortar brings out the essential oils more effectively than chopping them with a metal blade. The ingredients are the same in both.

3 cups fresh basil leaves, loosely packed
3 to 5 garlic cloves
4 tablespoons pine nuts
4 tablespoons freshly grated Parmesan
2 tablespoons freshly grated Pecorino Sardo or Romano
⅓ cup olive oil
salt and freshly ground pepper to taste

## *Pesto Made in a Mortar*

Place the leaves, a few at a time, in a mortar and grind them with a pestle until the leaves are turned into a paste. Remove from the mortar and set aside.

Peel and chop the garlic cloves and add them along with the pine nuts to the mortar. Grind until a smooth paste is obtained. Return the basil to the mortar and grind the ingredients together until well blended.

Mix in the Parmesan and Pecorino Sardo or Romano and, stirring constantly, pour in the olive oil. Season with salt and pepper. At this point, you must taste the sauce and determine what it needs, not according to any formula but according to your own taste buds. It will almost certainly need more oil, but again base the decision on your taste. The sauce is normally oily and has the consistency of thin porridge.

### Pesto Made in a Blender

Combine all the dry ingredients in a blender or food processor, blend or process until smooth, then with blender or processor running, add the oil in a thin stream until it is all used. Taste and adjust for seasoning and other ingredients.

### VARIATIONS

Substitute 2 tablespoons of butter at room temperature for 2 tablespoons of olive oil. The Genoese often omit the pine nuts.

*Pesto with Pasta:* Use ¾ cup of pesto sauce for 1 pound of spaghetti, trenette, or other pasta. Thin the pesto with 1 tablespoon of hot water, place 3 tablespoons of the sauce in the bottom of a heated serving bowl, and, when cooked, add the pasta, combine, and add the remaining sauce. Mix well and serve immediately.

### ♦ ♦ ♦ ♦ ♦
### Salsa di Prezzemolo con Noci

PARSLEY
SAUCE
WITH
WALNUTS

MAKES 1 CUP SAUCE

This sauce is similar to pesto and can be used in the same way. It has its own distinctive character, less aromatic than pesto but no less flavorful. And it has the great advantage that parsley, unlike basil, is available fresh twelve months of the year.

2 cups Italian parsley leaves without stems, loosely packed
meat of 6 walnuts
4 tablespoons cream
2 to 3 garlic cloves
6 tablespoons freshly grated Parmesan
½ cup olive oil
salt and freshly ground pepper to taste

Combine the parsley, walnuts, cream, garlic, and Parmesan in a blender or food processor and process until a smooth paste is formed. With the machine running, add the olive oil in a thin stream. Taste and correct for salt and pepper. You may need more oil. The sauce should have the consistency of thin porridge.

### VARIATION

Substitute 2 tablespoons of freshly grated Pecorino Sardo or Romano for 2 table-spoons of Parmesan. You can also use milk instead of cream.

♦ ♦ ♦ ♦ ♦

## Salsa di Peperoni

PEPPER
SAUCE

MAKES 1½ CUPS SAUCE

This is a marvelous sauce for polenta, and for short, stout pasta such as penne and rigatoni. We also use it as a filling for Schiacciata Sandwiches (see recipe).

3 tablespoons olive oil
½ medium onion, thinly sliced
1 garlic clove, chopped
6 large red, green, or yellow bell peppers or a
    combination, peeled (p. 257), seeded, and thinly
    sliced lengthwise
1 tablespoon chopped basil
½ teaspoon salt
freshly ground pepper to taste

Heat the oil in a large frying pan, add the onion, and sauté over a medium heat for 1 minute. Add the garlic and sauté for another minute. Stir in the pepper slices and cook over a medium to low heat, stirring frequently, for 5 minutes. Add the basil, salt, and pepper, combine well, and continue cooking for a few more minutes, until the peppers are tender.

♦ ♦ ♦ ♦ ♦

## Salsa di Funghi

MUSHROOM
SAUCE

MAKES 1½ CUPS SAUCE

This sauce can be used as filling for Schiacciata Sandwiches (see recipe), as a sauce for pasta, and for steamed vegetables such as string beans, asparagus, and broccoli. We also serve it with savory soufflés and vegetable puddings.

2 tablespoons butter
2 tablespoons olive oil
1 small onion, thinly sliced
2 garlic cloves, chopped

1 teaspoon chopped rosemary leaves
1½ pounds fresh mushrooms, trimmed and thinly sliced
1 tablespoon flour
½ teaspoon salt
freshly ground pepper to taste
1 tablespoon chopped parsley

Heat the butter and oil in a large frying pan, add the onion, and sauté over a medium heat for 2 minutes. Add the garlic and rosemary and sauté another minute, until the ingredients begin to brown. Blend in the mushrooms, and cook on a high heat, stirring constantly with a wooden spoon, for 3 or 4 minutes.

Stir in the flour to absorb the juices and thicken the sauce. Add the salt, pepper, and parsley, and combine thoroughly.

♦ ♦ ♦ ♦ ♦

## Salsa di Cipolle

ONION
SAUCE

MAKES 1 TO 1½ CUPS SAUCE

Cooking tends to bring out the natural sweetness in onions, which makes this sauce an ideal accompaniment for vegetable puddings or savory soufflés. We also use it as a filling for Schiacciata Sandwiches (see recipe).

2 tablespoons butter
1 tablespoon olive oil
2 pounds red onions, thinly sliced
¼ cup dry white wine
1 tablespoon chopped parsley
¼ teaspoon salt
abundant freshly ground pepper

Heat the butter and oil in a frying pan, add the onions, and cook over a medium to low heat until the onions begin to color, about 10 minutes. Add the wine, reduce by half, stir in the parsley, salt, and pepper, and combine well.

◆ ◆ ◆ ◆ ◆

## Salsa all'Aglio con Brie

### GARLIC SAUCE WITH BRIE

MAKES 1½ CUPS SAUCE, ENOUGH FOR 8 SERVINGS OF PASTA

French cheeses were once very expensive and relatively unknown in Italy, but the Common Market changed all that. They are now both commonplace and reasonably priced. This sauce, which we serve on pasta and on such steamed vegetables as broccoli and cauliflower, is one of the more delightful results of the decline in tariffs. You can also use Caprice de Deux, or, in a pinch, Bel Paese.

¼ cup butter
5 garlic cloves, minced
1½ tablespoons flour
⅔ cup milk or cream
¾ pound ripe but not overripe Brie, rind removed, cut
    into small pieces
salt and freshly ground pepper to taste

Melt the butter in a small saucepan, add the garlic, and sauté for 1 minute over a medium heat. Stir in the flour and cook, stirring, until the flour begins to color. Pour the milk or cream in slowly, stirring constantly, until a creamy sauce is formed. Add the cheese and cook, stirring constantly, until the cheese melts and combines with the sauce. Taste and adjust for salt and pepper. Use piping hot on pasta or vegetables. You may wish to pass the pepper grinder, since freshly ground pepper enhances the flavor of the sauce.

◆ ◆ ◆ ◆ ◆

## Salsa Verde

### PUNGENT GREEN SAUCE

MAKES 1½ CUPS SAUCE

This sauce, sometimes made with anchovies, is popular all over central and northern Italy. It has a strong, pungent flavor, perfect to serve with boiled new potatoes, steamed or boiled vegetables, or hard-boiled eggs. The sauce can be made in a blender or food processor or simply with a knife. We first give the hand-made version.

½ slice Homemade Italian Bread (see recipe) or good
    commercial bread, 3 by 3 by ½ inch thick
2 tablespoons wine vinegar
1 garlic clove
1 cup tightly packed parsley leaves, stems removed
2 tablespoons capers

1 hard-boiled egg yolk, creamed with a fork
1 cup olive oil
salt and freshly ground pepper to taste

Soak the bread in vinegar for 10 minutes, then chop it very fine and place it in a mixture bowl. Very finely chop the garlic, parsley, and capers, and add, with the creamed egg yolk, to the bread. Combine thoroughly. Pour the olive oil in a thin stream into the mixing bowl, stirring the ingredients constantly to mix with the oil. Taste and correct for salt and pepper. Set aside for at least 1 hour before using. The sauce can be kept covered in the refrigerator for 1 week.

If using a blender or food processor, place the bread, garlic, parsley, capers, and egg yolk in the machine and process until smooth. Add the oil with the machine running. Correct for seasoning.

### VARIATION

In Tuscany, the sauce is sometimes made with 2 tablespoons of pine nuts, lemon juice in place of vinegar, and ½ cup of fresh basil leaves and ½ cup of parsley.

♦ ♦ ♦ ♦ ♦

## Salsa d'Uovo all'Aceto

CREAMED
EGG
SAUCE
WITH
VINEGAR

MAKES ¾ CUP SAUCE

This sauce is more pungent and less rich than hollandaise but can be used for the same purposes. It is also less delicate and thus easier to work with. Serve hot over cooked vegetables and on poached eggs.

¼ cup butter
2 garlic cloves, minced
3 eggs
1 tablespoon flour
2 tablespoons wine vinegar
pinch of salt
freshly ground white pepper to taste

Heat the butter in a small saucepan, add the garlic, and sauté for 1 minute over a medium heat. Remove from the heat before the garlic begins to brown and set aside.

Place the eggs in a mixing bowl and beat with a wooden spoon or whisk until frothy. Add the flour, a little at a time, beating constantly. Beat in the vinegar, salt, and pepper, and pour into the saucepan that contains the garlic and butter. Return to a low heat and cook, stirring constantly, until the sauce thickens. Remove from the heat and continue to stir for 2 minutes.

If you do not use the sauce immediately, coat the surface with melted butter to prevent a crust from forming. It can be reheated and will keep for a couple of days in the refrigerator.

♦ ♦ ♦ ♦ ♦

## Salsa di Pomodoro con Aceto

TOMATO
SAUCE
WITH
VINEGAR

MAKES ½ TO ⅔ CUP SAUCE

A little of this pungent, highly flavored sauce will go a long way, so use it with discretion. It is excellent on pasta and such steamed or boiled vegetables as broccoli, string beans, potatoes, and cabbage. It is so tasty that we sometimes make up a batch and serve it on toasted bread (*crostini*).

¼ cup olive oil
⅔ cup fresh plum tomatoes, peeled, seeded, and
    chopped, or ½ cup canned Italian plum tomatoes,
    drained and finely chopped
½ cup mushrooms, finely chopped
2 tablespoons finely chopped parsley
1 tablespoon capers, finely chopped
pinch of salt
freshly ground pepper to taste
3 tablespoons wine vinegar or to taste

Place the oil, tomatoes, mushrooms, parsley, capers, salt, and pepper in a saucepan and bring to a boil. Lower the heat and simmer for 5 minutes. Add the vinegar and cook for another 2 minutes. Serve hot or cold.

♦ ♦ ♦ ♦ ♦

## Salsa agli Asparagi

ASPARAGUS
SAUCE

MAKES 1 CUP SAUCE

In late spring when asparagus are plentiful and relatively inexpensive, try this sauce with steamed or boiled vegetables, boiled potatoes, vegetable puddings, savory soufflés, and hard-boiled or poached eggs.

1 pound asparagus, prepared for cooking (p. 222)
2 hard-boiled egg yolks
¼ cup butter
⅓ cup thick cream

*1 tablespoon lemon juice*
*pinch of salt*
*freshly ground pepper to taste*

Steam the asparagus until very tender, about 15 minutes. Drain, cut off the tender tips, and purée in a blender, food processor, or food mill along with the egg yolks.

Place the butter in a small saucepan, add the asparagus purée and the cream, and cook, stirring constantly, over low heat for 3 minutes. Add the lemon juice, salt, and pepper, bring to a boil, and serve hot.

♦ ♦ ♦ ♦ ♦

## Salsa d'Olive con Capperi

OLIVE
AND
CAPER
SAUCE

MAKES ½ CUP SAUCE

We first had this delicious sauce in Florence served with a platter of mixed fried vegetables. It can also be served with a savory soufflé, or vegetable pudding, or on toast as an antipasto.

*1 tablespoon olive oil*
*3 tablespoons butter*
*1 small onion, finely chopped*
*¼ cup Italian black olives, pitted, rinsed under cold*
    *water if salty, and finely chopped*
*3 tablespoons capers, finely chopped*
*1 tablespoon finely chopped parsley*
*2 teaspoons water*
*1 teaspoon wine vinegar*
*1 teaspoon flour*

Heat the olive oil and 2 tablespoons of butter in a saucepan, add the onion, and sauté over medium heat for a few minutes, until transparent. Add the olives, capers, and parsley and continue cooking, stirring constantly, for another 2 minutes. Add the water and the vinegar, reduce the liquid by half, add the flour, and stir to thicken. Blend in the remaining tablespoon of butter. Serve hot or at room temperature.

# ANTIPASTI

A formal Italian meal consists of five courses: an antipasto, a pasta or soup, a main dish, a salad, and fruit or dessert. This may seem excessive to North Americans, but it is extremely modest when compared with the elaborate repasts that the wealthy Italians and French enjoyed in earlier centuries. It was not unusual to have eight or nine courses, including an antipasto, a pasta or soup, a *tramezzo*—a dish of minor importance that bridged the gap between more substantial courses—a course of fish or eggs, the main dish, another *tramezzo*, vegetables, salad, fruit, and dessert. Although much more modest today, the antipasto has retained its pride of place.

An antipasto, literally "before the meal," is generally very flavorful and served in modest amounts—its purpose is to stimulate the appetite, not to satiate it. The antipasti recipes we include fulfill a dual purpose. All can be served, as in Italy, at the table before the meal. But many, such as *crostini*, can also be served with cocktails. And, for weight-watchers, some of the antipasti can be substituted for pasta dishes, a not uncommon practice in Italy today.

## Crostini

*Crostini* are an Italian version of French canapés. They are essentially pieces of toast dressed with a sauce and served either at the table or before the meal, with drinks. Use white Italian bread, cut into ½-inch slices. Italians remove the crust, but if you like it by all means leave it. We find that the most suitable bread for *crostini* is the one made in long, thin loaves. Waste is minimized, and the diameter of the loaf is the perfect size for *crostini*. Naturally, if you have homemade bread, use it. Cut it into pieces 2 inches square by ½ inch thick, toast the pieces, add the topping, and serve.

You will need approximately eighteen 2-inch-square pieces of toast for the recipes that follow. If you prefer larger or smaller pieces of toast, adjust accordingly.

## Antipasto Misto

It is quite common in Italy to begin a meal with antipasto misto. In some cases, it even substitutes for pasta. There are no fixed rules about the right mix, but the greater the variety of dishes the better.

There are two ways to serve antipasto misto. The first is to arrange the various foods on one or two large platters and pass them among the guests. In Italy, there are large plates specially designed with separations for the various antipasti. Lacking such plates, divisions can be improvised using small bowls, or lettuce leaves.

The second is to prepare a dish for each guest with a selection of the antipasti. Don't forget that much of the pleasure of eating is visual. Antipasto misto can be a feast for the eyes as well as the palate.

Try to include at least four different antipasti. Olives, scallions, and raw vegetables can be used to add color and variety.

♦ ♦ ♦ ♦ ♦

## Crostini alla Paola

PAOLA'S CROSTINI

SERVES 6

These are a type of *crostini* found all along the Versilia coast from Viareggio to Massa. They go well with a chilled dry white wine or any other apéritif.

eighteen 2-inch-square pieces Italian bread, sliced ½ inch thick
Béchamel Sauce (see recipe) made with:
1 cup milk
3 tablespoons butter
3 tablespoons flour
¼ teaspoon salt
1 tablespoon butter
1 cup chopped onions
¼ cup thick cream
3 tablespoons freshly grated Parmesan
2 tablespoons peeled almonds, ground
2 egg yolks
¼ teaspoon dry mustard
salt and pepper

Toast the bread.

Make a thick béchamel sauce. Remove from the heat. In a small frying pan, melt the butter, and sauté the onions until lightly brown. Add them to the béchamel sauce, then stir in the cream, Parmesan, almonds, egg yolks, mustard, and salt and pepper to taste. Combine thoroughly. Return to the heat and warm through, stirring constantly. The sauce should be quite thick. Taste and correct for salt and pepper.

Spread the mixture thickly over the pieces of toast and brown the tops in a broiler. Serve hot.

◆ ◆ ◆ ◆ ◆

## Crostini al Gorgonzola

Any high-quality blue cheese will do for this recipe, but Gorgonzola is creamier and milder than most. A strong blue cheese requires more butter than indicated below to capture the delicate flavor of this dish.

GORGONZOLA
ON
TOAST

SERVES 6

*eighteen 2-inch-square pieces of Italian bread, sliced ½ inch thick*
*1 cup Gorgonzola*
*1 whole egg, beaten*
*1 tablespoon butter, softened*
*salt and pepper to taste*

Preheat oven to 400°F.

Toast the bread.

Combine in a mixing bowl the cheese, egg, and butter. Spread the mixture on the toast. Sprinkle with salt and pepper. Bake for 10 minutes or until the tops are golden. Serve immediately.

◆ ◆ ◆ ◆ ◆

## Crostini di Funghi alla Crema

MUSHROOMS
WITH
CREAM
ON
TOAST

SERVES 6

*¾ ounce dried wild mushrooms (Boletus edulis)*
*1 pound fresh mushrooms*
*3½ tablespoons butter*
*2 garlic cloves, finely chopped*
*1 teaspoon dry mustard*
*½ cup plus 1 tablespoon thick cream*
*salt and freshly ground pepper*
*eighteen 2-inch-square pieces Italian bread*

Soak the dried mushrooms in 1 cup of warm water for 20 minutes, remove carefully from the water, and rinse well under cold water to remove grit and sand. Drain and set aside.

Wash, trim, and thinly slice the fresh mushrooms. Chop the dried mushrooms and combine with the fresh ones.

Melt 2 tablespoons of the butter in a saucepan and add the garlic. Cook for 1 minute. Blend in the mushrooms and cook on a high heat, stirring frequently, for 2 to 3 minutes.

Combine the mustard with ½ cup of cream and heat through. Add the mustard-and-cream mixture to the mushrooms and cook until the cream has almost evaporated. Remove from the heat, add the additional tablespoon of cream, salt, and pepper to taste, and set aside.

Toast the bread and butter the pieces lightly. Heat the mushroom mixture and spread on top of the pieces of toast. Serve warm.

♦ ♦ ♦ ♦ ♦     We usually serve this with drinks before a meal.

## Crostini ai Capperi

CAPERS
ON
TOAST

SERVES 6

6 tablespoons butter
½ cup finely chopped red onion or scallions
2 tablespoons finely chopped parsley
2 tablespoons finely chopped fresh basil
½ cup water
1 tablespoon flour or cornstarch
¼ cup dry white wine
4 tablespoons capers, finely chopped
4 tablespoons black Italian olives, pitted, rinsed under
   cold water if very salty, and finely chopped
eighteen 2-inch-square pieces Italian bread, sliced ½
   inch thick
2 small tomatoes, thinly sliced

Heat 2 tablespoons of the butter in a saucepan and add the onion or scallions, parsley, and basil. Cook for 5 minutes or until the onion begins to color. Add ½ cup water and cook for another 5 minutes, until the water has completely evaporated, stirring frequently. Add 2 tablespoons of the butter and the flour or cornstarch and stir to thicken. Add the wine, capers, and olives, and continue cooking, stirring constantly for 2 minutes. Remove from the heat.

Toast and butter the bread with the remaining butter. Spread a thin layer of caper paste, either hot or cold, over each slice of toast. Cut the tomato slices in small pieces to garnish the top of the *crostini*.

◆ ◆ ◆ ◆ ◆

*Asparagi alla Maionese*

ASPARAGUS
WITH
MAYONNAISE

SERVES 6 TO 8

Bassano is famed throughout Italy for the quality of its asparagus. This dish, which combines these wonderful spring vegetables with a seasoned mayonnaise, comes from the heart of the asparagus-growing region.

2 pounds fresh asparagus
a few whole lettuce leaves
2 tablespoons Sott'aceti (see recipe), chopped
1 tablespoon finely chopped scallions, white parts only
1 tablespoon minced parsley
½ cup Homemade Mayonnaise (see recipe)
salt and freshly ground pepper to taste
6 to 8 strips pimento

Wash the asparagus, break off the tough ends, and steam until cooked but firm (p. 146). Place on lettuce leaves on a serving platter or on 6 to 8 individual dishes.

Make a sauce with the Sott'aceti, scallions, parsley, mayonnaise, salt, and pepper. Spread the sauce over the asparagus. Garnish with the strips of pimento. Chill for 30 minutes and serve.

◆ ◆ ◆ ◆ ◆

*Carciofi all'Uovo*

ARTICHOKES
WITH
EGG
SAUCE

SERVES 6 TO 8

12 medium artichokes, trimmed and cut in half
3 hard-boiled eggs, finely chopped
1 tablespoon capers, finely chopped
2 tablespoons finely chopped scallions, white parts only
1 tablespoon finely chopped fresh mint leaves, or dried leaves soaked for 10 minutes, drained, and finely chopped
½ teaspoon cayenne pepper, or to taste
2 tablespoons olive oil
juice of 1 lemon
salt and freshly ground pepper to taste
a few lettuce leaves, cucumber slices, tomato wedges, or pimento for garnish

Wash, trim, cut in half, and remove the chokes from the artichokes, as explained on p. 215. Place in acidulated water until ready to use. When ready, drain and steam them for 20 minutes, until cooked but still firm. Remove and let cool.

Meanwhile, combine the remaining ingredients (except garnish) in a mixing bowl. Arrange the artichoke halves on lettuce leaves on a serving platter or individual dishes. Spoon some of the egg mixture onto each of the artichoke halves. Garnish the dish with some cucumber slices, tomato wedges, or pimento. Chill for 30 minutes or serve at room temperature.

♦ ♦ ♦ ♦ ♦

## Pomodori alla Maionese

TOMATOES
WITH
HERBED
MAYONNAISE

SERVES 6

6 large ripe tomatoes
½ teaspoon salt
1½ cups Homemade Mayonnaise (see recipe)
1 heaping tablespoon Pesto (see recipe)
5 large basil leaves, crushed in a mortar or minced
10 fresh tarragon leaves, minced, or ¼ teaspoon dried leaves
freshly ground pepper to taste
slices of cucumber and green pepper and sprigs of parsley or basil for garnish

Cut the tomatoes in half, scalloping the edges with a sharp paring knife. Scoop out half the pulp with a serrated spoon. The pulp is not needed for this recipe, but can be saved for tomato sauce. Sprinkle the inside of the tomato halves with salt and turn them upside down on a dish to drain for 30 minutes.

Meanwhile combine the remaining ingredients (except garnish) with the mayonnaise. Fill the tomato halves with the mayonnaise mixture. Garnish and serve chilled or at room temperature.

♦ ♦ ♦ ♦ ♦

## Funghi con la Grana

MUSHROOMS
WITH
PARMESAN

SERVES 4

This dish originates in the region of Emilia, the home of Parmesan cheese. It is important to select Parmesan that is yellow and moist and therefore fresh. Do not be put off by the simplicity of this dish—it is excellent. Serve with a light dry red wine.

½ pound very fresh mushrooms
½ pound Parmesan cheese
freshly ground pepper
3 tablespoons good-quality olive oil
parsley sprigs

Wash carefully, trim, and slice the mushrooms thin. Slice the Parmesan very thin. Place in individual dishes, alternating slices of mushroom and cheese. Grind fresh pepper over the top and sprinkle with olive oil. Salt is not needed, since the Parmesan is salty. Garnish with parsley.

◆ ◆ ◆ ◆ ◆

## Funghi con Pesto

STUFFED
MUSHROOM
CAPS

SERVES 4 TO 6

12 large, very fresh mushrooms
1 teaspoon lemon juice
2 tablespoons bread crumbs
½ cup Pesto (see recipe)
5 tablespoons freshly grated Parmesan
1 tablespoon olive oil

Preheat oven to 375°F.
Remove the stems from the mushrooms, wash carefully, and rub the caps with lemon juice to prevent discoloration. Combine the bread crumbs with the pesto and fill each cap with a teaspoon of the mixture. Arrange on a baking dish and sprinkle with 3 tablespoons of Parmesan. Drizzle the olive oil over the caps and bake for 10 to 12 minutes until the cheese melts. Sprinkle with the remaining 2 tablespoons of Parmesan and serve hot.

◆ ◆ ◆ ◆ ◆

## Funghi Marinati

MARINATED
MUSHROOMS

MAKES 2 CUPS

1½ pounds small fresh mushrooms
4 tablespoons olive oil
3 garlic cloves, minced
1 bay leaf
1 teaspoon fresh rosemary, or ½ teaspoon dried
1 cup dry white wine
salt and freshly ground pepper to taste
2 tablespoons brandy
lettuce leaves for garnish (optional)

Wash and trim the mushrooms and place them in a mixing bowl. Heat the oil in a frying pan and cook the garlic for 1 minute. Do not allow the garlic to brown. Remove the pan from the heat and stir in the bay leaf, rosemary, wine, seasoning, and brandy. Return to the heat, bring the mixture to a boil, and pour it over the mushrooms. Toss to coat and let marinate in a cool place for at least 2 hours or overnight.

Drain off the liquid before serving. It can be reserved and used as a dressing for salads or vegetables. Serve the mushrooms on their own or on a bed of lettuce.

♦ ♦ ♦ ♦ ♦

## *Peperoni alla Griglia*

GRILLED
PEPPERS

SERVES 6

6 large bell peppers, green, red, or yellow, or a mixture
⅓ cup olive oil
3 tablespoons wine vinegar
¼ teaspoon salt
freshly ground pepper to taste
2 tablespoons finely chopped parsley
3 garlic cloves, finely chopped
pinch of oregano
pinch of cayenne pepper (optional)

Wash, grill, and peel the peppers according to instructions on p. 257. Cut in half lengthwise, remove the seeds, and cut in thin strips, approximately ½ inch wide. Place in a mixing bowl and set aside.

Mix the rest of the ingredients thoroughly in a small mixing bowl or a jar and pour over the pepper slices. Toss well to coat. Allow to marinate at least 1 hour. Serve chilled or at room temperature.

♦ ♦ ♦ ♦ ♦

## *Caviale di Olive Nere*

OLIVES
CAVIAR

SERVES 4

This may not be caviar, but if served as one serves caviar, garnished with chopped hard-boiled eggs, chopped onions, and slices of lemon, this dish matches it in elegance and flavor. Serve with a chilled dry white wine.

1 dried hot red pepper
½ pound dried black olives, pitted
1 teaspoon oregano, crushed
2 tablespoons olive oil
1 teaspoon lemon juice
eighteen 2-inch squares Italian bread, thinly sliced,
     crust removed, and cut into triangles, or plain
     Melba toast

8 *lemon wedges*

2 *hard-boiled eggs, finely chopped*

3 *tablespoons finely chopped onions*

Remove and discard the seeds from the pepper and grind it in a mortar. Add the olives and continue grinding until a rough paste is formed. If dried olives are unavailable, use salted ones, but rinse them very well under cold water. Add the oregano, oil, and lemon juice and mix thoroughly.

Toast the bread and place the pieces in a small basket or on a plate.

Serve the olive paste in a chilled bowl on crushed ice. Accompany with lemon wedges, chopped eggs, and onions.

♦ ♦ ♦ ♦ ♦

## Zucchini alla Virginia

ZUCCHINI,
VIRGINIA
STYLE

SERVES 4 TO 6

Although this way of preparing zucchini is traditional in Rome and throughout southern Italy, we call it "alla Virginia" because Virginia, our cook in Rome, introduced us to it.

Virginia likes people and loves to cook. From her point of view, there are never too many people for meals. If she encountered our friends while shopping in local markets in Vecchia Roma, she would insist they come for lunch. "There's plenty to eat," she'd say, "and guests are always welcome." And, then she'd clinch the invitation with a description of the specialty she intended to cook that day.

2 *pounds small zucchini*

¼ *cup olive oil*

1 *teaspoon salt*

3 *garlic cloves*

3 *tablespoons vinegar*

1 *tablespoon lemon juice*

3 *tablespoons minced parsley*

*freshly ground pepper to taste*

Wash, pat dry, and trim the ends of the zucchini. Slice lengthwise in thin strips, about ¼ inch thick. Place the slices on paper towels to dry. In a large frying pan, heat the oil and fry the zucchini, a few at a time, turning with a spatula to ensure that they brown on both sides. As the zucchini brown, transfer them to a platter with a slotted spatula, draining as much of the oil as possible back into the pan, but do not drain on paper towels. Sprinkle with salt.

When all the zucchini are fried, prepare the dressing. Grind the garlic cloves to a paste in a mortar, or mince. Combine with the vinegar, lemon juice, and parsley. Pour the dressing over the fried zucchini and toss them to coat. Allow to marinate 1 hour. Serve at room temperature, passing the pepper mill.

### VARIATION

The zucchini can be fried in seed oil. This will result in a lighter dish. If seed oil is used, drain the fried zucchini on paper towels and add ¼ cup of olive oil to the dressing.

♦ ♦ ♦ ♦ ♦

## Caponata Siciliana

SICILIAN
CAPONATA

SERVES 8 TO 10

This dish is always served cold, usually as an anti-pasto, but it is also an excellent addition to a cold buffet. A few words of caution. Eggplants soak up oil like a blotter absorbs ink. Try to add as little oil as possible when frying them. As an alternative, the eggplants can be broiled instead of fried. They will be less tasty, but lighter. Serve with a chilled dry white wine.

3 small eggplants, approximately 1 pound
2 teaspoons salt
1 tablespoon olive oil
2 large onions, chopped
1 celery heart, diced
2 pounds tomatoes, peeled, seeded, and chopped, or 2
    cups canned Italian plum tomatoes, drained
½ cup olive oil
4 red or green bell peppers, seeded and diced
½ cup green olives, pitted, rinsed in cold water if salty,
    and chopped
¼ cup capers, chopped
¼ cup wine vinegar
1 tablespoon sugar
salt and freshly ground pepper to taste

Peel the eggplants, cut in quarters, sprinkle with the salt, and allow to drain in a colander for half an hour.

Meanwhile, in a large frying pan heat the oil and sauté the onions until transparent. Add the celery and tomatoes, cooking until the liquid evaporates, about 10 minutes. Remove from the heat.

Rinse the salt from the eggplants, pat dry between paper towels, cut into ¾-inch cubes, and fry in the oil, a few at a time, until golden on all sides. As the pieces brown, remove them from the oil and drain them on paper towels. The eggplants should be browned, not cooked through. In the same oil fry the bell peppers until wilted. Remove from the oil and drain.

Add the fried eggplants and bell peppers to the tomato-onion-celery mixture. Add as well the olives, capers, vinegar, sugar, and salt and pepper. Cook over a low heat for 15 minutes, stirring occasionally. Serve cold.

♦ ♦ ♦ ♦ ♦

## Melanzane alla Calabrese

EGGPLANT, CALABRIAN STYLE

SERVES 6

During one of our trips to Calabria many years ago, we stopped for lunch in a small village by the Mediterranean. Mass tourism had yet to transform these southern villages into well-equipped resorts. The town had a single small trattoria—a few tables, a small kitchen, no menu. It seemed a most unpromising place to obtain a good meal, much less an outstanding one. Looks are often deceiving in such cases, as we quickly discovered. We ate what they had, and every dish was a treat. We started the meal with this dish. It goes well, as it did that day, with a Calabrian rosé wine.

6 small eggplants, approximately 2 pounds
3 teaspoons salt
2 tablespoons olive oil
3 cups chopped onions
2 garlic cloves, chopped
1 cup peeled and seeded fresh tomatoes, or 1 cup canned
    Italian plum tomatoes, drained and chopped
½ cup raisins
¼ teaspoon dried oregano
2 tablespoons capers, chopped
2 tablespoons pine nuts, chopped
¼ cup Italian black olives, pitted, rinsed in cold water
    if salty, and chopped
salt
about ½ teaspoon dried hot pepper

Preheat oven to 375°F. Oil a baking dish large enough to accommodate the eggplants in a single layer.

Cut the eggplants in half lengthwise and, with a serrated spoon or a curved knife, carefully remove the pulp without damaging the skin. Sprinkle the inside of the eggplants with 2 teaspoons of salt and place to drain upside down in a colander. Put the pulp in a strainer suspended over a mixing bowl, sprinkle with the remaining teaspoon of salt, and leave it to drain for 30 minutes.

Meanwhile, heat the oil in a frying pan, add the onions, and sauté over medium heat for a few minutes, until the onions are transparent. Add the garlic and sauté another minute. Remove from the heat.

Rinse the eggplant pulp, drain it, pat dry between paper towels, and chop roughly. Add 2 cups of the pulp to the onions. Return to the heat and sauté over medium heat for 2 minutes, stirring constantly. Add the rest of the ingredients (except salt and pepper) and continue cooking for another 10 minutes, until all the liquid has evaporated. Add salt and hot pepper to taste.

Rinse the eggplant skins. Pat them dry and fill with the pulp mixture. Place side by side in the oiled baking dish and add 1 cup of hot water to the baking dish. The water should come roughly halfway up the sides of the eggplants. Bake for 30 minutes, remove, and serve hot or at room temperature.

♦ ♦ ♦ ♦ ♦

## Insalata di Melanzane

EGGPLANT
SALAD

SERVES 4 TO 6

This dish can double as an antipasto or a salad—we prefer it as an antipasto. We recommend that you chop the vegetables by hand, not in a food processor or blender, since the final product should be coarsely textured, not smooth and creamy.

2 medium eggplants, approximately 2 pounds

1 large tomato, peeled, seeded, and coarsely chopped

6 scallions, coarsely chopped

1 garlic clove, minced

¼ cup olive oil

salt and freshly ground pepper to taste

a few leaves Boston lettuce

2 tablespoons chopped parsley

1 tablespoon black Italian olives, pitted, rinsed in cold
        water if salty, and chopped

1 tablespoon pine nuts, chopped

6 carrots, washed, peeled, and cut in thin strips

Preheat oven to 350°F.

Prick the eggplants with a fork in several places and put them in the oven until soft to the touch but not mushy, about 30 minutes. Remove, and when cool enough to handle, peel and chop coarsely.

In a large mixing bowl combine the tomato, scallions, garlic, and eggplant. Pour the olive oil into the bowl while stirring the ingredients. Taste and correct for salt and pepper, but remember that olives and capers are still to be added. Place the mixture in the refrigerator to chill. It can be kept overnight.

When ready to serve, distribute the eggplant salad on the leaves of Boston lettuce. Sprinkle the parsley, olives, and pine nuts over the top of the salad. Decorate the borders with carrot strips and serve.

♦ ♦ ♦ ♦ ♦

## *Fritto di Verdure Misto*

### FRIED VEGETABLES

SERVES 6

Artichokes, carrots, cauliflower, leeks, mushrooms, onions, fennel, and zucchini are all suitable for this dish. In Italy, especially in Rome, fried vegetables are often displayed on large platters in restaurants and served cold as antipasti. They are, however, much better, like all fried food, when served as soon as they are cooked. (You can vary the mixture of vegetables, but try to include at least two varieties.)

1¼ cups unbleached all-purpose flour
2 tablespoons butter, melted
1 whole egg, beaten
1 tablespoon brandy
1 cup carrots cut lengthwise into slices ¼ inch thick
1 cup zucchini cut lengthwise into slices ¼ inch thick
1 cup mushrooms, stems removed and halved
1 cup cauliflower cut into small flowerets
1 to 2 cups light seed oil
salt and freshly ground pepper to taste
sprigs of parsley
6 lemon wedges

Make a batter for frying by combining the flour, butter, egg, and brandy. Mix well and slowly add ¼ cup cold water to make a batter the consistency of thick cream. Let it sit for 1 hour. Meanwhile, prepare the vegetables for frying.

When the batter is ready, heat the oil in a pan suitable for deep frying, dip the vegetables into the batter, and fry them, a few at a time, until golden on all sides. Drain on paper towels. Sprinkle with salt and pepper and garnish with parsley sprigs. Serve hot with lemon wedges.

◆ ◆ ◆ ◆ ◆

## *Uova con Maionese*

STUFFED
EGGS

SERVES 6

6 hard-boiled eggs
2 tablespoons capers, chopped
2 tablespoons Sott'aceti (see recipe), chopped
½ cup Homemade Mayonnaise (see recipe)
1 teaspoon lemon juice
4 large basil leaves, finely chopped
salt and freshly ground pepper to taste
2 tablespoons capers

Peel the hard-boiled eggs and cut in half lengthwise. Gently remove the yolks without damaging the whites. Reserve the whites and place the yolks in a mixing bowl. Mash them to a smooth paste with a fork and add the remaining ingredients (except whole capers). Combine well and gently fill the cavity of the egg whites with one heaping tablespoon of the mixture. Garnish each egg half with whole capers. Serve at room temperature.

◆ ◆ ◆ ◆ ◆

## *Pan Bologna*

BOLOGNA
BREAD

SERVES 6

In northern Italy this dish is often eaten as a mid-morning snack, but it also makes an appetizing beginning to any meal. It can be served as a luncheon dish accompanied by eggs with mayonnaise or by an omelet with a crisp, green salad.

6 large slices Italian bread, ½ inch thick
1 or 2 garlic cloves, peeled
2 tomatoes
2 tablespoons finely chopped onion
1 teaspoon capers, chopped, plus 1 teaspoon, whole
¼ teaspoon fresh minced hot pepper or dried pepper
    flakes
¼ cup olive oil
1 teaspoon minced fresh basil or parsley
salt and freshly ground pepper to taste

Toast the bread lightly and rub with garlic. Cut the tomatoes in quarters and rub them over the toast, leaving as much of the pulp as possible on the bread. Sprinkle the onion, chopped capers, and hot pepper evenly on top of the tomato pulp. Drizzle with olive oil and evenly distribute the basil or parsley and a few whole capers over each slice of toast. Season with salt and pepper. Serve whole or cut in bite-size pieces.

♦ ♦ ♦ ♦ ♦

## *Fettunta*

GARLIC
BREAD

SERVES 6

After the olives were picked in December and January, the farmers piled them into large straw baskets, loaded them onto oxcarts, and brought them to the *frantoio*, the huge olive pressing room that was located under the south side of our villa. It was for me, as a child, a very special time, and I would spend as much of each day there as I could when the olive oil was being made, sitting with the farmers and listening to their stories and gossip—and to the sounds of the great stone grinding the olives into pulp. I would wait, impatiently, for snack time. It was then that a wood fire was made in a small brazier, thick slices of coarse Tuscan bread were toasted, garlic was rubbed on, and the great treat, the freshly pressed olive oil, green, thick, spotted still with pieces of olive pulp and skin, was slathered onto the toast. I would sit and munch my piece, convinced that there was nothing better to eat in all the world.

That way of preparing and eating *fettunta* (literally "oily slice") is, in fact, the origin of the dish.

> 6 slices coarse Italian bread, preferably homemade (p. 52)
> 3 garlic cloves
> ½ cup Tuscan olive oil (try to obtain olio extra vergine from Lucca)
> salt to taste

Toast the bread or, even better, roast it over an open fire. Rub the garlic generously over the bread. Arrange on a platter and pour the oil evenly over the slices. Sprinkle with salt and serve while still warm.

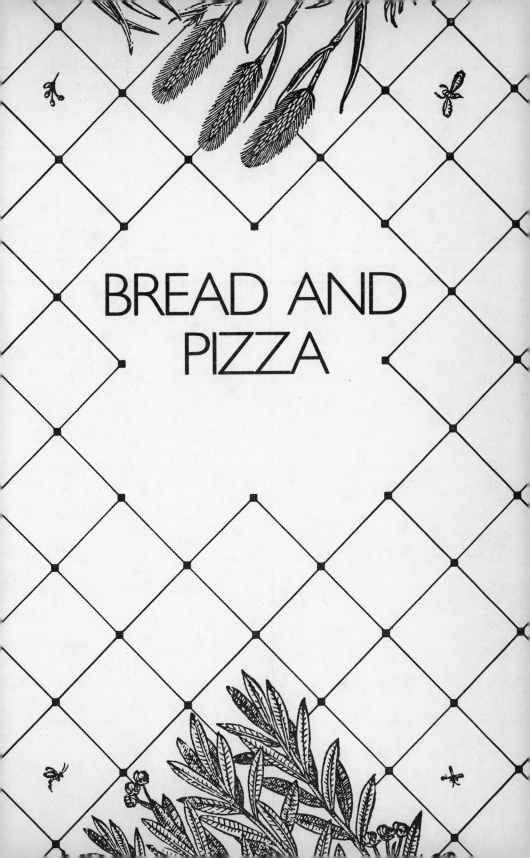

# BREAD AND PIZZA

Italians eat a great deal of bread. It is served with every meal; it is used in soups, with antipasti, and even in desserts. And as with every other type of Italian food, each area of the country has its own bread. The recipes we include here are for Tuscan bread, the kind we know best and prefer. It is relatively easy to make, and because it contains almost no salt and no oil, it is ideally suited for use in other dishes. We urge you to try these recipes and, particularly, to use this type of bread for Panzanella, Fettunta, Pappa di Pane, and Acquacotta soup. It makes a world of difference in the final results.

As for pizzas, they are probably as popular in North America as the ubiquitous hamburger, and justifiably so. They are tasty, nutritious, and varied. Pizzas are also popular in Italy today and, in fact, *pizzerie* are found the length and breadth of the peninsula. The similarity between the North American and Italian versions is striking, suggesting that the original Italian pizza made its way westward across the Atlantic with southern Italian immigrants, was modified to suit North American palates and dining habits, and made its way back again with tourists and returning emigrants.

The more or less original Italian version differs from its modified American descendant in that it is essentially a flat bread about 1 inch thick, cooked with a light tomato sauce on top. This is, at least, the classic Italian pizza that one finds in the bread shops in Rome and Naples. Farther north in Tuscany, there are *schiacciata* and *focaccia*, again flat breads baked most often with salt, oil, and rosemary or onions, with no tomato sauce or cheese at all. In Genoa, they also make a flat bread, cooked with cheese and no tomatoes. Some speculate that pizza is an Italian variant of pita, the Middle Eastern flat bread, and was a Saracen import into Italy. Others argue that the ancient Romans ate pizza, while some maintain that pizza hails from the area around Nice. Whatever its origins, the versatile pizza in its various guises has been around for a long time.

The selection of pizza recipes that follows is hardly exhaustive. It contains merely the ones that we find most satisfactory and interesting. As the history of pizza indicates, it is a dish that lends itself to creative variations, so don't hesitate to try your own modifications.

We first describe how to make Tuscan bread, both white and whole wheat varieties. We then tell how to make pizza doughs and give recipes for pizza toppings. We also include two recipes for Calzone and two for Panzerotti, first cousins of the pizza.

♦ ♦ ♦ ♦ ♦

## Pane Bianco Toscano

TUSCAN
WHITE
BREAD

A few years ago we reactivated the one remaining brick oven on our farm. We grew our own wheat, had it stone ground by a local miller, and used the flour to bake bread once a week for family and friends.

We prepared the dough and baked the bread according to traditional methods. The night before, we made a starter with a ball of dough reserved from the previous week and allowed it to rise overnight. The following day, early in the morning, we mixed the starter with more flour and warm water, kneaded it for 15 to 20 minutes, shaped it into loaves, reserving some for the bread next week and for *schiacciata*, and allowed the loaves to rise until doubled in bulk. We meanwhile heated the oven with wood pruned from olive and other trees on the farm. By the time the dough had risen, the oven was ready to receive the bread. We scattered the embers along the far inside wall of the oven, placed the bread inside, made one or two *schiacciate*, with oil, salt, and rosemary sprinkled on top, one or two pizzas, and sometimes Fagioli al Fiasco. The *schiacciate* cooked in about 20 minutes and we had these for breakfast while the loaves baked. When the loaves were ready—one could tell by the hollow sound they made when tapped on the bottom—we removed them with long-handled wooden spatulas, wrapped them in cotton blankets, and set them aside to cool slowly. Slow cooling allows the bread to be kept for a much longer time without going stale. The results, as you can imagine, were extraordinary.

We have discovered, fortunately, that it is possible with a little effort to bake very good Tuscan bread in North America with a conventional oven and readily available flour. Bricks are required. We use four rectangular fire bricks, 9 inches by 4½ inches by 1¼ inches thick, that we obtained at a local brickyard. Unbleached all-purpose flour is needed, and the dough must rise twice before baking, which means the whole process takes at least 4 hours. We give ingredients for one medium loaf, that is, a loaf that weighs about 1 pound. Increase quantities according to your requirements.

> 1 tablespoon (1 package) active dry yeast
> 1 cup warm water
> pinch of sugar
> 3 cups unbleached all-purpose flour

Dissolve the yeast in ¼ cup of the warm water with a pinch of sugar. Set aside and allow to activate for 5 to 10 minutes. In a large mixing bowl combine the yeast with ½ cup of flour, sprinkle a little flour on top, cover with a clean dish towel, and set aside to rise in a warm place until doubled in bulk, about 1 hour. This is the first rising.

Mound 2½ cups of flour on a work surface, and form a large well in the center. Place the risen starter in the center, add ¾ cup of water, and slowly combine the flour with the starter and water, drawing it from the inside wall of the well. The dough should be stiff but pliable. If it is too stiff, add warm water, a tablespoon at a time; if too wet, add flour, a tablespoon at a time. Knead for at least 10 minutes, until a homogeneous, smooth, and elastic dough is formed. Shape the dough into a loaf. We usually make it about 10 inches long and 4 inches wide. Flour a cookie sheet or a wooden board large enough to hold the bread. Place the bread on the board, score the top by making a large X about ⅛ inch deep with a sharp knife, sprinkle the top with flour, cover with a clean dish towel, and set aside to rise in a warm place until doubled in bulk, about 2 hours. This is the second rising.

Place the bricks in the oven preheated to 400°F. about 20 minutes before you intend to bake the bread.

When the dough has risen, uncover it and slide the bread off the board or cookie sheet directly onto the bricks.

Bake for about 50 minutes, or until done. The loaf is done if it sounds hollow when tapped on the bottom.

Remove the bread from the oven, wrap in a clean dish towel, and allow to cool slowly. Do not wrap the bread in plastic, as this will destroy the crust. Store in a bread box, in a paper bag, or wrapped in a dish towel. If you wish, freeze it wrapped in an airtight plastic bag.

NOTE: The preparation of the dough can be speeded up if you use a food processor. Dissolve the yeast in ¾ cup of warm water with a pinch of sugar as described above.

Place the metal blade in the food processor and add the 3 cups of flour. With the machine running, add the yeast-water mixture through the feed tube, and continue running for about 1 minute, until the dough clears the sides of the processor bowl. It may be necessary to add 2 to 3 tablespoons of warm water, one at a time, to the dough, depending on the water-absorbing capacity of the flour.

Remove the dough from the processor bowl. Place it in a large mixing bowl, sprinkle the top with flour, and cover with wax paper and a clean dry dish towel. Set aside in a warm place to rise until doubled in bulk, about 2 hours.

When risen sufficiently, place the dough on a floured work surface. Knead for a minute or two and shape into a loaf. Flour a cookie sheet or wooden board large enough to hold the bread and place the bread on the board. Score the top as described above, sprinkle with flour, cover with a clean dish towel, and set aside to rise in a warm place until doubled in bulk, about 2 hours. From this point, proceed as above.

◆ ◆ ◆ ◆ ◆

*Pane*

*Integrale*

*Toscano*

TUSCAN
WHOLE
WHEAT
BREAD

This recipe is identical to the previous one with two exceptions: substitute 1 cup of stone-ground whole wheat flour (hard or all-purpose) for 1 cup of white flour and increase the yeast by ¼ tablespoon. In Italy, we make our bread with stone-ground whole wheat flour that has not been sifted at all, so that it contains the germ and the bran.

We recently discovered, in an excellent article on breadmaking by Abby Mandel in *The Pleasures of Cooking*, March/April 1983, how to use a food processor to make *real* whole wheat bread. We describe the technique for whole wheat Tuscan bread below.

½ cup wheat berries
1 tablespoon (1 package) active dry yeast
¾ cup warm water
pinch of sugar
2½ cups unbleached all-purpose flour

Soak the wheat berries 8 hours or overnight in hot water to cover. When ready to use, drain well and dry on paper towels.

Dissolve the yeast in the warm water with the sugar and set it aside to activate for 5 to 10 minutes.

Insert the metal blade in the food processor, and add the wheat berries and 1 cup of flour. Process for 2 minutes, until you obtain a fine-textured whole wheat flour. Add the remaining 1½ cups of flour and, with the machine running, pour in the yeast-and-water mixture; continue to process until the dough clears the sides of the bowl. You may have to add 2 tablespoons of water, one at a time, to the dough, depending on the water-absorbing capacity of the flour.

Remove the dough from the processor, place in a large mixing bowl, sprinkle the top with flour, and cover with wax paper and a clean dish towel. Set aside to rise in a warm place until doubled in bulk, about 1½ hours.

When risen, knead for a minute or two on a heavily floured work surface and shape into a loaf about 10 inches long by 4 inches wide. Flour a cookie sheet or wooden board large enough to hold the bread and transfer the bread to the board. Score the top with a large X, using a sharp knife, sprinkle with flour, cover with a clean dish towel, and set aside to rise in a warm place until doubled in bulk, about 2 hours.

Place the bricks in the oven preheated to 400°F. about 20 minutes before you intend to bake the bread.

When the dough has risen, transfer immediately to the oven, placing the bread directly on the bricks. Bake for about 50 minutes, until the bread sounds hollow when tapped on the bottom.

Remove the bread from the oven, wrap in a clean dish towel, and cool slowly. Store as described in the previous recipe.

♦ ♦ ♦ ♦ ♦

*Pasta per Pizza*

PIZZA
DOUGH

We describe below three types of dough that we use for pizza. The first is the traditional bread dough, made with oil; the second includes whole wheat flour; and the third, made with baking powder instead of yeast, is what we call instant pizza dough.

Instant pizza dough has one supreme advantage over the others. It takes literally 5 minutes to prepare, and the results are quite satisfactory. You should be warned, however, that baking powder doughs, unlike yeast doughs, do not age well. Leftover pizza made with yeast dough can be reheated the following day with almost no deterioration in quality, while pizza made with baking powder dough is best eaten right away.

*Traditional Pizza Dough*

MAKES A 12- TO 14-INCH
PIZZA

1 tablespoon (1 package) active dry yeast
¾ cup warm water
pinch of sugar
2½ cups unbleached all-purpose flour
3 tablespoons olive oil
1 teaspoon salt

In a small mixing bowl, dissolve the yeast in the warm water with sugar, and allow to activate for 5 minutes.

Place the flour on a large working surface and shape it into a mound with a large well in the center. Pour the yeast, 1 tablespoon of olive oil, and the salt into the well and slowly add the flour from the inside of the well with your fingers. Continue until almost all the flour has been added, form into a ball, and knead until the dough becomes homogeneous and elastic, about 10 minutes. You may have to add ¼ cup of warm water as you work the dough, depending on the water-absorbing capacity of the flour. The dough should be somewhat soft but not wet or mushy.

Form the dough into a ball. Oil a large mixing bowl, place the dough in the bowl, and turn to coat with oil. Cover the bowl with wax paper and a clean dish towel and set the dough aside in a warm place, free from drafts, to rise until doubled in bulk, about 1½ hours.

Preheat the oven to 425°F.

Remove the dough and knead for a few minutes. Use 2 teaspoons of olive oil to coat a 12- to 14-inch pizza pan and roll out the dough with a rolling pin until approximately half its final size. Place the dough in the pan and spread it evenly to the borders with your fingers, leaving the indentation marks. The dough should be between ⅛ inch and ¼ inch thick. Dress with desired toppings and bake for 30 minutes until the crust begins to brown. Serve hot.

### Whole Wheat Pizza Dough

1¼ tablespoons (1¼ packages) active dry yeast
¾ cup warm water
pinch of sugar
1 cup whole wheat flour
1½ cups unbleached all-purpose flour
1 teaspoon salt
3 tablespoons olive oil

Combine the yeast, warm water, and sugar, and allow the yeast to dissolve and activate. Mix together the two types of flour, place on a large working surface, mound, and form a well in the center. Add the yeast-water mixture, salt, and 1 tablespoon of olive oil to the well and, with your fingers, combine the liquids with flour. Depending on the flour, you may have to add more warm water. Knead for 10 minutes, until the dough is elastic and smooth. From this point, follow directions given in the previous recipe.

### Instant Pizza Dough

2½ cups unbleached all-purpose flour
2¾ teaspoons double-acting baking powder
1 teaspoon salt
¾ to 1 cup water
2½ tablespoons olive oil

Sift the flour, baking powder, and salt into a large mixing bowl. Add ¾ cup of water and 2 tablespoons of olive oil. Stir with a fork or wooden spoon until the ingredients are combined. Add more water if the dough is too stiff. It should be soft and manageable but not wet. Remove from the bowl, place on a floured working surface, and knead until the ingredients are thoroughly combined, about 3 minutes. The dough is now ready to be rolled out, topped, and baked. (The remaining ½ tablespoon of olive oil is to be used to oil the pan.) There is no need to let this dough rise once the topping has been added.

NOTE: The first two recipes can be prepared in a food processor.

Prepare the yeast as described in the master recipes. Insert the metal blade in the food processor. Add the flour and salt and, with the machine running, pour in the olive oil through the feed tube, then the yeast-water mixture. Continue processing until the dough clears the sides of the bowl. Add an additional tablespoon or two of water to the dough if it is too dry.

Remove the dough from the processor and shape it into a ball. Oil a large mixing bowl, place the dough in the bowl, and turn to coat with oil. Cover the dough with wax paper and a clean dish towel and set it aside to rise in a warm place until doubled in bulk, about 1½ hours.

Preheat the oven to 425°F.

From this point, proceed according to the master recipe.

♦ ♦ ♦ ♦ ♦

## Schiacciata Toscana

TUSCAN SCHIACCIATA

SERVES 6 TO 8

This kind of bread, also called white pizza (*pizza bianca*), is found all over Tuscany. It is eaten as a snack or with meals, or for breakfast. It is good any time of day with practically anything.

*Traditional or Whole Wheat Pizza Dough (see recipes)*
2 tablespoons olive oil
3 to 4 tablespoons fresh rosemary, or 1 to 2 tablespoons dried
2 teaspoons coarse salt (or to taste)

Preheat oven to 425°F.

Make pizza dough and allow to rise until doubled in bulk.

Place on a working surface, knead for a few minutes, and set aside. Oil a 15-by-10-inch jelly roll pan or cookie sheet. Shape the dough into a rectangle and roll out with a rolling pin until roughly half the size of the pan. Place the dough in the pan and spread it evenly with your fingers to cover the entire surface. Leave the indentation marks on the *schiacciata*.

Spread the olive oil over the dough and sprinkle the rosemary and the salt on top. Allow to rise covered in a warm place for 20 minutes.

Place in the oven and cook until done, about 20 minutes. Remove, let cool, cut in pieces, and serve.

### VARIATION

A few years ago in Sardinia, we had a variation of the standard *schiacciata*. It was made with the following topping:

½ cup pecorino, grated (use Pecorino Sardo if available)
2 tablespoons olive oil
⅓ cup black olives, pitted, rinsed if very salty, and
    chopped
1 large onion, thinly sliced
pinch of salt and lots of freshly ground pepper

Prepare the *schiacciata* as above. Omit the rosemary and salt. Spread 1 table-spoon of olive oil evenly over the surface and bake for 15 minutes. Remove from the oven, spread the remaining ingredients evenly over the surface, drizzle the top with the remaining olive oil, and cook until done, another 10 to 15 minutes. Let cool and serve.

NOTE: If you use Instant Pizza Dough, knead for 1 minute, roll out, put the ingredients on top, and proceed as above. Instant dough does not have to rise outside of the oven at all, since it will do so in the oven.

♦ ♦ ♦ ♦ ♦

## Pizza Napoletana

NEAPOLITAN PIZZA

SERVES 6 TO 8

This is our version of the classic Italian pizza.

one of the three pizza doughs (p. 55)
¾ cup Tomato Sauce I (see recipe)
1 cup grated mozzarella cheese
1 medium onion, thinly sliced
1 teaspoon dried oregano
salt and freshly ground pepper to taste
1 hot pepper, seeded and finely chopped (optional)
2 tablespoons olive oil

Preheat oven to 425°F.

Make pizza dough, roll it out as directed, and spread the tomato sauce evenly over the surface. (It must be thick, with very little excess liquid, otherwise the top of the pizza will remain soft.) On top, sprinkle the cheese, onion slices, oregano, salt, pepper, and, if desired, the hot pepper. Drizzle the olive oil over the surface and bake until done, about 20 minutes. If the cheese begins to burn, cover the pizza with oiled aluminum foil and continue baking.

If, when you first make this, you find that the pizza is too soggy on top because of the tomato sauce, the next time try baking the pizza dough for 5 to 10 minutes with a light coating of olive oil (2 teaspoons), until a crust begins to form. Then add the topping and bake until done.

◆ ◆ ◆ ◆ ◆

## *Pizza alla Genovese*

### GENOESE PIZZA

SERVES 6 TO 8

An interesting variation on what is considered the "real" pizza. We sometimes serve it as a main dish for a light dinner.

*one of the three pizza doughs (p. 55)*
*1 tablespoon each chopped basil and parsley*
*1 teaspoon oregano*
*1 cup grated mozzarella*
*½ cup grated sharp pecorino or Romano*
*1 large onion, thinly sliced*
*salt and freshly ground pepper to taste*
*2 tablespoons olive oil*

Preheat oven to 400°F.

Make pizza dough and roll out as directed. Sprinkle the top of the pizza first with the basil, parsley, and oregano, cover with the cheeses, then the slices of onion. Add salt and pepper to taste, drizzle with the olive oil, and bake until done, about 20 minutes. If the cheese begins to burn, cover the pizza with oiled aluminum foil and continue baking.

◆ ◆ ◆ ◆ ◆

## *Pizza Capricciosa*

### CAPRICIOUS PIZZA

MAKES 6 INDIVIDUAL PIZZAS

There was a small pizzeria near our apartment in Rome that seemed to specialize in Pizza Capricciosa. It was, literally, a meal in a dish and, perhaps for that reason, had great appeal for the pizzeria's clientele, mostly artists and students, who needed to eat cheaply but wanted to eat well. It is indeed an excellent main dish for a light dinner.

*2 large onions, thinly sliced*
*3 tablespoons olive oil*
*2 bell peppers, peeled, seeded, and thinly sliced*
*one of the three pizza doughs (p. 55)*
*1 cup Tomato Sauce I (see recipe)*
*1 cup grated mozzarella*
*salt and freshly ground pepper to taste*
*6 eggs*

Preheat oven to 425°F.

Sauté the onions in 1 tablespoon of olive oil until transparent, add the peppers and cook until tender, about 10 minutes. Set aside.

Divide the pizza dough into 6 equal parts, shape each into a ball, pat down, and roll out on a floured working surface into a circle of approximately 8 inches in diameter. Transfer the circles to oiled cookie sheets and, on top of each, spread 2 tablespoons of tomato sauce and some of the onion-and-pepper mixture. Distribute the mozzarella in small clumps on the surface, leaving space on one side or in the center for an egg. Add salt and pepper to taste and drizzle with the remaining olive oil.

Place the pizzas in the oven and bake until done, about 20 minutes. Meanwhile fry the 6 eggs individually (sunny-side up) and keep warm. When the pizzas are done, remove from the oven, place an egg on each, and serve.

### VARIATION

An alternative way is to hard-boil the eggs, peel and slice them, and arrange the slices attractively all together on one side of the pizza.

♦ ♦ ♦ ♦ ♦

## Tramezzini di Schiacciata

SCHIACCIATA
SANDWICHES

SERVES 6 TO 8

When I was a child, I spent part of every summer at Forte dei Marmi, a small seaside resort on the Versilia coast. Each morning we went to our particular *bagno* (bathing concession) on the beach, where we remained until lunchtime. The great moment of these mornings came around noon when the vendors began to arrive, selling doughnuts, coconuts, *schiacciate* sandwiches, and other snacks. We describe here how to make the *schiacciata* for the sandwiches. The fillings are described on pp. 24–25.

FOR THE SCHIACCIATA:

*Traditional or Whole Wheat Pizza Dough (see recipes)*
*2 tablespoons olive oil*
*1 teaspoon salt*
*½ teaspoon freshly ground pepper*

FOR THE SANDWICHES:

*1 tablespoon fresh cream cheese, at room temperature*
*1 tablespoon butter, at room temperature*

Preheat oven to 425°F.

Make pizza dough and allow to rise until doubled in bulk. Place on a working surface and knead for a few minutes.

Oil two 10-inch pizza pans. Roll out the dough with a rolling pin until it is roughly ¼ inch thick and place in the pans. As an alternative, spread the dough with your fingers, leaving the indentations. Drizzle the surface of the pizzas with the olive oil, sprinkle with salt and pepper, cover with a clean dish towel, and allow to rise for 40 minutes in a warm spot.

Place the *schiacciate* in the preheated oven and cook until golden, about 25 minutes. Remove and let cool.

Prepare one or more fillings of your choice.

Cut the *schiacciate* into wedges as you would a pizza, then slice each wedge in half to form sandwiches. Combine the cream cheese and butter and spread a little on the inside of the bread. Add the filling, close, and serve.

NOTE: If you use Instant Pizza Dough, knead for 1 minute, roll out, put the ingredients on top, and proceed as above. Instant dough does not have to rise outside of the oven, since it will do so in the oven.

♦ ♦ ♦ ♦ ♦

## Schiacciata al Formaggio

SCHIACCIATA
WITH
CHEESES

SERVES 6 TO 8

This *schiacciata*, made with a rich dough that contains cheeses and eggs, can be eaten as a snack, can accompany a meal as an unusual and flavorful bread, or perhaps best of all, can be used for Schiacciata Sandwiches instead of the preceding, more conventional *schiacciata*. Use the same fillings as those described for Schiacciata Sandwiches, pp. 24–25.

1 tablespoon (1 package) active dry yeast
¼ cup warm water
2½ cups unbleached all-purpose flour
2 eggs, beaten
pinch of nutmeg
⅛ teaspoon salt
¼ teaspoon freshly ground pepper
½ cup grated fontina or Gruyère
⅓ cup freshly grated Parmesan
⅓ cup grated sharp pecorino or Romano
1 tablespoon oil

Dissolve the yeast in the warm water and allow to activate for 5 minutes. Combine with ½ cup of flour in a small mixing bowl, sprinkle the top with 1 teaspoon of flour, and allow to rise for 20 minutes.

Mound the remaining flour on a floured working surface and form a large well in the center. Combine the eggs, nutmeg, salt, pepper, and cheeses and place in the well. Add the risen dough to the well, mix with the cheeses, and slowly combine with the rest of the flour. Add more water if necessary to obtain a fairly soft but not sticky dough. Knead well until elastic and homogeneous. The dough will not be perfectly smooth because of the grated cheeses.

Dust the dough with flour, wrap loosely in a clean dish towel, and allow to rise in a warm place until doubled in bulk, about 2 hours.

When ready, remove the dough from the towel and knead for a few minutes. Oil a 15-by-12-inch jelly roll pan with 1 tablespoon of oil. Roll the dough out with a rolling pin to half its final size, place it on the oiled pan, and spread it with your fingers until it covers the surface of the pan. It should be between ⅛ inch and ¼ inch thick. Cover with a dish towel, set in a warm spot, and allow to rise again for 1 hour or until doubled in size.

Preheat oven to 425°F. Bake *schiacciata* until golden, about 20 minutes.

◆ ◆ ◆ ◆ ◆

## Calzone con Mozzarella e Salsa di Pomodoro

CALZONE
WITH
MOZZARELLA
AND
TOMATO
SAUCE

SERVES 6

A calzone is a pizza folded in half, filled, sealed, and baked. And, as with pizza, it is tasty, nutritious, and can serve as a first course or as a main dish for lunch or a light dinner.

1 cup diced mozzarella
1 cup Tomato Sauce I or II (see recipes)
½ cup freshly grated Parmesan
4 tablespoons chopped basil
1 hot pepper, seeded and chopped fine (optional)
salt and freshly ground pepper to taste
2 tablespoons olive oil
one of the three pizza doughs (p. 55)
1 egg, beaten with 1 teaspoon of water

In a mixing bowl, combine the mozzarella, tomato sauce, Parmesan, basil, hot pepper, salt, pepper, and 1 tablespoon of olive oil. Mix well and set aside.

When the pizza dough is ready, divide into 6 equal parts, shape each into a ball, pat down, then roll out on a floured board until it is very thin, approximately 7 inches in diameter. Place in the center of each disk about ½ cup of the filling, leaving ½ inch along the borders of the disks free of filling. Spread the water-egg mixture on the border of each disk, fold the disks in half, and seal the edges very well by pressing them together with a fork or your fingers. It is essential to seal the calzone; otherwise the stuffing will ooze out as they bake. Place on an oiled cookie sheet, brush the tops of the calzone with the remaining tablespoon of olive oil, and bake until golden, about 20 minutes. Serve hot.

◆ ◆ ◆ ◆ ◆

*Calzone con Verdure*

CALZONE WITH VEGETABLES

SERVES 6

In this delightful variation on the traditional calzone, in which vegetables are used as filling, it is important to use a green, leafy, slightly bitter vegetable such as *broccoletti*, collard greens, or escarole. The dish depends very much on the strong, pungent flavor of the green vegetable.

*1 pound* broccoletti *or the equivalent (see above)*
*3 tablespoons olive oil*
*2 medium onions, chopped*
*2 cups peeled, seeded, and chopped fresh tomatoes, or
     canned Italian plum tomatoes, drained and
     chopped*
*2 garlic cloves, chopped*
*pinch of rosemary and oregano*
*salt and freshly ground pepper to taste*
*one of the three pizza doughs (p. 55)*
*1 egg, beaten with 1 teaspoon water*

Wash and trim the *broccoletti* and simmer until tender, about 15 minutes. Remove from the saucepan and squeeze dry. Chop roughly and set aside. Heat 2 tablespoons of olive oil in a frying pan, add the onions, and cook until transparent. Add the tomatoes, garlic, rosemary, and oregano, and cook until the tomato sauce is thick and most of the liquid evaporated, about 20 to 30 minutes. Add the *broccoletti*, salt and pepper to taste, heat through, and set aside.

When the pizza dough is ready, divide into 6 equal parts, shape into balls, pat down, and roll out on a floured board until they are very thin and approximately 7 inches in diameter. Place about ½ cup of filling in the center of each disk, leaving ½ inch along the border free of filling. Spread the egg-water mixture on the border of each disk, fold, and seal the edges very well by pressing them together with your fingers or a fork. It is essential to seal the calzone; otherwise the stuffing will ooze out as they bake. Place on an oiled cookie sheet, brush the tops of the calzone with the remaining tablespoon of olive oil, and bake until golden, about 20 minutes. Serve hot.

♦ ♦ ♦ ♦ ♦

## *Panzerotti*

## *con*

## *Formaggio*

PANZEROTTI
WITH
CHEESE

SERVES 6

These *panzerotti* are small crescent-shaped pockets of dough made with an egg yolk and butter, filled with cheese stuffing, and fried. The dough is light and flaky. Serve these as a first course, instead of pasta, or as a main course for a luncheon.

FOR THE DOUGH:

2 cups unbleached all-purpose flour
1 egg yolk
¼ pound butter, at room temperature
pinch of salt
2 tablespoons warm water or milk

FOR THE FILLING:

⅓ cup grated mozzarella
⅓ cup freshly grated Parmesan
⅓ cup finely diced Gorgonzola
2 eggs, beaten
1 tablespoon finely chopped parsley
¼ teaspoon salt
¼ teaspoon freshly ground pepper
1 egg, beaten with 1 teaspoon water
½ cup light seed oil

The dough should be made first, since it needs to rest 20 minutes. Place the flour in a mound on a work surface and form a large well in the center. In the well place the egg yolk, the butter cut into small pieces, the salt, and 1 tablespoon of water or milk. Combine the flour with the ingredients in the well, drawing the flour initially from the inner wall of the mound. Add, if needed, an additional tablespoon of water or milk. Combine thoroughly and work until a smooth, fairly soft dough is obtained. Shape into a ball, place in a dish towel, and set aside to rest for 20 minutes.

Meanwhile prepare the filling. In a mixing bowl, combine well the mozzarella, Parmesan, Gorgonzola, eggs, parsley, salt, and pepper. Set aside.

When ready, remove the dough from the dish towel and roll out on a floured work surface to a thickness of ½ inch. Fold the dough in half, roll out again, and repeat one more time. Set aside for another 10 minutes. This extra working of the dough is not essential, but it does make the dough flakier when cooked.

After 10 minutes, roll out the dough until it is very thin, cut into circles approximately 3 inches in diameter with a cookie cutter or glass, and place in the center of each circle approximately 1 tablespoon of filling, leaving the border clear of filling. Spread the egg-water mixture along the border of each circle.

Fold the dough over and seal very well. A fork can be used to assist in this operation, since a good seal is absolutely essential.

Heat the seed oil in a pan suitable for deep frying, add the *panzerotti* a few at a time, and fry until golden, about 5 minutes. Remove and drain on paper towels. Keep warm until ready to serve.

♦ ♦ ♦ ♦ ♦

## *Panzerotti*
## *con Verdure*

PANZEROTTI
WITH
VEGETABLES

SERVES 6

These look quite similar to the Panzerotti with Cheese in the preceding recipe but are, in fact, quite different, since in this recipe one of the conventional pizza doughs is used.

1 pound spinach or escarole
2 garlic cloves, chopped
1 tablespoon capers, chopped
⅓ cup olives, pitted, rinsed in cold water if very salty,
    and chopped
1 teaspoon pine nuts, roughly chopped
1 tablespoon raisins, soaked for 10 minutes in ½ cup
    warm water, drained, and chopped
2 eggs, beaten
freshly ground pepper to taste
one of the three pizza doughs (p. 55)
1 egg, beaten with 1 teaspoon water
½ cup light seed oil

Wash and trim the spinach or escarole, place in a saucepan, and simmer, without adding water, over a low heat until cooked, about 5 minutes for spinach, 10 minutes for escarole. Remove from the heat when cooked, allow to cool, squeeze very dry, then chop fine and place in a mixing bowl. Add the garlic, capers, olives, pine nuts, raisins, eggs, and pepper. Combine well.

On a large floured work surface, roll the pizza dough until it is very thin. It may be easier to divide the dough into 2 balls and roll them out separately. Using a cookie cutter or glass, cut the dough into circles approximately 3 inches in diameter and place on each about 1 tablespoon of the filling, leaving the border clear of filling. Spread the beaten egg mixture along the border of each circle, fold in half, and seal very well. Use a fork to assist in this, since the seal must be perfect.

Heat the seed oil in a pan suitable for deep frying, add the *panzerotti*, and fry a few at a time until golden, about 5 minutes. Remove and drain on paper towels. Keep warm until ready to serve.

## ◆ ◆ ◆ ◆ ◆

# *Torta di Pomodori, Formaggio, e Olive*

## TOMATO, CHEESE, AND OLIVE FLAN

SERVES 6

In this recipe, capers, tomatoes, cheese, eggs, cream, and olives are combined and baked in a pastry shell. The dish actually falls between a pizza and a flan and can serve either as a substantial first course or as the main course for a light supper or luncheon.

FOR THE DOUGH:

*2 cups unbleached all-purpose flour*
*6 tablespoons butter*
*pinch of salt*
*6 tablespoons cold water*

FOR THE FILLING:

*3 tablespoons capers, chopped*
*⅓ cup thinly sliced Gruyère*
*1 cup canned Italian plum tomatoes, drained and chopped*
*2 eggs, beaten*
*½ cup milk*
*½ cup heavy cream*
*½ cup black Italian olives, pitted, rinsed in cold water if salty, and cut in half*

Sift the flour into a large mixing bowl, add the butter and salt, and combine with the flour, using your fingers or a pastry knife. The dough should have the texture of coarse oatmeal. Place the dough on a lightly floured work surface and add the water, 1 tablespoon at a time, mixing swiftly with your fingers, until a soft, pliable, but not sticky dough is obtained. Knead it a few times with the heel of your hand to combine the flour and butter. Roll the dough into a ball, wrap in wax paper, and place in the refrigerator for 30 minutes.

Preheat the oven to 375°F. Butter a 10-inch flan pan well and set aside.

When ready, roll the dough out to a thickness of ¼ inch and place it carefully in the flan pan, draping any extra dough over the edges of the pan. Press the dough firmly onto the bottom and sides of the pan, and cut off any extra dough. Prick the dough all over with the tines of a fork. Butter a sheet of aluminum foil and place it, buttered side down, on the dough. Place baking weights or dried beans on the foil to prevent the dough from buckling, and bake in the preheated oven for 10 minutes. At this point, remove the foil and weights, and bake for another 5 minutes. Remove the crust from the oven, and reset the oven to 350°F.

Spread the capers evenly on the bottom of the crust, distribute the cheese over the capers, then add the tomatoes. In a mixing bowl, combine the eggs, milk, and cream and pour the mixture over the ingredients in the pie shell. Place in the preheated oven and bake for 20 to 30 minutes, until the custard is firm.

Garnish the top of the flan with the olive halves and serve warm or at room temperature directly from the flan pan.

# FIRST
# COURSES

# Pasta

For most people, pasta, spaghetti, macaroni, tagliatelle, and other types of noodles made from wheat flour *are* Italian food. Although pasta dishes are today enjoyed throughout the peninsula, that is something of an exaggeration. Italians include, among dishes that serve as first courses, soups and other specialties that run the gamut from conventional pasta such as spaghetti through ravioli, lasagne, cannelloni, gnocchi, polenta, risotti, and timballi. In general, in the south *pasta asciutta* (dried pasta), especially the packaged dry variety made without eggs, is the primary first course. In the north, homemade egg noodles, dumplings, cornmeal, rice, and soups are also served.

The making of pasta could not be simpler. In one form or another, it has been made in areas of what is now modern Italy probably since Roman times. Essentially, it is wheat ground into flour, combined with water or some other liquid, rolled thin, cut into ribbons or some other shape, cooked immediately or at a later time in boiling water, and served with a sauce. Although commercial production of pasta dates back to the Renaissance, until relatively recently, especially in the north, most pasta was made at home. Given the simplicity of the process, the ingredients, and the delicacy of homemade varieties, this is hardly surprising.

A striking feature of both the homemade and packaged types is the enormous variety of shapes and sizes in which they come. Non-Italians are often puzzled by this variety. Pasta is, after all, pasta, whatever the shape or size. The essence of pasta, however, is not simply the ingredients that compose the dough but the way in which the cooked dough combines with a sauce or stuffing. And this is very much affected by the shape, size, and texture of the pasta, the ingredients of the sauce or stuffing, and the way in which they are prepared. As it turns out, and as a little experimenting on your own will confirm, some sauces are more suitable for certain types of pasta than for others. For example, delicate cream or cheese sauces go best with homemade fettuccine, while robust tomato or vegetable sauces are more suited to short, stout macaroni. Ribbed penne or rigatoni create more surface area for the sauce to attach itself than either unribbed varieties or flat noodles.

As you will see in the recipes, we link different sauces with different types of pasta. While there are some traditional combinations such as penne with spicy tomato sauce or pesto with trenette (similar to fettuccine in shape but made without eggs), there are no hard-and-fast rules that bind pastas and sauces. Additional sauces for pasta can be found in the Sauces chapter.

There are two principal types of pasta, the dry commercial variety and the fresh homemade type. The best of the commercial pasta comes from the south, from the Abruzzi and Campagna in particular, and is made with hard wheat flour and water. Although the wheat itself is mostly imported from the American Midwest and from Canada, the southern Italian brands are far superior to those made in North America, and we urge you to use them.

Fresh or homemade pasta is made with flour, usually all-purpose or hard wheat flour, eggs, oil, and salt. In Genoa, it is made with water instead of eggs; in Emilia-Romagna, oil is omitted. Fresh pasta made with eggs is now available commercially in Italy and in many metropolitan areas in North America. The commercial variety, however, is never quite as good as pasta made at home, so we strongly encourage you to make your own. As you will see once you've done it a few times, it really is a very simple process that takes less than an hour from laying out the ingredients to cleaning up.

## HOW TO COOK PASTA

Even the best pasta can be ruined through improper cooking. Although nothing could be easier than boiling noodles in salted water, it can be, and often is, done incorrectly. Here are simple rules to follow for foolproof results.

1. Use enough water to allow each noodle to cook separately. If the noodles are crowded, the starch in the wheat will cause them to adhere to one another with disastrous results. We calculate as a minimum 1 quart of water for ¼ pound of pasta. Also, use a large pot, an 8-quart stockpot for 1 pound of pasta.
2. Bring the water to a rapid boil, then add about 1 tablespoon of salt (coarse salt is preferable) for each pound of pasta. Salt flavors the pasta and also raises the boiling temperature of the water. Hotter water seals in the starch and improves the texture of the cooked pasta.
3. Add the pasta all at once to the rapidly boiling water, stir in long, dry noodles as they soften, and cook at a slow boil, stirring frequently with a wooden spoon, until done. Although some cooks add 1 tablespoon of oil to the water to prevent sticking, this is not necessary if the pasta is cooked in abundant water.
4. Most important of all, *do not overcook the pasta*. Italians like it al dente, which means one can feel the pasta between one's teeth, and this is the only way to eat it.

For commercial pasta, test it by removing a noodle and biting it after 5 to 7 minutes of cooking, depending on the thickness of the noodle, and at frequent intervals thereafter. The pasta is cooked when the hardness at the center of the noodle disappears. It will still be firm, that is al dente. Drain the pasta immediately by pouring it, water and all, into a colander placed in the sink. Do not rinse with cold water. Put the pasta at once into a heated serving bowl, add cheese if called for, add the sauce, combine well but quickly, and serve immediately. Some cooks add a cup of cold water to the stockpot before removing it from the stove to reduce the water temperature quickly. This is not necessary if you move fast. Some cooks also add butter, a tablespoon per pound of pasta, to the noodles before serving for all sauces made with butter. This is strictly a matter of taste.

Homemade pasta cooks much more rapidly than commercial pasta and the fresher, the faster. Test after 30 seconds of boiling and frequently thereafter. Otherwise, the process is the same for dry and fresh varieties.

The key features of good pasta cooking are: first, pasta that is cooked al dente; second, pasta that is combined with the sauce immediately after being drained; and third, pasta that is served as soon as it is combined with the sauce. In Italy, cooks will prepare many dishes ahead of time, but never the pasta.

## *Quantities*

In Italy, the general rule of thumb is 100 grams, a little less than ¼ pound, of pasta per person for a pasta course with other dishes to follow. We have given recipes calling for 1 pound of pasta for 6 people, based on the assumption, borne out by experience, that North Americans eat less pasta than Italians. However, adjust quantities to suit the appetite of your family and friends.

◆ ◆ ◆ ◆ ◆

## *Pasta Fatta*

## *in Casa*

### HOMEMADE
### PASTA

Some contend that the only homemade pasta worthy of the name is the kind kneaded by hand and rolled out with a rolling pin. Others argue that it doesn't matter how the pasta is kneaded or rolled out as long as it is cut by hand. From our point of view, the differences in results are relatively minor. What really matters are the ingredients. Use a good hard wheat or all-purpose flour, preferably unbleached, fresh eggs, and good olive oil and you will turn out high-quality homemade pasta whether you make it by hand, by hand-cranked machine, or by one of the new totally automatic pasta machines.

In the recipe that follows, we describe how to make pasta with a hand-cranked machine. The process is very simple and relatively quick once you get the knack. There are a few dishes for which the pasta must be hand-rolled, for example, Rotolo Verde, and, for these, we describe the process in the specific recipe. However, it should be stressed that while hand kneading and rolling takes more time than doing the same tasks by machine, it is not difficult. The dough must be kneaded until smooth and elastic, about 10 to 15 minutes, then rolled out paper thin and evenly on a floured board.

It is useful to prepare your work space properly and lay out your ingredients before you begin. An ideal work surface for making pasta is a kitchen table. The pasta machine can be clamped to the tabletop and the rolled-out pasta can be placed on the top to rest before cutting. If you do not have a kitchen table, a counter top is fine, but clear two spaces, each roughly 3 feet long, one for rolling out the dough, the other for laying out the sheets to rest before cutting.

The proportions given below are for 2 cups of flour, roughly ½ pound. That makes enough fettucine for about 3 people. To increase or decrease the amount of pasta, increase or decrease the ingredients in the exact ratios given below, that is, 1 cup of flour to 1 extra-large egg to 1 teaspoon of olive oil.

> 2 cups unbleached all-purpose or hard wheat flour
> 2 extra-large eggs
> pinch of salt
> 2 teaspoons olive oil
> water as necessary

Mound the flour on a work surface and form a large well in the center. Break the eggs into the well, add salt and oil, and stir with a fork until combined. Carefully draw the flour from the inside wall of the well with your fingers or a fork and combine with the liquid in the center. Continue until a soft dough is formed. Add the rest of the flour and knead for a few minutes until the ingredients are thoroughly mixed. The dough should be stiff but not unmanageable. If it is too dry, as it may be if you use hard wheat flour, add water and knead until incorporated; if it is too wet, add a little flour. Divide the dough into 2 or 3 balls, and cover with a dish towel.

Clamp the pasta machine to the work surface. Set the rollers on the widest setting, take one of the balls, flatten it with your hands, and pass it through the rollers. Fold in three, making the dough into a package the width of the machine and pass through the rollers again. Continue this process about eight to ten times until a smooth homogeneous dough has been obtained. If the dough is too wet or sticky, sprinkle flour on the surface before folding. Reduce the opening of the rollers and pass the dough through once, without folding. Continue this process, each time reducing the opening one notch, until you have obtained the desired thickness. Since egg pasta shrinks and thus thickens on cooking, the ultimate or penultimate setting usually makes the best pasta. Place the pasta sheet on a dry, lightly floured dish towel and repeat the process with the remaining dough. Allow the pasta to rest for 10 minutes.

Meanwhile, attach the cutter to the machine. With a knife cut the pasta into sheets approximately 18 to 20 inches long. When ready simply pass the pasta through the cutter, holding the dough with one hand while turning the crank with the other.

The pasta can be cooked at once or dried and cooked later. The easiest way to dry pasta is to place a broom handle or dowel between two chairs and drape the pasta over it. Once it is dried, it can be stored in a dry place for months.

Pasta kneaded and rolled out by machine can also be cut by hand. For example, if you want to make *pappardelle*—broad flat noodles—simply flour the rolled-out pasta, roll it up on itself, choose the width you want, and cut it with a sharp knife. Each cut produces a noodle.

NOTE: The flour, eggs, salt, and oil can be combined and partially kneaded in a food processor. It is, however, necessary to alter quantities. Place the metal blade in the processor, add 2¼ cups of flour and a pinch of salt to the processor bowl, and, with the machine running, add 2 teaspoons of olive oil through the feed tube, then, one at a time, 3 whole extra-large eggs. Continue running the processor until the dough clears the sides of the bowl. Remove the dough from the processor, divide into 2 or 3 balls, and cover with a clean dish towel. Clamp the pasta machine to the work surface and proceed as described in the above recipe.

If you want less rich pasta, substitute approximately 1 tablespoon of water for the third egg.

♦ ♦ ♦ ♦ ♦

## Pasta Verde

GREEN
SPINACH
PASTA

MAKES ½ POUND PASTA

5 to 6 ounces fresh spinach
2 cups unbleached all-purpose flour
2 extra-large eggs
2 teaspoons olive oil
pinch of salt
water as necessary

Trim the spinach, wash it very well, place in a saucepan without water, and cook until tender, about 10 minutes. Drain, rinse with cold water, squeeze as dry as possible, and chop very fine or process in a food processor or blender.

Mound the flour on a work surface, form a large shallow well in the center, add the eggs, oil, spinach, salt, and combine the ingredients. Carefully mix the flour with the liquid ingredients, drawing the flour from the inside of the well until a moist dough is formed. Then combine with the remaining flour and knead until the ingredients are mixed and a fairly stiff but manageable dough is obtained. Add more water or flour as necessary.

From this point proceed as directed for Homemade Pasta (see recipe).

NOTE: The flour, eggs, spinach, oil, and salt can be combined in a food processor, but the proportions must be altered. Prepare the spinach as described above. Place the metal blade in the processor, add to the processor bowl 2¼ cups of flour, the spinach, and the salt. With the machine running, add through the feed tube 2 teaspoons of olive oil and, one at a time, 3 extra-large eggs. Continue running until the dough clears the sides of the bowl. Remove from the processor, divide into 3 balls, and cover with a clean dish towel. Clamp the pasta machine to the work surface and proceed according to the master recipe.

If you want a less rich pasta, substitute approximately 1 tablespoon of water for the third egg.

♦ ♦ ♦ ♦ ♦

## Pasta Rossa

RED

PASTA

MAKES ½ POUND PASTA

The coloring in this case is tomato paste. It is, otherwise, identical to green pasta.

2 cups unbleached hard or all-purpose flour
2 extra-large eggs
2 teaspoons tomato paste
pinch of salt
2 teaspoons olive oil
water as necessary

The process is exactly the same as that described for Homemade Pasta (see recipe), with the addition of 2 teaspoons of tomato paste to the liquid ingredients in the well. You can also use a food processor to combine the ingredients as indicated in the note to the preceding recipe.

♦ ♦ ♦ ♦ ♦

*Spaghetti con Aglio, Olio, e Peperoncino*

SPAGHETTI
WITH
GARLIC,
OIL, AND
HOT PEPPER

SERVES 4 TO 6

This dish relies on absolutely basic ingredients, could not be simpler to prepare, and is delicious. In fact, it's so tasty that it can be served for almost any occasion, from an "instant" meal to planned dinner parties.

⅓ cup olive oil
3 to 4 garlic cloves, roughly chopped
½ teaspoon dried hot pepper, roughly chopped
pinch of salt
1 pound spaghetti or spaghettini
½ teaspoon freshly ground black pepper
3 tablespoons chopped parsley

Heat the oil in a small frying pan and sauté the garlic and hot pepper until the garlic begins to color. Remove immediately from the heat, since the garlic will continue to brown slightly in the hot oil. Add salt and keep warm, or reheat just before combining with the pasta.

Cook the pasta in 4 quarts of rapidly boiling salted water, until al dente, stirring occasionally with a wooden spoon. Drain well and place in a warm serving bowl. Immediately pour the garlic and pepper sauce over the pasta. Add the black pepper and parsley and mix well.

♦ ♦ ♦ ♦ ♦

*Spaghetti con Melanzane*

SPAGHETTI
WITH
EGGPLANT

SERVES 4 TO 6

The secret to success with this dish is to complete the cooking of the pasta and the eggplant at the same time, so that the fried eggplant is added to the hot pasta immediately after being cooked.

2 medium eggplants, approximately 2 pounds
1 tablespoon salt
2 tablespoons flour
1 pound spaghetti
⅓ to ½ cup light seed oil
¼ cup freshly grated Parmesan cheese
¼ cup freshly grated pecorino or Romano
4 tablespoons butter

Peel the eggplants and cut them into ¼-inch-thick strips about 2 inches long. Sprinkle with salt and let drain in a colander for 30 minutes, then rinse, pat dry between paper towels, and dredge with flour.

At this point bring 4 quarts of salted water to a boil, drop in the spaghetti, and cook until al dente, stirring occasionally with a wooden spoon.

While the spaghetti cooks, heat the oil in a pan suitable for deep frying and rapidly fry the eggplant strips until golden. Drain on paper towels and keep warm.

Drain the spaghetti and combine with the Parmesan, pecorino or Romano, and butter. Add the fried eggplant. Mix well and serve immediately.

♦ ♦ ♦ ♦ ♦

*Spaghetti con Melanzane e Pomodori*

SPAGHETTI
WITH
EGGPLANT
AND
TOMATO
SAUCE

SERVES 4 TO 6

Although the ingredients in this dish and the previous one are similar, they are not identical, and the addition of tomato sauce makes a world of difference. The two dishes are quite distinct, and both are excellent.

2 medium eggplants, approximately 2 pounds
1 tablespoon salt
2 tablespoons olive oil
2 garlic cloves, chopped
2 pounds tomatoes, peeled, seeded, and roughly
    chopped, or 2 cups canned Italian plum tomatoes,
    drained and chopped
salt and freshly ground pepper to taste
2 tablespoons flour
⅓ to ½ cup light seed oil
1 pound spaghetti or spaghettini
¼ cup freshly grated pecorino or Romano
1 tablespoon chopped parsley

Peel the eggplants and cut them into ¼-inch-thick strips about 2 inches long. Sprinkle with salt and let drain in a colander for 30 minutes.

Heat the oil in a frying pan and sauté the garlic. When it begins to color add the tomatoes, and cook over medium heat for about 20 minutes until the sauce thickens. Add salt and pepper to taste (remembering that pecorino and Romano are both salty cheeses). Take off the stove and keep warm.

Meanwhile, rinse the eggplants, pat dry between paper towels, and dredge with the flour. Heat the seed oil and fry the eggplants until golden. Remove with a slotted spoon, drain on paper towels, and keep warm.

Cook the spaghetti or spaghettini in 4 quarts of rapidly boiling salted water, stirring occasionally with a wooden spoon. Cook until al dente. Drain and place in a warm serving bowl. Sprinkle with the pecorino or Romano, add the tomato sauce, the fried eggplants, and the chopped parsley. Combine and serve immediately.

◆ ◆ ◆ ◆ ◆

*Spaghetti al Gorgonzola*

SPAGHETTI
WITH
GORGONZOLA

SERVES 4 TO 6

This is a simple but excellent pasta dish. The exact ratio of butter to Gorgonzola must be adapted to the sharpness of the cheese and the taste of the chef.

½ cup crumbled Gorgonzola cheese
2 tablespoons unsalted butter (more if the Gorgonzola is strong)
1 pound spaghetti or spaghettini

Combine the Gorgonzola and butter in a heated serving bowl. Cream them together with a fork.

Cook the spaghetti or spaghettini in 4 quarts rapidly boiling salted water, stirring occasionally with a wooden spoon, until al dente.

Drain and transfer the pasta immediately to the serving bowl that contains the cheese-and-butter mixture. Toss to coat the pasta with the sauce and serve hot.

VARIATION

Our son Lorenzo has a variation of this sauce that he prefers. It is lighter, less sharp, and creamier. Combine ½ cup of crumbled Gorgonzola with 1 tablespoon of unsalted butter, 5 tablespoons of thick heated cream, and 3 tablespoons of freshly grated Parmesan in the serving bowl. Then proceed as above.

♦ ♦ ♦ ♦ ♦

## Fettuccine Verdi alla Ricotta

### GREEN FETTUCCINE WITH RICOTTA

SERVES 4 TO 6

Since the flavor of this dish depends on the quality of the cheeses, make an effort to obtain good, fresh creamy ricotta and a strong aged pecorino or Romano. If the ingredients are first-rate, the results are mouth-watering.

FOR THE GREEN FETTUCCINE:

*use 4 cups flour (see recipe)*

FOR THE SAUCE:

*1 cup fresh whole milk ricotta*
*½ cup freshly grated well-aged pecorino, preferably from Sardinia, or Romano*
*3 tablespoons butter, melted*
*¼ cup milk or cream*
*¼ teaspoon freshly ground black pepper*
*¼ teaspoon cayenne pepper or a few drops of Tabasco sauce*
*1 tablespoon finely chopped parsley*
*1 tablespoon finely chopped fresh chives or scallions (white parts only)*
*¼ cup freshly grated Parmesan*

Place the ricotta and the pecorino or Romano in a large mixing bowl and combine thoroughly with a wooden spoon. Add the melted butter, milk or cream, black pepper, and cayenne and mix well. The sauce should have the consistency of thick sour cream. If it is too dense, add more milk or cream.

Prepare the green fettuccine according to the master recipe and cook in 4 quarts of rapidly boiling salted water, stirring occasionally with a wooden spoon, until al dente.

Place half the sauce in a heated serving bowl, drain the cooked pasta, and combine it with the sauce. Add the remaining sauce and sprinkle the parsley and chives or scallions and the Parmesan on top. Combine and serve immediately.

♦ ♦ ♦ ♦ ♦

*Fettuccine*

*alla Crema*

FETTUCCINE
WITH
CREAM

SERVES 4 TO 6

Simple, elegant, delicious—there is no other way to describe this dish made famous by the Ristorante Alfredo in Rome.

*Homemade Pasta (see recipe), using 4 cups flour*
*1 cup butter*
*⅔ cup heavy cream*
*2 cups freshly grated Parmesan*
*pinch of nutmeg*
*salt and freshly ground pepper to taste*

Make the pasta, following instructions for preparation of fettuccine.

Melt the butter in a small saucepan, add the cream, 1½ cups of Parmesan, nutmeg, salt, and pepper, and simmer over low heat (do not boil) for 5 minutes. Keep the sauce warm.

Cook the pasta in 4 quarts of rapidly boiling salted water, stirring occasionally with a wooden spoon, until al dente.

Drain the pasta and place in a warm serving dish. Pour the warm cream sauce over the fettuccine, toss gently until coated, and serve immediately.

Freshly ground pepper is often added to the pasta at the table. Serve with freshly grated Parmesan.

♦ ♦ ♦ ♦ ♦

*Paglia e*

*Fieno*

STRAW
AND
HAY

SERVES 4 TO 6

We first ran across this pasta dish, a mixture of green and white egg noodles served with a cream sauce, many years ago in a small trattoria in Vecchia Roma, the area of Rome around the Piazza Navona. At the time, the dish was quite unusual, perhaps even unique to that trattoria, and although it is much more commonplace in Rome and elsewhere today, it has lost none of its appeal. Paglia e Fieno makes a most attractive and elegant first course for a dinner party. Use fresh noodles if at all possible.

FOR THE PASTA:

*Homemade Pasta (p. 73), made into white fettuccine*
*Green Spinach Pasta (p. 75), made into fettuccine*

FOR THE SAUCE:

4 *tablespoons butter*

3 *tablespoons finely chopped onion*

1 *teaspoon cornstarch*

1 *cup heavy cream*

1½ *cups washed, trimmed, and thinly sliced mushrooms*

⅓ *cup fresh or frozen cooked peas*

1 *cup freshly grated Parmesan*

Make the pasta.

In a small saucepan melt 3 tablespoons of butter, add the onion, and sauté until golden. Add the cornstarch, stirring constantly. Stir in the cream, bring to a simmer, remove from the heat, and set aside.

In a frying pan, melt 1 tablespoon of butter, add the mushrooms, and sauté for 2 minutes over high heat. Add the peas and heat through. Blend the mushrooms and peas into the cream sauce, stir in ½ cup of Parmesan, combine well, and keep warm.

Cook the pasta in 4 quarts of rapidly boiling salted water, stirring occasionally with a wooden spoon, until al dente. Drain the noodles, place them in a heated serving bowl, add the sauce, combine well, and serve immediately. Pass the remaining ½ cup of Parmesan at the table.

♦ ♦ ♦ ♦ ♦

## Bucatini Briganteschi

BUCATINI HIGHWAYMAN

SERVES 4 TO 6

When I was a child, my folk hero was a southern Italian Robin Hood–type outlaw called the bandito Giuliano. Although I now find it incomprehensible, I was for a time a poor eater, and my grandfather, clever man that he was, told me that this was the favorite sauce of my hero. Naturally I could never get enough of this particular dish. Whatever the real origin of this recipe, the name has stuck and so has the pleasure in eating it.

2 *tablespoons butter*

6 *tablespoons olive oil*

4 *medium tomatoes, peeled, seeded, and coarsely*
   *chopped, or 1½ cups canned Italian plum*
   *tomatoes, drained and chopped*

½ *fresh or dried hot pepper, seeded and chopped*

1 *tablespoon whole capers*

¼ cup black Italian olives, pitted, rinsed in cold water
if salty, and chopped
½ teaspoon oregano
1 garlic clove, chopped
1 teaspoon freshly ground black pepper, or to taste
1 pound bucatini (spaghetti-type noodles with a hole
down the center)
3 tablespoons freshly grated Parmesan
2 tablespoons chopped parsley

Place the butter and 3 tablespoons of olive oil in a saucepan and heat. Add the
tomatoes and cook for 3 minutes. Add the hot pepper, capers, olives, oregano,
and garlic. Simmer, stirring occasionally, for 20 minutes or until the sauce thickens. Add the black pepper and keep warm.

Cook the bucatini in 4 quarts of rapidly boiling salted water, stirring occasionally with a wooden spoon, until al dente. Drain and place in a warm serving
bowl. Add the Parmesan and the sauce and combine. Add 3 tablespoons of olive
oil and the parsley and serve immediately.

♦ ♦ ♦ ♦ ♦

*Fusilli ai*

*Capperi*

FUSILLI
WITH
CAPERS

SERVES 4 TO 6

This sauce, like pesto, has a base of fresh basil
leaves, but, unlike pesto, it includes capers and
prepared mustard, thus giving it a special zest. It
can be made in a blender or food processor, but the
flavor is stronger and the texture smoother if made
with a mortar and pestle. Try to obtain fusilli, a
pasta similar to spaghetti but twisted like long cork-
screws to catch the sauce. If fusilli are unavailable,
use spaghetti or fettuccine.

½ cup packed fresh basil leaves
1 to 2 garlic cloves
3 tablespoons capers
3 tablespoons prepared mustard
salt and freshly ground black pepper to taste
½ cup olive oil
1 pound fusilli
½ cup freshly grated Parmesan (optional)

Place the basil leaves, garlic, and capers in a mortar and mash with a pestle until
a smooth paste is obtained. (If using a blender or food processor, put in the basil,

garlic, and capers all at once and process until smooth but not liquid.) Add the mustard, salt, and pepper, and, while stirring vigorously with a spoon, or while processing, add the olive oil a little at a time until all of it is incorporated.

Cook the pasta in 4 quarts of rapidly boiling salted water, stirring occasionally with a wooden spoon, until al dente. Drain and place in a warm serving bowl. Pour the sauce over the pasta, mix well, and serve immediately.

Some may wish to add grated Parmesan, but the dish is also good without it.

### ♦ ♦ ♦ ♦ ♦
### *Linguini con Fiori di Zucca*

The large yellow flowers of the zucchini plant make an excellent, exotic pasta sauce. They are hard to come by if you don't grow your own, but not necessarily impossible. Ask your friends who have gardens, try your local greengrocers, and scan Italian markets. The results, we think, are well worth the effort.

**LINGUINI WITH ZUCCHINI FLOWERS**

SERVES 4 TO 6

3 garlic cloves, finely chopped
3 tablespoons finely chopped parsley
3 tablespoons olive oil
3 cups zucchini flowers, loosely packed (handle gently— they are delicate)
½ cup dry white wine
2 tablespoons Tomato Sauce I (see recipe)
salt and freshly ground pepper to taste
1 pound linguini or spaghettini
freshly grated Parmesan (optional)

Sauté the garlic and parsley in the olive oil for 1 or 2 minutes over medium heat until the garlic browns. Remove from the heat.

Carefully rinse the zucchini flowers. Drain them on a kitchen towel. Remove and discard the stem and the firm pollen-bearing stalk from each flower and cut the flowers into thin slices, including the hard portion just above the stem.

Add the sliced flowers to the oil and garlic, return to the heat, and simmer gently for 2 or 3 minutes. Add the wine and let evaporate another 2 or 3 minutes. Stir in the tomato sauce, heat through, and add salt and pepper to taste. Keep warm.

Cook the linguini or spaghettini in 4 quarts of rapidly boiling salted water, stirring occasionally with a wooden spoon, until al dente. Drain well.

Place 4 tablespoons of the sauce in a heated serving bowl. Add the pasta and mix well. Top with the rest of the sauce. Combine and serve with or without grated Parmesan.

♦ ♦ ♦ ♦ ♦

*Conchiglie*

*Primavera*

*alla Virginia*

VIRGINIA'S
SHELLS
WITH
FRESH
VEGETABLES

SERVES 6

*4 tablespoons olive oil*
*½ cup roughly chopped onion*
*4 garlic cloves, chopped*
*½ cup roughly chopped zucchini*
*½ cup washed, trimmed, and thinly sliced mushrooms*
*½ cup roughly chopped broccoli flowerets*
*½ cup roughly chopped red or green bell pepper*
*1 medium tomato, roughly chopped*
*½ teaspoon salt*
*pepper to taste*
*½ cup Tomato Sauce I or II (see recipes)*
*1 pound shells, wheels, or short, stout pasta*
*2 tablespoons butter*
*⅓ cup freshly grated Parmesan*
*1 tablespoon chopped basil*
*1 tablespoon chopped parsley*

Heat the olive oil and sauté the onion until transparent. Add the garlic and sauté 1 minute, stirring constantly. Stir in the zucchini, mushrooms, broccoli, and bell pepper and sauté over medium heat for 5 minutes, until the vegetables begin to soften but are still crisp. Blend in the tomato and warm through. Add the salt and pepper. Keep warm.

In a separate pan warm up the tomato sauce.

Cook the pasta in 4 quarts of rapidly boiling salted water, stirring occasionally with a wooden spoon, until al dente. Drain and place in a heated serving bowl. Dot the pasta with the butter, sprinkle with the Parmesan, basil, and parsley, and add the tomato sauce. Combine, top with the sautéed vegetables, and serve immediately.

### VARIATION

As an alternative, instead of topping the pasta with the vegetables, place them in the center of a heated dish, surround them with the pasta, and serve.

♦ ♦ ♦ ♦ ♦

## Penne all'Arrabbiata

PENNE
WITH
SPICY
TOMATO
SAUCE

SERVES 4 TO 6

Almost every Roman trattoria serves some version of this pasta dish, a very simple way to enliven a commonplace tomato sauce. The name literally means "angry," and in Rome, if you like it really hot (as we do), you ask for it very angry, *molto arrabbiata*.

1 pound penne
3 tablespoons olive oil
2 to 3 garlic cloves, crushed in a mortar or minced
1 or 2 teaspoons hot pepper flakes or 1 small fresh, hot
    pepper, seeded and finely chopped
1½ cups Tomato Sauce I (see recipe)
¼ teaspoon salt
½ teaspoon pepper
3 tablespoons chopped parsley
½ cup freshly grated Parmesan

Cook the pasta in 4 quarts of rapidly boiling salted water, stirring occasionally with a wooden spoon, until al dente.

While the pasta cooks, prepare the sauce. Heat the olive oil in a saucepan. Add the garlic and hot pepper and sauté for 1 minute, stirring constantly. Add the tomato sauce, salt, and pepper and cook for 5 minutes. Drain the penne when cooked. Put 3 tablespoons of the sauce on the bottom of a heated serving dish. Add the pasta and top it with the rest of the sauce. Combine, sprinkle with the chopped parsley, and serve immediately. Pass Parmesan at the table for those who want it.

♦ ♦ ♦ ♦ ♦

## Penne al Forno

BAKED
PENNE

SERVES 4 TO 6

This is one of our favorite dishes. Its flavor is delicate but distinctive, its appearance is elegant and impressive, and it is surprisingly easy to prepare.

1 pound penne or rigatoni
Béchamel Sauce (see recipe) made with:
    3¼ cups milk
    7 tablespoons butter
    8 tablespoons flour
    ¾ teaspoon salt
    ¼ teaspoon white pepper
1 cup freshly grated Parmesan

Preheat the oven to 375°F.

Cook the pasta in 4 quarts of rapidly boiling salted water, stirring occasionally with a wooden spoon, until al dente.

While the pasta cooks make the béchamel sauce. Just before the sauce is done add the Parmesan and continue cooking until the ingredients are well blended.

Generously butter an attractive 9-by-15-inch baking dish, and add the pasta. Spread the béchamel sauce evenly over the pasta. Allow some of the sauce to penetrate by moving the pasta gently with a wooden spoon. Most of the sauce should, however, remain on top.

Place in the oven for 45 minutes or until the top is browned. Serve directly from the baking dish.

♦ ♦ ♦ ♦ ♦

## *Rigatoni Puttanesca*

RIGATONI
WITH
RAW
TOMATO
SAUCE

SERVES 4 TO 6

1 pound ripe tomatoes, or 1½ cups canned Italian plum
    tomatoes, drained
3 garlic cloves, minced
3 tablespoons olives, pitted, rinsed in cold water if salty,
    and chopped
1 tablespoon capers, chopped
3 tablespoons chopped basil
⅓ cup olive oil
salt to taste
1 teaspoon freshly ground pepper
1 pound rigatoni or other short, stout pasta

Remove seeds and excess liquid from the tomatoes and chop fine. Put in a bowl and add the rest of the ingredients (except pasta). You may not need additional salt if the olives are salty.

Cook the pasta in 4 quarts of rapidly boiling salted water, stirring occasionally, until al dente. Drain very well, shaking the colander to remove excess water, and place the pasta in a warm serving bowl. Add the sauce, combine, and serve immediately.

### VARIATION

The *puttanesca* sauce can also be cooked. Cook the tomatoes with oil and garlic until a thick sauce is obtained, about 25 minutes. Mix in the rest of the ingredients (except pasta). Warm through and pour over the pasta when cooked.

♦ ♦ ♦ ♦ ♦

### Maccheroni allo Zafferano

MACARONI
WITH
CAULIFLOWER
AND
SAFFRON

SERVES 4 TO 6

2 tablespoons butter
1 large onion, finely chopped
2 garlic cloves, finely chopped
1 medium cauliflower, coarsely chopped
¼ teaspoon saffron, soaked in ¼ cup warm water
¼ cup currants, soaked in warm water to cover for 20
    minutes and drained
2 tablespoons pine nuts
pinch of salt
freshly ground pepper to taste
2 tablespoons olive oil
1 pound macaroni shells, rigatoni, or penne

In a large saucepan, melt the butter, add the onion, and sauté over a medium heat until transparent. Add the garlic and cook 1 more minute. Blend in the cauliflower and continue cooking until the cauliflower is tender, about 20 minutes. Use more butter as required.

Add the saffron and the water in which it soaked to the cauliflower. Add the currants, pine nuts, salt, and pepper, and combine the ingredients over a low heat. Blend in the olive oil. Keep the sauce warm.

Cook the pasta in 4 quarts of rapidly boiling salted water, stirring occasionally with a wooden spoon, until al dente. Drain, place in a heated serving bowl, add the sauce, combine quickly, and serve immediately. Do not serve with Parmesan.

♦ ♦ ♦ ♦ ♦

### Bucatini al Finocchio

BUCATINI
WITH
FENNEL
SAUCE

SERVES 4 TO 6

We first had this dish many years ago when a friend from southern Italy promised us a most unusual pasta sauce. It is not only unusual—a combination of fennel, pine nuts, currants, saffron, and almonds—but also exquisitely flavored.

1 large fennel, leaves and bulb
4 tablespoons olive oil
1 medium onion, coarsely chopped
2 tablespoons pine nuts
3 tablespoons currants, soaked in warm water to cover
    for 20 minutes and drained

*pinch of saffron, soaked in 2 tablespoons warm water*
*salt and freshly ground pepper to taste*
*1 pound bucatini (a long thin noodle with a hole down*
*        the center)*
*2 to 3 tablespoons peeled, toasted, and chopped*
*        almonds*

Remove the stems and leaves from the fennel bulb, chop them coarsely, and cook them in 4 quarts of salted boiling water until tender, about 15 minutes. Drain but do not discard the water in which the fennel tops were cooked.

Heat the olive oil in a medium saucepan.

Coarsely chop the fennel bulb, combine with the onion, and sauté together in the olive oil until the onion begins to brown. Add the pine nuts, currants, saffron, salt, pepper, and the previously boiled fennel tops. Heat through and keep warm.

Bring the water in which the fennel tops were cooked to a boil. Add more water, if necessary, to make at least 4 quarts. Add the pasta and cook, stirring occasionally with a wooden spoon, until al dente. When cooked, drain and place in a heated serving bowl. Add the sauce, combine well, sprinkle the almonds on top, and serve immediately.

◆ ◆ ◆ ◆ ◆

*Rigatoni con*

*Carciofi*

RIGATONI
WITH
ARTICHOKES

SERVES 4 TO 6

*8 medium artichokes*
*2 tablespoons butter*
*1 large onion, finely chopped*
*1 tablespoon flour*
*¾ cup dry white wine*
*2 tablespoons chopped parsley*
*⅓ cup freshly grated Parmesan plus ½ cup to serve with*
*        the pasta*
*1 pound penne, rigatoni, or tufoli*

Trim the artichokes, remove the chokes, and cut into very thin wedges, about ⅛ inch thick, as explained on p. 215. Place in acidulated water until ready to use.

Heat the butter in a large saucepan, add the onion, and sauté until transparent. Add the flour and cook, stirring constantly, for 1 minute. Pour in the wine slowly in a thin stream and continue stirring. Add the artichokes and the parsley, cover, and simmer over a low heat until the artichokes are tender, about 15 minutes. Add water as necessary. Blend in ⅓ cup Parmesan and keep warm.

Bring 4 quarts of salted water to a rapid boil. Add the pasta and cook, stirring occasionally with a wooden spoon, until al dente. Drain, place in a heated serving bowl, add the sauce, combine well, and serve immediately. Pass the ½ cup of freshly grated Parmesan for those who want it.

### VARIATION

Two 14-ounce cans of artichokes can be used in place of fresh ones.

◆ ◆ ◆ ◆ ◆

## Bombolotti con Funghi

BOMBOLOTTI
WITH
MUSHROOMS

SERVES 4 TO 6

This is a long-time favorite of ours, a scrumptious blend of creamy béchamel, earthy mushrooms, and crisp peas. Use short, thick, macaroni-type noodles, such as rigatoni, penne, or tufoli. The sauce can be prepared ahead of time, kept covered, and reheated just before combining with the pasta.

2 tablespoons olive oil
2 garlic cloves, chopped
2 tablespoons chopped parsley
1 cup peas, fresh or frozen, cooked but still crisp
¼ teaspoon freshly ground pepper
Béchamel Sauce (see recipe) made with:
   1¾ cups milk
   5 tablespoons butter
   5 tablespoons flour
   ½ teaspoon salt
2 cups washed, trimmed, and thinly sliced fresh
   mushrooms
1 cup freshly grated Parmesan
1 pound short macaroni

Heat the olive oil in a saucepan, add the garlic and parsley, and sauté until the garlic begins to color. Add the peas and pepper, combine, and set aside.

Make the béchamel sauce, add the mushrooms, ½ cup of Parmesan, the peas-and-garlic mixture, and keep warm.

Bring 4 quarts of salted water to a rapid boil. Add the pasta and cook, stirring occasionally with a wooden spoon, until al dente. Drain, place in a heated serving bowl, add the sauce, combine, and serve immediately. Pass the remaining ½ cup of freshly grated Parmesan at the table.

VARIATION

Soak 1 ounce of wild mushrooms *(Boletus edulis)* in 1 cup of warm water until tender, about 20 minutes. Remove the mushrooms from the soaking liquid with a slotted spoon, reserving the soaking liquid. Rinse the mushrooms, chop coarsely, sauté with the garlic and parsley, and proceed as described above. Strain the soaking liquid through a coffee filter or cheesecloth and combine ½ cup of it with 1½ cups of milk. Use this mixture instead of the 1¾ cups of milk to make the béchamel sauce.

♦ ♦ ♦ ♦ ♦

## *Orecchiette con Broccoletti*

PASTA
WITH
BROCCOLETTI

SERVES 4 TO 6

In this exceptionally good pasta dish from southern Italy, the *broccoletti* are cooked along with the pasta. If available, use orecchiette pasta ("little ears"); if not, use macaroni shells. The greens must be bitter, for it is this quality in combination with the blandness of the pasta that brings out the unique flavor of the dish. If you are unable to obtain *broccoletti* (sometimes called *rapini*), use collard greens.

⅓ *cup olive oil*
6 *garlic cloves, roughly chopped*
1 *hot pepper, fresh or dried, seeded and chopped*
3 *tablespoons Tomato Sauce I (see recipe)*
1 *pound broccoletti or collard greens*
1 *pound orecchiette or shells*
½ *cup freshly grated Parmesan*

Heat the olive oil in a saucepan and sauté the garlic and hot pepper for 1 minute or until the garlic begins to color. Add the tomato sauce, stir, and bring to a simmer. Remove from the heat.

Wash, drain, and finely chop the *broccoletti* or collard greens. Bring 6 cups of salted water to a boil and add the *broccoletti* and the pasta at the same time. Cook until the pasta is al dente. Drain the pasta and greens together in a colander and place in a warm serving bowl.

Combine the pasta and *broccoletti* with the tomato sauce, stir, and serve, passing Parmesan on the side.

# INTRODUCTION TO RAVIOLI, AGNOLOTTI, TORTELLINI

It is often claimed, especially by the Genoese, that they invented ravioli, the master recipe from which all other stuffed pasta dishes derive. Whether or not the claim has merit, anyone who has traveled in Italy knows that today some form of ravioli is found all over the country. They vary in shape, size, texture, and flavor but adhere to the general principle of being dough made with flour, eggs and/or water or milk, rolled out thin, stuffed with a meat, cheese, or vegetable filling, usually boiled, and served with a light sauce. They are also used in soup, a traditional and excellent way to serve them.

In the recipes that follow, we recommend that for ravioli, agnolotti, and tortellini you use the recipe for Homemade Pasta. However, feel free to vary the ingredients: substitute milk or water for the eggs (this will make the pasta dough somewhat less rich); omit the oil (this will produce a lighter but less elastic dough). The only way you can discover which you prefer is to experiment.

We describe here how to make ravioli, agnolotti, and tortellini and how to cook them. Then we give recipes for stuffings, any one of which is suitable for the three shapes. If you make more than you can use immediately, freeze the extra and use them when required.

## How to Make Ravioli

FOR THE DOUGH:

*Homemade Pasta (see recipe), using 3 cups flour*

FOR THE RAVIOLI:

*1 egg beaten with 1 tablespoon water*
*stuffing of your choice (see pp. 94–96)*

Make the pasta according to the master recipe. Take one long sheet of pasta, cut it in half across the width, and place it on a lightly floured work surface. Cut each of the halves in half again, thus obtaining 4 sheets of pasta of equal size. Most hand-cranked pasta machines make sheets 5½ inches to 6 inches wide.

Using a pastry brush, paint one side of each sheet of pasta with the egg-water mixture. On two of the sheets, place mounds of 1 heaping teaspoon of stuffing in two rows with roughly 2 inches separating the center of each mound. Place the other sheets over the ones with the stuffing and with your fingers press the dough together firmly between the mounds of stuffing and along the borders, removing as much air as possible. Cut into squares with a sharp knife or a scalloped pastry wheel. Each one of the ravioli should be approximately 2 inches square. Make sure all the edges are well sealed.

Repeat until all the pasta is used or until you have as many ravioli as you require.

## How to Make Agnolotti

The same ingredients are used for agnolotti and ravioli. Cut the pasta into 2½-inch-diameter disks using a scalloped cookie cutter or the equivalent. Place 1 heaping teaspoon of stuffing in the center of each disk, leaving the edges free of stuffing, wet the edges with the egg-water mixture, fold the disk in half to form a half circle, and seal the edges well.

## How to Make Tortellini

Follow the above procedure for agnolotti. Take an agnolotto and hold one end of it between your thumb and index finger with the curved side facing upward. Grasp the other end with your other hand, then bend it around the index finger until the two sides join. Press the ends together to seal. You will then have a small, oddly shaped doughnut. This is a tortellino. Repeat with all the other agnolotti.

## How to Cook Ravioli, Agnolotti, and Tortellini

Allow the stuffed pasta to rest on a clean, dry dish towel for at least 30 minutes. Turn over once to ensure that they dry evenly on both sides. Cook in 4 quarts of boiling water with 1 tablespoon of salt, 10 to 12 at one time, for 5 to 7 minutes. The cooking time will vary with the thickness of the pasta and the length of time the pasta has dried. As they cook they will rise to the surface. When cooked, remove with a large, slotted spoon, drain well, and keep warm until ready to serve.

♦ ♦ ♦ ♦ ♦

## Ravioli con Spinaci

RAVIOLI
WITH
SPINACH
AND
RICOTTA

SERVES 4 TO 6

These ravioli are found throughout central and northern Italy. They are called *ravioli di magro*, that is, ravioli made without meat, thus suitable for those days on which, for religious reasons, Catholics did not eat meat. They are now so popular that they are no longer relegated to special days. They make an elegant beginning for any meal.

Prepare the stuffing first, then the pasta.

FOR THE STUFFING:

*1½ pounds fresh spinach*
*1 tablespoon butter*
*½ pound fresh ricotta*
*½ cup freshly grated pecorino or Romano*
*¼ cup freshly grated Parmesan*
*2 eggs plus 1 egg yolk, beaten*
*pinch of saffron*
*½ teaspoon salt*
*freshly ground pepper to taste*
*pinch of nutmeg*

FOR THE PASTA:

*Homemade Pasta (see recipe), using 3 cups unbleached*
*all-purpose flour*

FOR THE SAUCE:

*1 tablespoon butter*
*1 cup freshly grated Parmesan*
*1 cup Tomato Sauce I (see recipe)*

Wash the spinach well and remove the stems. Steam until done, about 10 minutes. Place in a strainer and let cool. When cool enough to handle, divide into 2 equal parts and squeeze very dry with your hands or press the vegetable against the sides of a colander with a wooden spoon. Whatever method you use, make sure all the water is squeezed out. Chop it fine.

Melt 1 tablespoon of butter in a saucepan, add the spinach, sauté for 3 to 5 minutes, then set aside.

In a large mixing bowl, combine the ricotta, pecorino or Romano, and Parmesan. Add the beaten eggs and saffron to the cheeses, combine well, add the spinach, salt, pepper, and nutmeg and mix thoroughly. Place in the refrigerator.

Make the pasta, prepare the sheets for ravioli, then prepare the ravioli according to the master recipe, p. 92. The ravioli can be cooked immediately or *kept up to 1 hour* laid out on a dish towel. If kept longer than 1 hour, the stuffing may become too liquid. Make sure to turn them once to ensure that they dry evenly.

Cook according to instructions in the master recipe, p. 92. As they cook, place them on a heated serving dish, dot with butter, sprinkle with Parmesan, and keep warm until all are cooked and ready to serve.

Heat the tomato sauce, spread it over the ravioli, and serve at once, passing freshly grated Parmesan.

♦ ♦ ♦ ♦ ♦

## *Agnolotti ai Tre Formaggi*

### AGNOLOTTI WITH THREE CHEESES

SERVES 4 TO 6

FOR THE STUFFING:

1 pound fresh ricotta
½ cup freshly grated Parmesan
½ cup grated Gruyère
1 extra-large egg, beaten
1 teaspoon minced fresh sage, or ½ teaspoon dried
pinch of nutmeg
¼ teaspoon salt
freshly ground pepper to taste

FOR THE PASTA:

Homemade Pasta (see recipe), using 3 cups flour, or
    Green Spinach Pasta (see recipe)

FOR THE SAUCE:

3 tablespoons freshly grated Parmesan
5 tablespoons melted butter

Combine all the ingredients for the stuffing in a large mixing bowl. Mix well with a wooden spoon and set aside.

Make the pasta, cut into disks for agnolotti, and shape them according to directions in the master recipe, p. 93. Bring the water to a boil and cook the agnolotti according to the same recipe.

Remove from the water when cooked and keep warm on a serving dish until all are done. Sprinkle with the Parmesan, pour on the melted butter, and serve at once.

♦ ♦ ♦ ♦ ♦

## *Tortellini con Odori*

TORTELLINI
WITH
HERBS

SERVES 4 TO 6

This very delicately flavored stuffing combines the mildness of ricotta with the fresh pungent tastes of the basil and parsley. These tortellini go well with a light cream sauce. Prepare the stuffing first, then the pasta.

FOR THE STUFFING:

*5 tablespoons finely chopped fresh parsley*
*5 tablespoons finely chopped basil*
*¾ pound fresh ricotta*
*2 extra-large eggs, beaten*
*pinch of nutmeg*
*¼ teaspoon salt*
*freshly ground pepper to taste*

FOR THE PASTA:

*Homemade Pasta (see recipe), using 3 cups flour*

FOR THE SAUCE:

*5 tablespoons butter*
*1 cup heavy cream*
*1 cup freshly grated Parmesan*

Combine the chopped herbs with the ricotta, eggs, nutmeg, salt, and pepper. Blend well with a wooden spoon and set aside.

Make the pasta, cut it for agnolotti, stuff it, and shape into tortellini, p. 93. Let them rest for at least 30 minutes. Make sure they dry evenly. Make the sauce by melting the butter in a saucepan. Add the cream and simmer over medium heat for 30 seconds. Lower the heat, add ½ cup of Parmesan, and cook, stirring constantly, for 1 minute. Remove from the heat but keep warm.

Cook the tortellini according to the master recipe. As they cook, drain them with a large slotted spoon and place them in a heated serving bowl. Sprinkle with a tablespoon of the cream sauce and keep warm until all are cooked.

Pour the remaining cream sauce over the tortellini and turn them gently to coat. Serve immediately. Pass additional Parmesan to those who want it.

## INTRODUCTION TO CANNELLONI

The name cannellone comes from the Italian word for cane, and indeed the pasta rolls that are stuffed with a variety of mixtures do resemble sections of cane.

They are usually topped with a tomato, béchamel, or cheese sauce and baked until brown. Cannelloni are elegant and impressive and deserve pride of place at a dinner party.

Cannelloni can be assembled a few hours before they are needed, covered with foil or wax paper, and stored in the refrigerator. When ready, coat them with the appropriate sauce and bake. They should be served hot.

## How to Prepare and Cook Cannelloni

Although cannelloni may appear to be a complicated dish to those who prepare it for the first time, it is, in fact, quite easy to make and certainly much too good to avoid because of its apparent complexity. The key to success is proper order of preparation.

It is preferable to prepare the filling first, then make the pasta. In this way, the pasta can be parboiled as soon as it is made, then stuffed and baked. If the pasta is prepared before the stuffing, cut it into the proper shape (see below) and set it aside to dry on a dish towel or draped over a broom stick or dowel, suspended between chairs. Whatever order you choose, *do not parboil the pasta until the filling is made and you are ready to stuff it.*

Plan on two cannelloni per person as a first course. For six people, we find a 9-by-15-inch baking dish ideal.

Make the stuffing first and set aside.

Make the Homemade Pasta (see recipe) and cut the sheets across their length with a sharp knife or pizza cutter the width of the baking dish you wish to use. For example, if you plan to use a 9-inch-wide baking dish, each sheet of pasta for a cannellone should be 9 inches long by 5 inches wide. (The width of course is determined by the size of the hand-cranked pasta machine.)

Place next to the stove a large mixing bowl filled with cold water. Lay out on a work surface two damp dish towels. Bring to a rapid boil 4 quarts of water, add 2 teaspoons of salt and 1 tablespoon of oil, and cook the pasta, 2 sheets at a time, until half done, about 30 seconds, depending on the freshness of the dough.

Remove the sheets of pasta from the boiling water with a slotted spoon, place immediately in the cold water, remove, let drain, and lay out on the dish towels until ready to use.

Butter the baking dish generously. Place one of the pasta pieces on a work surface, spread 2 or 3 tablespoons of the stuffing along the 9-inch edge, and roll to the opposite side. Place the cannelloni in the baking dish and repeat with the other pieces of pasta. The cannelloni should be packed closely together in the baking dish.

Spread on top of the cannelloni the appropriate sauce and bake for 20 minutes in a hot oven.

Cannelloni can also be made with packaged, commercial cannelloni or manicotti shells. The process is simple. Cook the shells until almost done, drain, stuff, and bake as described above.

NOTE: In Italy cannelloni are sometimes made using a *crespelle* (crêpes) dough. Made in this way, they are richer and more substantial and, we think, more suitable as a main dish.

◆ ◆ ◆ ◆ ◆

## Cannelloni alla Napoletana

CANNELLONI, NEAPOLITAN STYLE

SERVES 6

These cannelloni, as the name indicates, are characteristic of Naples and the south and have all the ingredients that conjure up the southern Mediterranean—basil, mozzarella, ricotta, and tomatoes.

FOR THE STUFFING:

1 pound mozzarella, grated
1 pound fresh ricotta
¼ cup freshly grated Parmesan
1 extra-large egg plus 1 egg yolk, beaten
½ cup finely chopped mushrooms
¼ cup finely chopped basil
¼ cup finely chopped parsley
¼ teaspoon salt
freshly ground pepper to taste
Béchamel Sauce (see recipe) made with:
   1¼ cups milk
   3 tablespoons butter
   3 tablespoons flour
   pinch of salt

FOR THE PASTA:

Homemade Pasta (see recipe), using 3 cups unbleached
   all-purpose flour

FOR THE SAUCE:

1 cup Tomato Sauce I (see recipe)
¼ cup freshly grated Parmesan

In a large mixing bowl, combine the mozzarella, ricotta, Parmesan, eggs, mushrooms, basil, parsley, salt, and pepper.

Make the béchamel sauce, add it to the cheese mixture, and combine thoroughly.

Prepare the pasta. Cut, cook, and stuff the cannelloni according to instructions in the master recipe. Place in a buttered 9-by-15-inch baking dish, spread the tomato sauce on top, sprinkle with Parmesan, and bake for 20 minutes, until the Parmesan begins to brown. Let cool for 5 minutes, then serve.

◆ ◆ ◆ ◆ ◆

## Cannelloni con Funghi

CANNELLONI
WITH
MUSHROOMS

SERVES 6

Mushroom lovers will certainly appreciate these cannelloni stuffed with a delicate blend of mushrooms and béchamel sauce. Serve it with freshly grated Parmesan.

FOR THE STUFFING:

1 medium onion, minced
2 tablespoons butter
1 pound very fresh mushrooms, washed, trimmed, and
    thinly sliced
Béchamel Sauce (see recipe) made with:
    3 cups milk
    6 tablespoons butter
    8 tablespoons flour
    ½ teaspoon salt
freshly ground pepper to taste
1 tablespoon chopped parsley

FOR THE PASTA:

Homemade Pasta (see recipe), using 3 cups unbleached
    all-purpose flour

FOR THE SAUCE:

¼ cup milk
½ cup freshly grated Parmesan

Sauté the onion in the butter until golden.

Place the mushrooms in a large mixing bowl and add the onion.

Make the béchamel sauce and, when ready, add half of the sauce to the mushrooms, combining carefully to avoid breaking them. Season with pepper and parsley and set aside.

Preheat the oven to 375°F.

Prepare the pasta for the cannelloni, cook and stuff according to the master recipe, p. 96, with the mushroom-béchamel mixture, and arrange them side by side in a buttered 9-by-15-inch baking dish.

Stir ¼ cup milk into the remaining béchamel sauce for the topping. Combine this sauce with the Parmesan and spread it evenly over the cannelloni.

Bake for 20 minutes, until the sauce begins to brown. Let cool 5 minutes before serving.

♦ ♦ ♦ ♦ ♦

## Cannelloni con Peperoni

CANNELLONI
WITH
BELL
PEPPERS

SERVES 6

This unusual but very successful stuffing for cannelloni combines fresh crisp bell peppers, tomato sauce, and creamy béchamel.

FOR THE STUFFING:

*5 large bell peppers*
*1 cup Tomato Sauce I (see recipe)*
*¼ teaspoon salt*
*freshly ground pepper to taste*

FOR THE PASTA:

*Homemade Pasta (see recipe), using 3 cups unbleached*
    *all-purpose flour*

FOR THE TOPPING:

*Béchamel Sauce (see recipe) made with:*
    *2¼ cups milk*
    *6 tablespoons butter*
    *6 tablespoons flour*
    *¼ teaspoon salt*
*1 cup freshly grated Parmesan*

Wash and peel the peppers (p. 257). Core them and discard the seeds. Slice very thin in long julienne strips.

Prepare the tomato sauce and set aside.

Preheat the oven to 375°F.

Make the pasta. Cook and prepare the squares for stuffing according to the master recipe, p. 96. Along one edge of each square, evenly spread a tablespoon of tomato sauce. Arrange the julienned peppers on top of the tomato sauce. The peppers should be piled approximately 1 inch high along the edge. Season with salt and pepper. Roll up the cannelloni and place in the baking dish.

Make the béchamel sauce for the topping. When cooked, spread evenly over the cannelloni. Sprinkle ½ cup grated Parmesan on top and bake until golden, about 20 minutes. Let cool 5 minutes and serve with the remaining freshly grated Parmesan.

# INTRODUCTION TO LASAGNE

Lasagne are usually eaten in Italy as a first course, but they are substantial and nutritious, so we often serve them as a main dish, especially for a light dinner. Lasagne are also ideal for parties, since they can be assembled ahead of time. You can use either fresh homemade pasta or the dry commercial variety, but of course the former, which virtually melts in your mouth, makes far superior lasagne.

We will first give some general tips on preparation and cooking of lasagne and then follow with two recipes.

## *How to Prepare and Cook Lasagne*

Make the stuffing for lasagne according to one of the two recipes that follow.

Make Homemade Pasta (see recipe) and roll out the dough to the penultimate setting on the machine. It should not be paper thin. Cut the sheets of pasta into sections roughly half the length of the dish in which the lasagne will be baked. Set aside for 30 minutes on a dry floured dish towel to rest.

Meanwhile, bring 4 quarts of water to a boil in a large saucepan or stockpot; add 1 tablespoon of salt and 1 tablespoon of oil. Fill a large mixing bowl with cold water and place it near the stove. Lay out damp dish towels (2 or 3) on a work surface.

Cook the pasta, 2 sheets at a time, in the boiling water until half cooked, about 1 minute for fresh pasta. Remove from the water with a slotted spoon, place in the cold water, remove, drain, and lay out on the damp dish towels.

Assemble the lasagne according to one of the following recipes.

## ◆ ◆ ◆ ◆ ◆

## Lasagne alla Fiesolana

LASAGNE,
FIESOLE
STYLE

SERVES 6

This is our standard and favorite lasagne recipe. Make the lasagne with either green or white pasta.

½ ounce dried wild mushrooms (Boletus edulis)
1½ pounds fresh ricotta
1 pound fresh mushrooms
2 tablespoons chopped basil
2 tablespoons chopped parsley
3 cups Tomato Sauce I or II (see recipes)
Béchamel Sauce (see recipe) made with:
    4 cups milk
    8 tablespoons butter
    ½ cup flour
    ¾ teaspoon salt
freshly ground pepper
¾ cup freshly grated Parmesan
Homemade Pasta (see recipe)

Soak the dried mushrooms in 1 cup of warm water for 20 minutes, remove carefully from the water, and rinse well under cold water to remove all grit and sand. Drain and set aside.

Place the ricotta in a large mixing bowl and beat with a fork or wooden spoon until creamy.

Wash and trim the fresh mushrooms, slice thin, and sprinkle with the basil and parsley. Chop the wild mushrooms and combine with the fresh.

Prepare the tomato sauce and keep warm over low heat.

Prepare the béchamel sauce, add 2½ cups to the ricotta mixture, and reserve the rest for later use. Add pepper to taste.

Preheat oven to 400°F.

Make the pasta, cook it (p. 101), butter a 9-by-12-inch baking dish, and begin to assemble the lasagne.

Cover the bottom of the baking dish evenly with 3 tablespoons of béchamel sauce. Place on top a layer of pasta, overlapping the edges about ¼ inch. Spread on top of the pasta a thin layer of the ricotta mixture, some of the mushrooms, some of the tomato sauce and sprinkle with 2 tablespoons of Parmesan. Repeat the process, making 3 or 4 layers until all the ingredients are used. End with a layer of pasta.

Spread the remaining béchamel on top of the pasta. Sprinkle with the remaining Parmesan and bake for 20 minutes, until the top begins to brown. Remove the lasagne from the oven, allow to rest for 5 minutes, and serve from the baking dish.

♦ ♦ ♦ ♦ ♦

*Lasagne di*
*Melanzane*

These lasagne are made with a combination of eggplant and pasta. The eggplant can be either fried (as we indicate in the recipe) or broiled. It is much tastier if fried, but lighter and more digestible if broiled.

LASAGNE
WITH
EGGPLANT

SERVES 6

3 medium eggplants, approximately 3 pounds
1 tablespoon salt
1 cup Tomato Sauce I (see recipe)
seed oil for deep frying
Béchamel Sauce (see recipe) made with:
   3 cups milk
   6 tablespoons butter
   6 tablespoons flour
   pinch of salt
Homemade Pasta (see recipe)
2 tablespoons finely chopped basil
2 tablespoons finely chopped parsley
½ cup freshly grated Parmesan
freshly ground pepper to taste

Peel the eggplants, cut into thin lengthwise slices, sprinkle with 1 tablespoon salt, and place in a colander to drain for 30 minutes.

Meanwhile, prepare the tomato sauce.

When the eggplants are ready, rinse in cold water and pat dry with a dish towel or paper towels. Heat the seed oil in a pan suitable for deep frying, add the slices of eggplant, and fry until golden. When cooked, drain the eggplant slices on paper towels and set aside.

Make the béchamel sauce and keep warm. Prepare the pasta, cook, drain, and place on damp dish towels.

Preheat the oven to 400°F.

Butter a baking dish approximately 9 by 12 inches. Place 3 tablespoons of béchamel sauce on the bottom. Cover with a layer of pasta, overlapping the pasta pieces about ¼ inch. On top of the pasta, spread a layer of eggplant, a thin layer of tomato sauce, sprinkle with some of the basil and parsley, cover with 2 tablespoons of Parmesan and some pepper, and end with a thin layer of béchamel. Start the process again, beginning with the pasta and continue until all the ingredients are used, approximately 3 or 4 layers, ending with a layer of pasta. Cover the top with the remaining béchamel sauce, sprinkle with Parmesan, and bake for 20 minutes until the top begins to brown. Let rest for 5 minutes at room temperature and serve from the baking dish.

# Rice

Although it may come as a surprise to some, Italy is the largest producer of rice in Europe and one of the largest consumers. The rice is grown almost exclusively in the north, in the flat fertile plain of the Po valley. Rice is not indigenous to Italy. It was introduced by the Arabs in the late Middle Ages, but Italians have managed over the years to develop an extremely varied and impressive array of rice dishes.

As a first course, rice is prepared as a risotto, used to stuff vegetables, or served with a sauce. In each recipe we give detailed instructions on preparation, but it may be useful to give some general tips on how to cook risotto. First, it is important to use the right kind of rice. The best is Arborio, but most Italian varieties, such as Originario or Fino, are perfectly acceptable. Carolina long-grain rice is adequate but, because it is less starchy, it makes a less creamy risotto. Never use an instant (precooked) rice—the results will be disastrous.

Second, and equally important, the risotto must be cooked correctly. A risotto is not a boiled rice dish. The rice is first sautéed in butter to coat the kernels and seal them. Then over medium heat, while stirring constantly, hot broth (or water) is added to the rice a little at a time until the liquid is absorbed and the rice cooked. It takes 20 to 25 minutes for the rice to cook. A risotto should be creamy, dense, and moist. And, as with pasta, the rice must be al dente, tender on the outside with a firm, but cooked, center.

In most risotti, Parmesan is added after the rice is cooked and before serving. It is important to add the cheese while the rice is steaming hot so that the Parmesan melts and combines completely with the rice.

As everyone knows, the wine used in cooking is almost as important as the wine served with the meal. In fact, it is best if you use the same wine for both. We suggest where wine is called for that you use a dry white wine such as Pinot Grigio or Soave.

A risotto is usually cooked and served immediately, but if absolutely necessary, it can be made an hour or so ahead of time. If so, undercook by 5 minutes and just before serving complete the cooking process on top of the stove or in a medium oven, adding liquid as required.

♦ ♦ ♦ ♦ ♦

## *Risotto alla Milanese*

RISOTTO,
MILANESE
STYLE

SERVES 6 TO 8

This is the great classic risotto of Lombardy. It is an absolute delight to the eye and palate, a golden bowl of saffron-flavored rice. For a memorable feast, if you are able to obtain white or black truffles, slice them over the risotto with a truffle slicer before serving.

6 tablespoons butter
1 medium onion, finely chopped
3 cups Arborio rice
½ cup dry white wine
a generous pinch of saffron
8 cups hot Vegetable Broth (see recipe)
¾ cup freshly grated Parmesan
pinch of salt
truffles (optional)
parsley or watercress

Heat 3 tablespoons of butter in a large, heavy saucepan, add the onion, and sauté until transparent. Add the rice and sauté, stirring constantly, for 2 to 3 minutes. Add the wine and cook, stirring, until it evaporates. Add the saffron and combine well. Add the hot vegetable broth, ½ cup at a time, and continue cooking, stirring constantly, until the risotto is creamy, smooth, moist, and cooked al dente.

Remove from the heat, add the remaining 3 tablespoons of butter and the Parmesan, and combine. Correct for seasoning. Slice truffles over the top if you like, and serve immediately on a heated serving platter decorated with parsley or watercress.

### VARIATIONS

1. Prior to cooking the Risotto alla Milanese, sauté 1 medium onion, finely chopped, in 2 tablespoons of butter until transparent, add 2 tablespoons of chopped parsley and ½ pound of fresh mushrooms, washed and thinly sliced. Sauté for another 3 minutes, then set aside but keep warm. Make the risotto, butter a 9-inch ring mold, place the risotto in it, unmold it on a serving platter, and serve immediately, piling the mushrooms in the center.
2. Substitute for the mushrooms, peas sautéed with onions and butter.

♦ ♦ ♦ ♦ ♦

## Risotto con Carciofi e Funghi

RISOTTO
WITH
ARTICHOKES
AND
MUSHROOMS

SERVES 6

The combination of mushrooms and artichokes cooked with rice makes a hearty, substantial risotto. When preparing the artichokes, make sure that all the tough, inedible parts are removed.

*8 medium-size artichokes*
*6 tablespoons butter*
*1 medium onion, finely chopped*
*1 cup dry white wine*
*½ pound mushrooms, washed, trimmed, and thinly*
   *sliced*
*2½ cups Arborio rice*
*7 cups hot Vegetable Broth (see recipe)*
*½ teaspoon freshly ground pepper*
*pinch of salt*

Clean, trim, and remove the chokes from the artichokes as explained on p. 215 and cut into very thin wedges, about ⅛ inch thick. Place them in acidulated water until ready to use. Heat 3 tablespoons of butter in a large, heavy saucepan, add the onion, and sauté until transparent. Drain the artichokes, blend with the onion, and sauté for a few minutes to coat. Pour in the wine, cover, and simmer until the artichokes are almost cooked, about 10 minutes. Remove the cover, add the mushrooms, and cook, stirring, for 3 minutes.

Combine the rice with the mushrooms and artichokes and sauté for 2 to 3 minutes. Ladle in the hot vegetable broth, ½ cup at a time, and continue cooking, over a medium heat, stirring constantly, until the risotto is creamy, smooth, moist, and the rice is cooked al dente. Remove from the heat, add the remaining 3 tablespoons of butter and the seasoning, combine, and serve the risotto immediately.

♦ ♦ ♦ ♦ ♦

## Risi e Bisi

RISOTTO
WITH
PEAS

SERVES 6 TO 8

Any dish that maintains its appeal for centuries must have something special and, indeed, Risi e Bisi does. This great Venetian risotto was enjoyed by the Doges when Venice was at the apex of its power and glory and is still enormously popular today. And, surprisingly, it is little more than the happy combination of rice and peas.

Since the peas will disintegrate if cooked with the rice, they must be prepared separately and combined with the rice just before it is served.

7 *tablespoons butter*
1 *medium onion, finely chopped*
1 *cup fennel or celery, finely chopped*
2 *tablespoons chopped parsley*
2 *cups fresh or frozen peas*
*pinch of sugar*
*pinch of salt*
2½ *cups Arborio rice*
7 *cups hot Vegetable Broth (see recipe)*
½ *cup freshly grated Parmesan*

Melt 2 tablespoons of butter in a saucepan, add half the onion, and sauté until transparent. Stir in the fennel or celery, sauté for 3 to 5 minutes, add the parsley, peas, a pinch each of sugar and salt, and cook until almost done. Do not over-cook. Add water as necessary to prevent the peas from sticking. Set aside.

Melt 3 tablespoons of butter in a large, heavy saucepan, add the remaining onion, and sauté until transparent. Blend in the rice and sauté 2 to 3 minutes, stirring constantly. Ladle in the hot vegetable broth, ½ cup at a time, and continue cooking over a medium heat, stirring constantly, until the risotto is almost cooked, about 20 to 25 minutes. Add the peas, combine well, and finish cooking the risotto.

Remove from the heat, add the remaining butter and the Parmesan, combine, and serve immediately.

♦ ♦ ♦ ♦ ♦

*Risotto al Pomodoro*

RISOTTO
WITH
TOMATOES

SERVES 6

3 *tablespoons butter*
⅓ *cup minced onion*
1 *tablespoon minced parsley*
2 *tablespoons capers, minced*
2 *garlic cloves, minced*
2 *tomatoes, peeled, seeded, and chopped, or 1 cup*
  *Italian canned plum tomatoes, drained*
4 *tablespoons Tomato Sauce I or II (see recipes)*
2½ *cups Arborio rice*
½ *cup dry white wine*
6½ *cups Vegetable Broth (see recipe)*
*pinch of salt*
*freshly ground pepper to taste*
⅔ *cup freshly grated Parmesan*

Melt the butter in a large, heavy saucepan. Add the onion, parsley, capers, and garlic, and sauté, stirring, over a medium heat for 2 to 3 minutes. Combine with the tomatoes and tomato sauce and cook for 5 to 8 minutes, until the moisture evaporates.

Stir in the rice and combine to coat with the tomato sauce. Add the wine and cook, stirring, until the wine is absorbed. Ladle in the vegetable broth or water, ½ cup at a time, and continue cooking over a medium heat, stirring constantly, until the risotto is cooked al dente. Remove from the heat. Taste and correct for salt and pepper. Blend in ⅓ cup of Parmesan, cover, and let stand for a few minutes. Pass the remaining Parmesan on the side.

♦ ♦ ♦ ♦ ♦

## Risotto con Funghi

RISOTTO
WITH
MUSHROOMS

SERVES 6

One of the more traditional ways to prepare risotto is with mushrooms. It is wonderfully aromatic, delicately flavored, and very elegant. The addition of the dried wild mushrooms is like the call of the wild to the cultivated ones, bringing out in them the rich, earthy taste of the fields and woodlands.

½ ounce dried wild mushrooms (Boletus edulis)
5 tablespoons butter
½ medium onion, finely chopped
1 tablespoon finely chopped parsley
1 stalk celery, finely chopped
1 small carrot, finely chopped
1 pound fresh mushrooms, cleaned, trimmed, and
    thinly sliced
2½ cups Arborio rice
pinch of salt
6 cups Vegetable Broth (see recipe)

Soak the dried mushrooms in 1 cup of warm water, remove carefully from the water, reserving the liquid, rinse under cold running water to remove grit and sand, drain, chop coarsely, and set aside. Strain the soaking liquid through a thick layer of cheesecloth or a coffee filter and set aside.

Melt 3 tablespoons of butter in a large, heavy saucepan, add the onion, parsley, celery, and carrot, and sauté over a medium heat for 5 minutes. Add the fresh and dried mushrooms and sauté for another 2 minutes. Stir in the rice and salt and cook, stirring, for 2 minutes. Pour in the liquid in which the dried mushrooms were soaked, then the broth, ½ cup at a time, stirring constantly until the rice is cooked al dente. Do not overcook. Add the remaining 2 tablespoons of butter, combine well, and serve immediately.

♦ ♦ ♦ ♦ ♦

*Riso con*

*Finocchio*

RICE
WITH
FENNEL

SERVES 6

In this recipe, be sure not to overcook the fennel—
the secret lies in the blend of textures, the crisp
fennel with the creamy rice.

4 tablespoons butter
2 tablespoons olive oil
¼ cup minced onion
¼ cup minced celery
6 cups chopped fennel
½ teaspoon salt
2½ cups Arborio rice
½ cup dry white wine
3 tablespoons chopped parsley
1 cup freshly grated Parmesan cheese

Heat together 3 tablespoons of butter and the olive oil in a saucepan. Add the
onion and celery, sauté for 3 minutes over a high heat, stirring constantly, then
add the fennel. Reduce the heat to medium and continue cooking for 5 minutes,
until the fennel begins to brown but is still firm. Remove from the heat.

Bring 5 cups of water to a boil in a large saucepan, add the salt and the rice,
and cook covered over a low heat until all the water is absorbed. Stir in the fennel
and wine, combine well, replace the cover, and cook for 5 minutes more or until
the rice is cooked al dente. Add more water if necessary. Remove from the heat
and mix in the parsley, 1 tablespoon of butter, and ⅓ cup of Parmesan. Serve on
a heated serving platter, passing the remaining Parmesan for those who want it.

♦ ♦ ♦ ♦ ♦

*Riso*

*all'Uovo*

RICE
WITH EGGS

SERVES 6

Rice with eggs is considered by many Italians as an
ideal first course to any dinner, simple to prepare,
easy to digest, yet elegant and delicately flavored.

3 cups Italian or Carolina long-grain rice
3 egg yolks
juice of 1 lemon
3 tablespoons melted butter
½ cup freshly grated Parmesan
2 tablespoons chopped parsley

Cook the rice in 8 cups of boiling salted water until al dente. While the rice
cooks, combine the egg yolks, lemon, melted butter, and ⅓ cup of Parmesan in a
warm serving bowl.

When the rice is cooked, drain it and place immediately in the serving bowl. Mix carefully to coat the rice in the egg-lemon sauce. Sprinkle with parsley and the remaining Parmesan. Serve immediately.

♦ ♦ ♦ ♦ ♦

## *Riso con Salsa Cruda*

RICE
WITH
RAW
VEGETABLE
SAUCE

SERVES 6

This dish always brings back childhood memories of summers at Forte dei Marmi, a small seaside resort on the Tyrrhenian coast then and now very popular with Florentines. My mother, I'm convinced, thought this was a very healthful dish, probably because of all the raw vegetables included in the sauce. Thus, we had it as a first course two or three times a week. As the summer progressed, the dish changed subtly as different vegetables came into season. It is important to combine the steaming hot rice with the raw sauce and to serve immediately. The heat of the rice brings out the flavor of the vegetables.

2½ cups Italian or Carolina long-grain rice
4 tomatoes, peeled and seeded
1 cup finely chopped celery
1 cup finely chopped carrots
½ cup sliced red or yellow onion, soaked for 30 minutes
    in cold water to cover and drained
1 garlic clove, finely chopped
⅓ cup finely chopped parsley
⅓ cup finely chopped fresh basil
½ cup olive oil
salt and freshly ground pepper to taste
a few drops of Tabasco sauce or ½ teaspoon minced fresh
    hot pepper (optional)

Cook the rice al dente in 5 cups of boiling salted water and drain.

Meanwhile, prepare the sauce by combining all the remaining ingredients in a bowl. If using a food processor, process a small amount of the vegetables at a time to ensure that they remain finely chopped, not puréed. They should be crunchy under the teeth to contrast with the softness of the rice.

When the rice is cooked, place it in a glass serving bowl and pour the raw vegetable sauce over it. Mix well and serve. You can also put half the sauce over the rice and pass the other half in a sauceboat to be added individually.

♦ ♦ ♦ ♦ ♦

*Pomodori
Ripieni di
Riso alla
Virginia*

TOMATOES
STUFFED
WITH
RICE,
VIRGINIA
STYLE

SERVES 6

Tomatoes stuffed with rice are very popular with Romans as a first course in the summer. They can be served hot or at room temperature. Since the flavor depends on the tomatoes, use large, firm, and tasty ones.

6 *large tomatoes*
3 *tablespoons Tomato Sauce I (see recipe)*
2 *garlic cloves, finely chopped*
8 *large basil leaves, finely chopped*
1 *tablespoon finely chopped parsley*
3½ *tablespoons olive oil*
6 *tablespoons Arborio rice*
*salt and freshly ground pepper to taste*

Wash the tomatoes, place them on a cutting board, stem side down, and with a sharp knife slice a ¼-inch cap off of each tomato. Reserve the caps, which will serve as tops for the stuffed tomatoes. With a paring knife or serrated spoon, carefully remove the pulp from the tomatoes, taking care to keep the bottoms intact, and set them aside. Eliminate the seeds from the pulp, chop, and place in a mixing bowl.

Add to the tomato pulp 1 tablespoon of tomato sauce, the garlic, basil, parsley, 2 tablespoons of olive oil, the rice, and salt and pepper. Combine well.

Preheat the oven to 375°F.

Oil an 8-by-10-inch baking dish (large enough to hold the tomatoes without crowding), and place the tomatoes in the dish. Sprinkle the inside of the tomatoes with olive oil and a pinch of salt, and fill each tomato two-thirds full with the rice and tomato mixture. Replace the caps and drizzle with the remaining olive oil. Add to the pan a mixture of 2 tablespoons of tomato sauce and enough water to come halfway up the sides of the tomatoes. Bake, basting once or twice, until rice is cooked, about 35 to 40 minutes.

Transfer the tomatoes carefully from the baking dish to a serving platter. Serve hot or at room temperature.

◆ ◆ ◆ ◆ ◆

## Peperoni Imbottiti di Riso

PEPPERS
STUFFED
WITH
RICE

SERVES 6

*3 large bell peppers (red or yellow is preferable)*
*¼ teaspoon salt*
*1 cup Arborio rice*
*2 tablespoons capers, chopped*
*2 garlic cloves, finely chopped*
*2 tablespoons chopped parsley*
*2 tablespoons pine nuts*
*3 tablespoons olive oil*
*freshly ground pepper to taste*

Wash, peel, cut in half lengthwise, and seed the peppers as described on p. 257. Set aside.

Bring 3 cups of water to a boil in a saucepan, add the salt and rice, and cook for 10 minutes. Drain and place in a mixing bowl. Add to the rice the capers, garlic, parsley, pine nuts, 2 tablespoons of olive oil, and pepper. Combine well.

Preheat oven to 375°F.

Oil an 8-by-10-inch baking dish, and place the peppers in the dish. Fill the peppers with the rice mixture, sprinkle the stuffing with 1 tablespoon of olive oil, add approximately 1 cup of water to the baking dish (enough to cover the bottom of the dish), and bake for 20 minutes. Serve hot or at room temperature.

◆ ◆ ◆ ◆ ◆

## Riso Gratinato

RICE
AU
GRATIN

SERVES 6

Although the essence of simplicity, rice baked with saffron-flavored béchamel sauce, golden and aromatic, is ideal for dinner parties. It has the added attraction that it can be prepared ahead of time and baked just before serving.

*2½ cups Italian or Carolina long-grain rice*
*salt and freshly ground pepper to taste*
*pinch of nutmeg*
*Béchamel Sauce (see recipe) made with:*
  *¼ cup finely chopped onion*
  *4 tablespoons butter*
  *4 tablespoons all-purpose flour*
  *2 cups milk*

*generous pinch of saffron soaked for 10 minutes in ¼*
*cup warm milk*
*6 tablespoons freshly grated Parmesan*
*2 tablespoons butter*

Cook the rice in 8 cups boiling salted water until al dente. Drain and combine in a mixing bowl with the pepper and nutmeg. Set aside.

Make the béchamel sauce, first sautéing the onion in the butter until it wilts and then adding the flour and milk. Add to the béchamel sauce the soaked saffron with the ¼ cup of milk. Add the Parmesan and mix well.

Preheat oven to 400°F.

Blend together in the mixing bowl the béchamel sauce and the rice. Place the rice mixture either in 6 individual buttered baking dishes or in a single 9- or 10-inch-diameter buttered baking dish. Dot with butter, place in the oven for 20 minutes until the top browns, and serve.

# Dumplings and Cornmeal

## Gnocchi

Gnocchi, the Italian word for dumplings, are made from a dough, usually of flour, potatoes, or semolino, that is first cooked with milk or water, combined with eggs, butter, and sometimes cheese, then baked, boiled, or fried. They are most often served with an herb-flavored butter and cheese sauce or with a light tomato sauce.

Gnocchi, when correctly prepared, are wonderfully light and creamy with a mild but distinctive flavor. They literally melt in your mouth. The secret to their success is to minimize the amount of flour used to bind the other ingredients, except, of course, when making flour dumplings. Excessive flour makes the dumpling heavy, tasteless, and chewy. Preparation of dumplings does take time, but you will be well rewarded. Your guests will love them and so will you.

## Polenta

Polenta, made in Italy today of coarsely ground cornmeal, has a curious history. The name comes from the Latin *pulmentum*, a mush made from coarsely ground grains that the Romans adopted from the Etruscans. The use of corn came much later. The grain was first introduced into Europe from America at the end of the fifteenth century, but initially received little attention. Two centuries later, however, it was reintroduced, this time from Turkey, met with much greater success, and became known in Italy as *granturco*, Turkish grain.

By the nineteenth century, in fact, polenta had become something of a health hazard. Corn, an otherwise nutritious grain, lacks one of the B vitamins, nicotinic acid. Many poor northern Italian peasants ate a diet that relied heavily on polenta and thus suffered from pellagra, a disease caused by an acute vitamin deficiency.

Conditions, of course, have vastly improved since then, and today polenta is very popular, especially in the north. There is nothing subtle about most polenta dishes. They tend to reflect their humble peasant origins. This is not to say that they are without art, but it is the unpretentious art of the peasant household, not the refined art of the noble's court. We tend to reserve polenta dishes for the winter when hearty fare is most appreciated. If possible try to obtain freshly ground cornmeal or find a store that will grind it for you. The fresher the cornmeal, the more flavorful the polenta.

A word on preparation will help those new to these dishes. In a number of them, it is necessary to spread out the dumpling or cornmeal dough on a work surface to cool and dry after first cooking. It is useful to prepare the surface in advance. For these dishes, butter generously or wet with water an 18-by-24-inch work surface of marble, Formica, or wood. The dough is generally very sticky when warm and spreads easiest if the spreader, usually a kitchen knife or metal spatula, is kept wet with cold water. It is therefore necessary to place the work surface near the kitchen sink or place a bowl of cold water near the work surface.

♦ ♦ ♦ ♦ ♦

## Gnocchi di Patate

POTATO
DUMPLINGS

SERVES 6 TO 8

3 pounds potatoes (preferably mealy ones)
1 egg, beaten
¼ teaspoon salt
1½ to 2 cups unbleached all-purpose flour
3 tablespoons butter
½ teaspoon finely chopped fresh sage or dried sage
    soaked in water for 10 minutes, drained, and
    chopped
½ cup freshly grated Parmesan

Cook the potatoes, unpeeled, until tender. Cool, peel, mash, and place them in a mixing bowl. Add the egg and salt and mix thoroughly. Blend in the flour, a little at a time, stirring vigorously with a wooden spoon until a soft, light dough is formed. Try to add as little flour as possible.

Lightly flour a work surface and knead the dough on it for 1 minute. Divide the dough into 6 equal parts and roll each into sticks, roughly ¾ inch in diameter. Cut on a diagonal into pieces 1 inch long. With your hands lightly floured, take a dumpling and press it with your thumb against the inside tines of a fork or against a cheese grater. The dumpling should have the shape of a shell, smooth on the concave side with ridges on the convex side to hold the sauce. When made, place the dumpling on a lightly floured board and repeat the process with the remaining dough.

Bring 4 quarts of unsalted water to a gentle boil. Add the dumplings to the water, 5 or 6 at a time, and cook until they rise to the surface, about 2 to 3 minutes. (Taste one to make sure it is cooked—if not, allow them to cook a minute or two longer.) Remove with a slotted spoon, drain well, place in a heated serving dish, dot with butter, and keep warm until all the dumplings are cooked.

Melt the butter that remains, add the sage, sauté for 1 minute, and pour over the dumplings. Sprinkle the Parmesan on top and serve immediately.

### VARIATIONS

1. After boiling the dumplings as described above, place them in a buttered baking dish, sprinkle ¼ pound shredded fontina or Gruyère on top, dot with butter, and bake in a preheated 400°F. oven for 5 minutes, until the cheese melts and begins to brown.
2. Make the dumplings as described above, *but do not boil*. Instead, deep fry them in a light seed oil until golden, remove with a slotted spoon, drain well on absorbent paper, and keep warm on a serving platter until all are cooked. Sprinkle them with salt and pepper and serve immediately.

◆ ◆ ◆ ◆ ◆

## Gnocchi di Farina al Forno

### BAKED FLOUR DUMPLINGS

A few preparatory steps will facilitate the making of these dumplings. You will need a large (approximately 24-by-18-inch) wooden, marble, Formica, or similar work surface. Butter it before you begin. You will also need a large kitchen knife that you wet constantly with cold water to spread the batter on the work surface. Either place a bowl with cold water near the work surface or place the work surface near the sink. From this point on, preparation is easy. Make sure you bake the dumplings until

SERVES 4 TO 6

they are golden and crisp. The dumplings can be prepared ahead of time and baked before serving.

*½ pound plus 4 tablespoons butter*
*2¾ cups milk*
*1½ cups unbleached all-purpose flour*
*pinch of salt*
*pinch of nutmeg*
*3 tablespoons grated Gruyère*
*7 tablespoons freshly grated Parmesan*
*5 eggs, beaten*

Place ½ pound of butter and milk in a saucepan and heat at a low temperature until the butter melts. Add the flour, a little at a time, stirring constantly with a wire whisk or wooden spoon to prevent lumps from forming. Add salt and nutmeg and continue cooking, stirring constantly, for 5 minutes. The batter must be very dense, the consistency of mashed potatoes. If it is too liquid, add flour; if it is too thick, add milk.

Remove from the heat, add the Gruyère and 3 tablespoons of Parmesan, and slowly incorporate the eggs, stirring constantly. Place the dough on the buttered work surface and spread evenly with a kitchen knife, wetting the blade occasionally with cold water, to a thickness of ¼ inch or less. Allow to cool.

Heat the oven to 450°F.

Butter a 9-by-12-inch baking dish. When the batter has cooled, cut into disks roughly 2 inches in diameter with a cookie cutter or the equivalent, and place them in the baking dish, overlapping them so that they all fit.

Melt 4 tablespoons butter and pour it over the dumplings. Sprinkle with 4 tablespoons Parmesan, place in the oven for 20 minutes, or until they are golden and crisp, and serve.

◆ ◆ ◆ ◆ ◆

## Gnocchi di Zucca

SQUASH
DUMPLINGS

SERVES 4 TO 6

These make an interesting variation from more traditional dumplings. In Italy, they are made with a squash similar in shape but not flavor or texture to American pumpkins. We have had success with golden Hubbard and butternut squash. Try to obtain a very flavorful squash. The success of the dish depends on it.

*2 pounds butternut or golden Hubbard squash*
*3 tablespoons butter*

water
1½ cups unbleached all-purpose flour
5 eggs, beaten
pinch of nutmeg
pinch of salt
1¼ cups freshly grated Parmesan
1 tablespoon cream
½ cup freshly grated mozzarella

Peel the squash, remove the seeds, and cut into 1-inch cubes. Melt 1 tablespoon of butter in a frying pan, add the squash and ¼ cup of water, and cook uncovered for 15 minutes until the squash disintegrates. Add water as needed but only enough to prevent the squash from sticking. It must be as dry as possible.

Remove the squash from the heat and add flour, a little at a time, mixing vigorously with a wooden spoon or wire whisk. Add the eggs, nutmeg, salt, and ¾ cup of grated Parmesan. Combine thoroughly.

In a small saucepan, heat the cream, add the mozzarella, and continue cooking until the mozzarella melts. Add it to the squash. Continue working the mixture until a smooth, homogeneous batter is obtained.

Flour your hands, shake off any excess, and shape the batter into dumplings as described in the recipe for Potato Dumplings, p. 114. Add more flour to the batter if it is unworkable, but try to use as little flour as possible. Place the dumplings on a dry dish towel until all are made.

Bring 4 quarts of unsalted water to a boil. Add the dumplings, about 6 to 8 at a time, and cook until they float to the surface, about 2 to 3 minutes. Remove with a slotted spoon, place in a serving bowl, and keep warm until all are cooked.

Melt 2 tablespoons of butter, pour it over the dumplings, add ½ cup of Parmesan, and serve immediately.

♦ ♦ ♦ ♦ ♦

*Gnocchi di Semolino alla Romana*

BAKED
SEMOLINA
DUMPLINGS

Similar in preparation to Baked Flour Dumplings (see recipe), although the use of semolina gives a richer flavor and a coarser texture, these also make an excellent first course for dinner parties or for family affairs. Before you begin cooking, butter a 24-by-18-inch wooden, marble, Formica, or similar work surface. Place a large bowl of cold water near the work surface or, alternatively, place the work surface near the sink. These dumplings are best if baked until golden and crusty. They can be prepared ahead of time and baked before serving.

SERVES 4

FOR THE DUMPLINGS:

*3¾ cups milk*
*1½ cups semolina (Italian semolino, if available)*
*⅓ cup butter*
*⅓ cup freshly grated Parmesan*
*2 eggs plus 2 egg yolks, beaten*
*pinch of salt*
*pinch of nutmeg*

FOR THE SAUCE:

*3 tablespoons butter*
*½ cup freshly grated Parmesan*

Place the milk in a saucepan and bring to a boil over medium heat. Add the semolina slowly in a thin stream, stirring constantly with a wooden spoon. The semolina will thicken very quickly and should be thick enough to support the wooden spoon. If it is too thin, add semolina; if too thick, add milk. Continue cooking over a low heat for 7 minutes, stirring constantly.

Remove from the heat, add the ⅓ cup butter, ⅓ cup Parmesan, eggs, salt, and nutmeg. With a large kitchen knife, spread the batter evenly on the buttered work surface, wetting the blade occasionally with cold water, to a thickness of ¼ inch. Allow to cool.

Heat the oven to 450°F.

Butter a 9-by-12-inch baking dish. Cut the dumplings into 2-inch disks with a cookie cutter or the equivalent and place them in the baking dish, overlapping them so that they all fit.

Melt the 3 tablespoons of butter and drizzle over the dumplings. Sprinkle the ½ cup Parmesan on top and bake until golden, about 20 minutes. Serve hot.

◆ ◆ ◆ ◆

*Gnocchi di*
*Semolino*
*con Ricotta*

SEMOLINA
DUMPLINGS
WITH
RICOTTA

SERVES 4 TO 6

These are among our favorite dumplings. They are also very nourishing and can serve as a main course for a luncheon or light dinner. Prepare a working surface as in Baked Flour Dumplings, p. 115, before cooking begins.

FOR THE DUMPLINGS:

3¾ cups milk
pinch of saffron
1½ cups plus 2 to 3 tablespoons semolina (Italian
    semolino, if available)
2 eggs plus 2 yolks, beaten
3 tablespoons butter
⅓ cup freshly grated Parmesan
pinch of nutmeg
pinch of salt
¾ cup fresh ricotta

FOR THE SAUCE:

4 tablespoons butter
¾ pound fresh mushrooms, thinly sliced
¼ cup freshly grated Parmesan

Place the milk in a saucepan, add the saffron, and bring the milk to a boil over medium heat. Add the semolina slowly in a thin stream, stirring constantly with a wooden spoon. Cook 5 to 7 minutes, stirring constantly. The semolina should be thick enough to support the wooden spoon. Remove from the heat, add the eggs, butter, Parmesan, nutmeg, salt, and ricotta, and combine thoroughly.

Place the semolina batter on a buttered work surface and spread with a large kitchen knife, wetting the blade occasionally with cold water, to a thickness of ½ inch. Allow to cool for 10 minutes.

Meanwhile, melt the butter for the sauce in a large frying pan. When very hot, add the mushrooms and cook for 1 minute. Remove from the heat and set aside.

Sprinkle 2 tablespoons of semolina over the batter and combine well. Divide into 6 equal parts, shape each into a ball, and, on a working surface floured lightly with 1 tablespoon of semolina, roll and draw out each ball into a roll approximately 18 inches long and ¾ inch thick. Cut the rolls into pieces ½ inch to ¾ inch long, shape into dumplings (see recipe for Potato Dumplings), and place on a dry dish towel.

Bring 4 quarts of unsalted water to a boil and add the dumplings, about 6 to 8 at a time, and cook for 3 to 4 minutes. Remove with a slotted spoon and keep warm in a heated serving bowl until all are cooked.

Heat the mushroom sauce and add it to the dumplings. Sprinkle the Parmesan on top, mix gently, and serve at once.

♦ ♦ ♦ ♦ ♦

## Gnocchi di Polenta al Forno

CORNMEAL
DUMPLINGS

SERVES 6

Before beginning, butter an 18-by-24-inch wooden, marble, or Formica work surface. Place it near the sink or place a large bowl of cold water near the work surface. These dumplings can be served with either a tomato sauce (as described below) or a béchamel sauce. We prefer the former, but both are good. These dumplings can be prepared ahead of time and baked before serving.

FOR THE DUMPLINGS:

*4 cups water*
*pinch of salt*
*1½ cups coarse cornmeal*
*1 tablespoon butter*
*4 tablespoons freshly grated Parmesan*
*pinch of nutmeg*

FOR THE SAUCE:

*2 cups Tomato Sauce I (see recipe)*
*½ cup freshly grated Parmesan*

Bring the water to a boil in a saucepan, add salt, and pour the cornmeal into the water in a thin stream, stirring constantly with a wooden spoon. Continue cooking over low heat for 30 minutes, stirring frequently. Remove from the stove, add the butter, 4 tablespoons Parmesan, and nutmeg, and combine thoroughly.

Place the batter on the buttered work surface and spread evenly with a large kitchen knife, wetting the blade occasionally with cold water, to a thickness of ¼ inch. Allow to cool.

Preheat oven to 400°F. Meanwhile heat the tomato sauce.

When the dumpling batter has cooled, cut into disks with a 2-inch cookie cutter or the equivalent. Butter a 9-by-12-inch baking dish and place the dumplings in the dish, overlapping them so that they all fit. Spread the tomato sauce evenly over the dumplings, sprinkle the Parmesan on top, and bake in the preheated oven for 15 minutes. Serve hot.

◆ ◆ ◆ ◆ ◆

# *Gnocchi alla Fiorentina*

## FLORENTINE DUMPLINGS

### SERVES 3 TO 4

Dumplings made with ricotta and spinach are today very popular in northern Italy, especially in Florence, where they are sometimes called naked ravioli (*ravioli nudi*)—that is, ravioli stuffing without the pasta. These light, mildly flavored dumplings are usually served as a pasta dish, but they are lovely as a main course for a light supper. If done correctly, they are really very easy to prepare. At least the first time, follow the recipe closely.

FOR THE DUMPLINGS:

1½ *pounds fresh spinach*
½ *pound fresh ricotta, drained of excess water through a*
    *fine sieve or cheesecloth for 30 minutes*
2 *tablespoons butter, at room temperature*
¼ *cup plus 1 tablespoon flour*
1 *egg plus 2 egg yolks, beaten*
½ *cup freshly grated Parmesan*
*pinch of salt*
*freshly ground pepper to taste*
*pinch of nutmeg*

FOR THE SAUCE:

3 *tablespoons butter*
⅓ *teaspoon dried sage*
1 *cup freshly grated Parmesan*

Wash the spinach very well and discard the hard stems. Drain the spinach and cook in a saucepan without adding water until done, about 5 minutes for young, tender leaves. Drain and squeeze the spinach dry, either with your hands or by pressing the spinach with a spoon against the sides of a sieve. The drier the spinach, the less flour is needed, and the lighter the dumplings. Chop and put aside.

In a medium-size saucepan combine the ricotta, 2 tablespoons butter, flour, eggs, ½ cup Parmesan, salt, pepper, and nutmeg. Add the spinach, mix thoroughly, and cook over medium heat for 3 minutes, stirring constantly with a wooden spoon. Remove from the heat and allow to cool.

Take 1 heaping tablespoon of the ricotta-spinach mixture and shape it into a sausage-shaped roll 2 inches long by 1 inch thick on a lightly floured board. Shake off any excess flour. Continue until all the mixture is used.

When ready to serve, bring 4 quarts of unsalted water to a boil, then reduce the heat to a simmer. Place the dumplings, 4 at a time, in the simmering water and cook until they rise to the surface, about 3 minutes. Remove with a slotted spoon to a serving dish, and keep warm until all the dumplings are cooked.

Melt 3 tablespoons of butter, add the sage, sauté for 1 minute, and pour over the dumplings. Sprinkle 3 tablespoons of Parmesan on the dumplings and serve immediately. Pass the rest of the Parmesan for those who wish to add it.

### VARIATION

As an alternative, serve with 6 tablespoons of tomato sauce and grated Parmesan.

♦ ♦ ♦ ♦

## Polenta con Funghi e Peperoni

CORNMEAL
WITH
MUSHROOMS
AND
PEPPERS

SERVES 6

Polenta's mild, slightly nutty taste is a perfect foil for a rich, flavorful sauce such as the one given in this recipe, in which mushrooms and peppers are combined with tomato sauce.

1 teaspoon salt
freshly ground pepper to taste
2 cups coarse cornmeal
2 tablespoons butter
1 medium onion, thinly sliced
2 garlic cloves, chopped
½ pound fresh mushrooms, washed, trimmed, and
    thinly sliced
3 red or green bell peppers, seeds removed, thinly sliced
    lengthwise
1½ cups Tomato Sauce I or II (see recipes)
2 tablespoons chopped parsley
2 tablespoons chopped basil
2 tablespoons capers, chopped
3 tablespoons freshly grated Parmesan

Place 8 cups of water in a large, heavy saucepan, add salt and pepper, bring the water to a boil, and add the cornmeal slowly in a thin stream, stirring constantly with a wooden spoon to prevent lumping. Reduce the heat to low and cook, stirring occasionally, for at least 30 minutes.

Meanwhile generously butter a 10-inch-square baking dish or the equivalent and, when the cornmeal is cooked, pour it into the baking dish. Set aside.

Preheat the oven to 350°F.

Melt the butter in a frying pan, add the onion, and sauté over a medium heat for a few minutes. Add the garlic, sauté another minute, stir in the mushrooms and peppers, and continue to cook, stirring frequently, for 10 minutes, until the peppers are tender. Spread the vegetables evenly over the cornmeal.

Heat the tomato sauce in a small saucepan, add the parsley, basil, and capers, adjust for seasoning, and pour over the peppers and mushrooms. Sprinkle the top with Parmesan and bake in the preheated oven until the top begins to brown, about 20 minutes. Serve hot.

### VARIATION

Make a sauce: Cook the mushrooms and peppers and combine with the tomato sauce, herbs, and capers. Cook the cornmeal as described, place it on a heated serving platter, top with the sauce, sprinkle with Parmesan, and serve immediately.

♦ ♦ ♦ ♦ ♦

## Polenta Grassa

CORNMEAL
WITH
FONTINA

SERVES 6

In this delicious, rich specialty of the Piedmont, the cornmeal is cooked almost to completion, then fontina and Parmesan are added. If fontina is unavailable, use Gruyère. This is a substantial dish that can be served as a main course for a luncheon or light dinner.

*8 cups milk*
*1 teaspoon salt*
*freshly ground pepper to taste*
*4 tablespoons butter*
*1¾ cups coarse cornmeal*
*2 cups fontina or Gruyère, diced*
*½ cup freshly grated Parmesan*

Place the milk in a large, heavy saucepan, season with salt and pepper, add the butter, and bring the milk to a boil. Add the cornmeal slowly in a thin stream, stirring constantly with a wooden spoon to prevent lumping. When all the cornmeal is incorporated, reduce the heat to low and cook, stirring occasionally, for 30 minutes. Add the cheeses, blend thoroughly, and continue cooking until the cheeses are melted, about 5 minutes. Serve immediately in a heated serving bowl.

### VARIATION

Cook the cornmeal, add the cheese, and spread the mixture ½ inch thick on a wet work surface with a wet knife blade or spatula. Set aside until cooled and firm. Cut the cornmeal into small squares or disks and fry in butter or light seed oil until golden on both sides. Drain and serve hot.

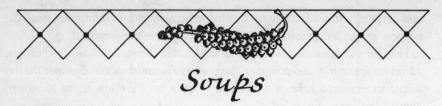

# *Soups*

Aside from a few famous exceptions, such as minestrone and Pasta e Fagioli, Italian soups are not well known outside of Italy. This is indeed unfortunate, since in variety, quality, and inventiveness they are second to none. The recipes included here give some idea of the range and originality of these soups and, of course, also represent our favorites. Some, such as Crêpes in Broth, are light and delicate—suitable as a first course for an elegant dinner party—while others, hearty and substantial like Minestrone Toscano, are ideal served with a salad, cheese, and fruit for a luncheon or light supper.

As you will see some soups are called *zuppe* and others *minestre. Zuppe* include bread as a main ingredient and are usually thick, while in *minestre*, which range from thick minestrone to pure broth, bread is not an ingredient.

It should be emphasized that in Italy soup, like pasta, is served as a first course and the two are never served together at the same meal.

We give only one recipe for vegetable broth. It can be used on its own or as the base for other soups. You can, of course, concoct your own broth by altering the ingredients—there are no hard-and-fast rules for broths. It is also possible to purchase powdered vegetable broth or broth cubes in health food shops and quality groceries. You can, with these, make a reasonably good vegetable broth in minutes instead of hours. And, with a few exceptions, instant vegetable broth can be substituted for the homemade variety in these recipes without any significant loss in flavor or quality.

♦ ♦ ♦ ♦ ♦

## *Crostini per Minestra*

CROUTONS
FOR
SOUP

Croutons are very easy to make at home and infinitely better than packaged varieties. Serve them in a straw basket or an attractive pottery dish along with the soup. They can be prepared in advance and will keep for a few days if stored in an airtight container.

*6 slices Italian bread, cut ½ inch thick*
*⅓ to ½ cup light seed oil for frying*

Remove and discard the crusts from the bread and cut into ½-inch cubes. Heat the oil in a frying pan, add the bread cubes, a few at a time, and fry, turning frequently, until golden on all sides. Remove with a slotted spoon and drain on paper towels. Do not cook at too high a heat—the bread cubes burn easily.

### VARIATION

As an alternative, toast 6 slices of Italian bread, crust removed, rub with a clove of peeled garlic, and cut into ½-inch cubes.

♦ ♦ ♦ ♦ ♦

## *Brodo Vegetale*

VEGETABLE
BROTH

MAKES 10 TO 13 CUPS

Use this broth on its own, strained or unstrained, or add rice or soup pasta. Use strained in recipes that require vegetable broth. For a light cream of vegetable soup, purée the vegetables, add cream, and serve. The broth will keep up to a week in the refrigerator or may be frozen.

4 tablespoons butter
3 onions, chopped
2 celery stalks with leaves, chopped
2 leeks, white and green parts, chopped
3 carrots, chopped
2 cups shredded cabbage
½ cup lentils
1 cup peeled and diced potatoes
½ teaspoon dried thyme
½ cup chopped parsley
¼ cup chopped basil
8 to 10 whole peppercorns
3 garlic cloves
2 bay leaves
½ teaspoon salt
pinch of nutmeg

Melt the butter in a stockpot, and sauté together the onions, celery, leeks, and carrots for a few minutes, until the onions begin to color. Stir in all the remaining ingredients, add 3 quarts of water, and bring to a boil. Reduce the heat and simmer covered for 2 hours. Remove from the heat and use as required.

♦ ♦ ♦ ♦ ♦

## *Minestrone Toscano*

### TUSCAN VEGETABLE SOUP

SERVES 6 TO 8

Every region in Italy has its minestrone, or hearty vegetable soup, and each has features that distinguish it from its relatives elsewhere. The Tuscan minestrone does not include potatoes or rice but relies instead on small pasta or stale bread for starch. If you opt for bread, use either good whole wheat bread or Italian bread, homemade if possible. Italians serve minestrone hot or, in the summer, at room temperature.

Florentines do not add Parmesan to Tuscan minestrone. They insist that it ruins the dish, especially when served at room temperature.

Minestrone improves with age and is, among Tuscans, as popular the second day as it is the first. When we make minestrone, we always try to make extra so that we can enjoy it again a day or so later. It will keep for 3 or 4 days in the refrigerator and should be reheated and stirred well before serving. Serve with a light dry red wine.

2 cups dried white beans
1 tablespoon flour
3 tablespoons olive oil
1 cup chopped onions
3 garlic cloves, minced
2 tablespoons chopped parsley
1 teaspoon dried thyme
1 tablespoon fresh rosemary, or 1 teaspoon dried
½ cup coarsely chopped celery
1 cup coarsely chopped carrots
1 bay leaf
1 cup canned Italian plum tomatoes, undrained and
    chopped
½ cup Tomato Sauce I (see recipe)
2 cups chopped zucchini
2 cups shredded cabbage
2 cups shredded Swiss chard
salt and freshly ground pepper to taste
1 cup small soup pasta
¾ cup freshly grated Parmesan (if desired)
6 slices Italian bread (optional)
1 garlic clove (optional)

Soak the beans for 8 hours, or overnight, in 4 cups of water to which 1 table-spoon of flour has been added. The flour softens the skin of the beans. Rinse the soaked beans and cook them in 5 cups of water for 1 hour, until cooked but still firm. As an alternative, cook them in a pressure cooker for 20 minutes. Drain the beans, reserving the liquid for use later. Set the beans aside.

While the beans are cooking, heat the olive oil in a large, heavy saucepan and sauté the onions until they begin to color. Add the 3 cloves of minced garlic, parsley, thyme, and rosemary and sauté for 1 more minute. Add the celery, carrots, and bay leaf and cook for 3 minutes, stirring. Add the tomatoes and tomato sauce and simmer over a low heat for 30 minutes.

Mash or process in a food processor 1 cup of the cooked beans to a smooth pulp and add this, together with the liquid in which the beans were cooked, to the tomato mixture. Combine and simmer for 15 minutes. Add the zucchini, cabbage, chard, and the whole beans and simmer for 20 minutes, until the vegetables are tender. Add more water or vegetable stock as required to make approximately 6 cups of liquid. Taste and correct for salt and pepper.

Ten minutes before serving, add the small soup pasta and simmer until the pasta is cooked al dente. Blend in the Parmesan if desired and serve.

## VARIATION

As an alternative, do not add the pasta but instead place a thick slice of toasted or stale bread rubbed with garlic in each individual soup bowl and ladle the soup over it.

♦ ♦ ♦ ♦ ♦

*Minestrone*

*alla*

*Milanese*

MILANESE
VEGETABLE
SOUP

SERVES 6 TO 8

The Milanese vegetable soup is distinguished from its Tuscan cousin by the addition of rice instead of pasta, peas instead of beans, and vegetables that are finely chopped, shredded, or even puréed instead of coarsely chopped. The Milanese minestrone is thus denser, but no less flavorful, than the Tuscan one. And, as with all minestrone, it is just as good, if not better, the second day as the first. Serve hot or at room temperature.

2 tablespoons butter
2 tablespoons olive oil
1 cup finely chopped or shredded onions
2 cups finely chopped or shredded leeks
2 cups finely chopped or shredded carrots
1 cup finely chopped or shredded celery
1 cup finely chopped or shredded potatoes
3 cups shredded escarole
3 cups shredded cabbage
2 tablespoons chopped parsley
2 tablespoons chopped basil
1 teaspoon crushed sage
2 bay leaves
¼ teaspoon cayenne pepper (optional)
1 cup seeded, peeled, and chopped fresh tomatoes, or 1
    cup chopped canned Italian plum tomatoes
½ cup Arborio rice
1 cup fresh or frozen peas
salt and freshly ground pepper to taste
½ cup freshly grated Parmesan

Heat the butter and olive oil in a large saucepan, add the onions and leeks, and sauté until they begin to color. Stir in the carrots and sauté another few minutes. Add the remaining vegetables, except the peas and tomatoes, one at a time in the order listed above, sautéing each for a few minutes before adding the next one.

When all the vegetables have been added, blend in 6 to 7 cups of water, the parsley, basil, sage, bay leaves, and cayenne pepper (if desired), and simmer, covered, for 1 hour, stirring occasionally. Add water as required.

After cooking the vegetables for an hour, add the tomatoes and simmer another 15 minutes.

Stir in the rice and peas and cook until the rice is done. Adjust for salt and pepper. Serve with grated Parmesan for those who want to add it.

♦ ♦ ♦ ♦ ♦

*Minestrone*

*al Pesto*

VEGETABLE
SOUP
WITH
PESTO

SERVES 6 TO 8

The addition of pesto sauce to this dish transforms it into a wonderfully aromatic, richly flavored, and altogether unforgettable vegetable soup. Serve this minestrone with a chilled dry white wine.

1½ cups dried white beans
1 tablespoon flour
½ ounce dried wild mushrooms (Boletus edulis)
¾ pound green beans, trimmed and cut into 1-inch
    segments
2 carrots, diced
2 cups diced butternut or golden Hubbard squash
3 cups shredded cabbage, escarole, Swiss chard, or
    spinach
1 leek, chopped
⅓ pound short, stout pasta such as penne or elbow
    macaroni
salt and freshly ground pepper to taste
2 tablespoons butter
1 fresh tomato, peeled, seeded, and chopped
4 tablespoons Pesto (see recipe)
½ cup freshly grated Parmesan

Soak the beans for 8 hours or overnight in 4 cups of water with 1 tablespoon of flour. The flour softens the skin of the beans. Then rinse the beans, combine them with 6 cups of water in a large saucepan, and simmer covered for 1 hour, until tender but still firm, or cook for 20 minutes in a pressure cooker.

Soak the dried mushrooms in 1 cup of warm water for 20 minutes and remove carefully from the water, reserving the soaking liquid. Rinse under cold running water to remove grit and sand, drain, chop fine, and set aside. Strain the liquid in which the mushrooms were soaked through thick cheesecloth or a coffee filter and set aside.

When the white beans are cooked, stir in the mushrooms, green beans, carrots, squash, leafy vegetables, and leek. Add 2 cups of water plus the water in which the mushrooms were soaked, bring to a boil, and simmer, covered, for 30 minutes, stirring occasionally. Bring the soup mixture to a rapid boil, pour in the pasta, and cook, uncovered, until the pasta is al dente. Taste and correct for salt and pepper and add the butter.

While the pasta cooks, mash the tomato with a fork in a small mixing bowl and add the pesto, a little at a time, combining the ingredients thoroughly. Add the pesto mixture to the vegetable soup, mix well, cover, and allow to steep for 5 minutes before serving. Pass the Parmesan for those who wish it.

♦ ♦ ♦ ♦ ♦

*Zuppa di Cavolo*

HEARTY
CABBAGE
SOUP

SERVES 6

This thick soup, made with cabbage and beans, resembles onion soup and can, like onion soup, be served in individual ovenproof terra cotta bowls. It makes a substantial first course and, accompanied with a fresh salad, serves nicely as a main dish for a light dinner or for a luncheon.

½ cup dried white beans
2 teaspoons flour
3 tablespoons olive oil
1 cup thinly sliced leeks
1 cup thinly sliced carrots
1 cup thinly sliced turnips, cut in strips
3 garlic cloves, chopped
1 tablespoon chopped parsley
1 tablespoon chopped basil
1 teaspoon oregano
2 whole bay leaves
1 small cabbage, thinly sliced
salt and freshly ground pepper to taste
6 small slices Italian bread, crust removed, and toasted
¼ cup grated Gruyère
¼ cup freshly grated Parmesan

Soak the beans for 8 hours or overnight in 3 cups of water to which 2 teaspoons of flour have been added. The flour softens the skin of the beans. When ready to use, rinse, and cook for 1 hour in 4 cups of water. As an alternative, cook in a pressure cooker with 2 cups of water for approximately 20 minutes. The beans should be cooked but firm.

While the beans are cooking, heat the oil in a large saucepan, add the leeks, and sauté until they begin to color. Add the carrots, turnips, garlic, and herbs. Sauté a few minutes more, then add 1 cup of water and simmer covered for 20 minutes. Add 1 cup of cooked beans, the water in which the beans were cooked, and additional water, if necessary, to make approximately 6 cups. Add the cabbage. Cover and simmer for another 20 minutes, adding salt and pepper to taste.

Meanwhile preheat the oven to 375°F.

If you wish to make individual servings, put the soup in 6 ovenproof soup bowls and place on top of each a slice of toast. Combine the Gruyère and Parmesan in a small mixing bowl, and sprinkle 2 tablespoons of the cheese mixture on each slice of toast. Place the bowls in the oven for 10 to 15 minutes, until the cheese melts and a crust forms.

If you prefer to serve the soup from a large tureen, select a large ovenproof bowl or casserole, add the soup, place the bread slices on top, sprinkle with the cheeses, and put in the oven for 10 to 15 minutes until the cheeses melt and begin to form a crust. Serve immediately.

♦ ♦ ♦ ♦ ♦

## *Minestrone di Risʊ e Rape*

RICE
AND
TURNIP
SOUP

SERVES 6

This is a miraculous soup—even inveterate turnip haters love it. The combined flavors of turnips and rice in broth is extraordinarily good. Serve this soup on any occasion, from elegant dinners to simple family meals.

3 tablespoons butter
4 cups peeled young turnips, cut into ½-inch cubes
6 cups Vegetable Broth (see recipe)
½ cup Italian or Carolina long-grain rice
salt and freshly ground pepper to taste
2 tablespoons chopped parsley
¾ cup freshly grated Parmesan

Heat the butter in a large saucepan and sauté the turnips over high heat, turning frequently, until browned. Add the broth and cook covered for 10 minutes. Blend in the rice and cook until the rice is al dente, about 15 minutes. Taste and correct for salt and pepper. Just before serving mix in the parsley and ¼ cup of Parmesan. Serve hot. Pass ½ cup of Parmesan for those who wish to add it.

♦ ♦ ♦ ♦ ♦

## *Minestra di Piselli con Risʊ*

RICE
AND
PEA
SOUP

SERVES 4 TO 6

½ ounce dried wild mushrooms (Boletus edulis)
3 tablespoons butter
½ cup finely chopped celery
1 onion, chopped fine
2 cups fresh or frozen peas
5 cups Vegetable Broth (see recipe)
¾ cup Italian or Carolina long-grain rice
salt and freshly ground pepper to taste
¼ cup freshly grated Parmesan
3 tablespoons roughly chopped parsley

Soak the dried mushrooms in 1 cup of warm water for 20 minutes and remove carefully from the water, reserving the soaking liquid. Rinse the mushrooms under cold water to remove grit and sand, drain, chop fine, and set aside. Strain the soaking liquid through thick cheesecloth or a coffee filter and set aside.

Melt the butter in a large saucepan, add the celery and onion, and cook over high heat for 2 to 3 minutes. Stir in the mushrooms, add the fresh peas, the liquid in which the mushrooms were soaked, and vegetable broth. Bring to a boil, add the rice, combine, and cook, covered, until the rice is al dente, about 15 to 20 minutes. If using frozen peas, add 5 minutes before the rice is cooked. Taste and correct for salt and pepper.

Just before serving, blend in the Parmesan and the parsley.

♦ ♦ ♦ ♦ ♦

## Minestra di Cavolfiore

CAULIFLOWER
SOUP

SERVES 4 TO 6

3 tablespoons olive oil
1 large onion, finely chopped
1 carrot, finely chopped
1 celery stalk, finely chopped
2 garlic cloves, chopped
1 cup canned Italian plum tomatoes, drained and
    chopped, or ½ cup Tomato Sauce I or II (see
    recipes)
1 small cauliflower, washed, trimmed, and cut into
    small pieces
5 cups Vegetable Broth (see recipe)
1 bay leaf
1 dried hot pepper, whole
salt and freshly ground pepper to taste
⅓ pound small pasta such as orecchiette or small
    macaroni
½ cup freshly grated Parmesan

Heat the oil in a large, heavy saucepan, add the onion, carrot, and celery, and sauté for 5 minutes. Add the garlic and sauté for another minute. Stir in the tomatoes or tomato sauce, add the cauliflower, and combine well. Simmer for 5 minutes, stirring frequently. Pour in the broth, add the bay leaf and hot pepper, and simmer covered for 30 minutes. Taste and correct for salt and pepper.

Ten minutes before serving, bring the soup to a boil, add the pasta, and cook until the pasta is al dente.

Remove the bay leaf and the hot pepper and serve hot. Pass the Parmesan for those who wish to add it.

♦ ♦ ♦ ♦ ♦

## Minestra di Spinaci

COLD
SPICY
SPINACH
SOUP

SERVES 4 TO 6

This zesty combination of spinach, chili pepper, lemon juice, and yogurt is served chilled. It is ideal for lunch on a hot summer's day.

*¼ to ½ teaspoon dried or fresh hot pepper, seeded and*
*    chopped*
*2 cups finely shredded spinach*
*2 egg yolks*
*juice of 1 lemon*
*½ cup peeled and chopped cucumber*
*1 cup plain yogurt*
*1 garlic clove, minced*
*salt and freshly ground pepper to taste*
*12 thin slices cucumber*

Bring 5 cups of water to a boil in a large saucepan, add the hot pepper and the spinach, and cook covered for 5 minutes. Meanwhile, combine the egg yolks and lemon juice in a large serving bowl and add to the hot soup, a little at a time, beating constantly. Chill for 2 hours.

When ready to serve, add the chopped cucumber, yogurt, and garlic. Taste and correct for salt and pepper and serve the soup garnished with the slices of cucumber.

♦ ♦ ♦ ♦ ♦

## Zuppa di Asparagi

ASPARAGUS
SOUP

SERVES 6

*6 tablespoons butter*
*1 tablespoon flour*
*6 cups Vegetable Broth (see recipe)*
*1 pound fresh asparagus, washed and cut into 1-inch*
*    sections, the tough parts of the stems removed*
*6 small slices bread, roughly 3 inches square by ½ inch*
*    thick*
*½ cup freshly grated Parmesan*
*salt and freshly ground pepper to taste*

In a saucepan melt 2 tablespoons of butter, add the flour, and stir for 30 seconds over low heat. Add the vegetable broth, a little at a time, stirring constantly with a whisk or wooden spoon. The broth should be slightly thick and creamy.

Bring the broth to a simmer and add the asparagus pieces. Cover and simmer gently for 10 minutes or until the asparagus is tender.

Meanwhile, melt the remaining butter in a frying pan, add the slices of bread a few at a time, and fry on both sides until golden. Add more butter if necessary. Place one slice of the fried bread in the bottom of each of 6 individual soup bowls and sprinkle 1 tablespoon of Parmesan on each slice.

Taste the soup and correct for salt and pepper. Ladle the soup, boiling hot, into the individual soup bowls and serve immediately. Pass additional Parmesan for those who want it.

♦ ♦ ♦ ♦ ♦

## *Zuppa di Cipolle*

ONION
SOUP

SERVES 6

*¼ pound butter*
*4 large red onions, thinly sliced*
*1 tablespoon flour*
*½ teaspoon salt*
*1 teaspoon freshly ground pepper*
*½ cup dry white wine*
*9 slices coarse Italian bread, ¼ inch thick by 3 inches square, lightly toasted*
*¼ cup freshly grated Parmesan*
*¼ cup freshly grated Gruyère*

Melt the butter in a large, heavy saucepan, add the onions, and simmer covered, stirring occasionally, for 10 minutes. If you wish to brown the onions, cook uncovered until golden, stirring frequently. If cooked this way, the soup will be a little stronger in flavor and the onions less sweet. We prefer the former method.

When ready, add the flour and salt and pepper, and cook uncovered 2 to 3 minutes, stirring constantly.

Stir in 6 cups of boiling water, enough to cover the onions completely. Cover and cook slowly over a low heat for 1½ to 2 hours, stirring occasionally. Ten minutes before serving, taste and adjust for seasoning and blend in the white wine.

Butter the toasted bread lightly, place 4 to 5 slices on the bottom of a heated tureen, and sprinkle on half the cheeses. Add the remaining bread slices and cover with the rest of the cheeses. When cooked, pour the soup, boiling hot, into the tureen or casserole, cover, allow to steep for 5 minutes, then serve. Make sure that some of the bread and cheeses from the bottom of the tureen are included with each serving.

♦ ♦ ♦ ♦ ♦

*Acqua Cotta*

COOKED
WATER

SERVES 4 TO 6

This delicious soup with the unappetizing name was invented by the shepherds of the Maremma, an extensive, sparsely populated area between Siena and Grosseto. During their long sojourn in the hills with their flocks, they had to rely on stale bread, garlic, onions, oil, and whatever wild herbs and mushrooms they could find to make soup. They called the soup Acqua Cotta for the simple reason that the main ingredient was water. The recipe that follows is a modern adaptation. Serve with a chilled dry white wine.

3 tablespoons olive oil
1 medium onion, thinly sliced
4 garlic cloves, thinly sliced
1 pound fresh mushrooms, washed, trimmed, and thinly sliced
3 cups peeled, seeded, and chopped fresh tomatoes, or 3 cups canned Italian plum tomatoes, drained and chopped
¼ teaspoon dried oregano
¼ teaspoon dried or fresh thyme
1 bay leaf
½ teaspoon dried rosemary, or 1 teaspoon fresh
salt and freshly ground pepper to taste
6 thick slices Italian bread, preferably homemade, either stale or toasted
1 garlic clove, peeled
2 tablespoons freshly grated Parmesan

Heat the olive oil in a large, heavy saucepan, add the onion and the sliced garlic cloves, and sauté until the garlic begins to color. Stir in the mushrooms and sauté over medium heat for 3 minutes. Blend in the tomatoes and simmer for 5 minutes, stirring frequently.

Add the oregano, thyme, bay leaf, rosemary, and 5 cups of water. Bring to a boil, reduce the heat, and simmer, covered, for at least 30 minutes. Taste and adjust for salt and pepper.

When ready to serve, rub the slices of bread with the clove of garlic and place one slice in each of 6 individual soup bowls. Remove the bay leaf, add the Parmesan, and serve.

♦ ♦ ♦ ♦ ♦

## Pappa di Pane

BREAD
SOUP

SERVES 6

A favorite among Florentines, this is a delicious combination of tomatoes, bread, garlic, and oil. It is easy to prepare, inexpensive, and very tasty. The bread should be dry and hard, the more stale the better. Pass olive oil for those who wish to add a tablespoon to the Pappa.

¼ cup olive oil

4 garlic cloves, roughly chopped

6 leaves fresh or dried sage

2½ cups canned Italian plum tomatoes, roughly chopped with their own juice

3 cups very stale, coarse bread, cut into ½-inch cubes

5 cups Vegetable Broth (see recipe)

salt and pepper

Heat the olive oil in a large saucepan, add the garlic and sage, and sauté for 30 seconds. Blend in the tomatoes and simmer over a medium heat, stirring occasionally, until a dense tomato sauce is obtained, about 25 minutes.

Add the bread and continue cooking, stirring frequently, for 3 minutes. Stir in the vegetable stock and simmer over a low heat for 15 minutes. Taste and adjust for salt and pepper. The soup should have the consistency of thick cornmeal.

Serve hot or at room temperature in individual soup bowls.

♦ ♦ ♦ ♦ ♦

## Crema di Cetriolo Fredda

COLD
CREAM
OF
CUCUMBER
SOUP

SERVES 4 TO 6

This is in every way a marvelous soup for a hot summer's day. It is easy to prepare, light, and fresh. For those who want a strong garlic flavor, do not cook the garlic with the other ingredients, but instead add it raw to the blender.

5 cups Vegetable Broth (see recipe)

2 cucumbers, peeled and coarsely chopped

1 potato, peeled and coarsely chopped

3 leeks, coarsely chopped, or 2 cups coarsely chopped onions

2 garlic cloves

1 cup thick cream

salt and freshly ground pepper to taste

2 tablespoons chopped chives

12 thin slices cucumber

Place the broth in a large saucepan and bring to a boil. Add the chopped cucumbers, potato, leeks or onions, and garlic. Simmer until tender, about 30 minutes. Transfer the soup to a blender, food processor, or food mill and blend until smooth. Refrigerate until cold, at least 1 hour.

Just prior to serving, stir in the cream and correct for salt and pepper. Pour the soup into a chilled bowl, preferably glass, garnish with the chives and cucumber slices, and serve.

♦ ♦ ♦ ♦ ♦

## Crema di Pomodori

·

CREAM
OF
TOMATO
SOUP

SERVES 4 TO 6

3 tablespoons butter
¾ cup roughly chopped onions
½ cup roughly chopped carrots
1 tablespoon flour
1 pound ripe tomatoes, peeled, seeded, and roughly chopped, or 1½ cups canned Italian plum tomatoes, chopped with their juice
2 cups milk
2 cups water
¼ teaspoon sugar
½ cup Italian or Carolina long-grain rice
salt and freshly ground pepper to taste

Over medium heat, melt the butter in a saucepan, add the onions and carrots, and sauté until the onions wilt. Do not allow them to brown. Add the flour and stir until blended with the vegetables. Add the tomatoes and cook for 2 minutes. Then add the milk, a tablespoon at a time in the beginning, stirring constantly. Add 2 cups of water and the sugar. Simmer, covered, over low heat, stirring occasionally, for 30 minutes.

Remove the soup from the heat, let cool for a few minutes, transfer to a blender or processor, and purée until smooth. Return the soup to the saucepan, add the rice, and simmer over low heat until the rice is cooked, about 15 to 20 minutes. Add milk if the soup is too thick. Taste and correct for salt and pepper.

♦ ♦ ♦ ♦ ♦

## Crema di Piselli

CREAM
OF
PEA
SOUP

SERVES 4 TO 6

3 tablespoons butter
3 leeks, washed and sliced
½ head romaine lettuce, washed and shredded
2 cups fresh or frozen peas
½ teaspoon sugar
5 cups water or Vegetable Broth (see recipe)
½ teaspoon salt
2 egg yolks
1 tablespoon minced parsley
1 teaspoon chopped fresh or dried mint
¾ cup thick cream

Heat the butter in a large saucepan, add the leeks and lettuce, and cook covered over moderate heat, stirring occasionally, for 5 to 7 minutes. Blend in the peas and sugar and cook for 2 minutes. Add water or broth and the salt. Simmer covered until the peas are tender, 5 minutes for frozen peas, 15 for fresh.

When the peas are cooked, transfer the soup to a blender or food processor and purée. Return the soup to the saucepan, heat through, and set aside.

When ready to serve, combine the egg yolks, parsley, mint, and cream in a heated tureen or casserole. Bring the soup to a boil and, beating the egg-and-cream mixture constantly, pour 1 cup of the boiling soup into the tureen slowly in a thin stream. It is important to beat the egg-and-cream mixture as you add the soup. This way the egg yolks will cook but remain smooth. Add the rest of the soup. Serve hot.

♦ ♦ ♦ ♦ ♦

## Crema di Funghi

CREAM
OF
MUSHROOM
SOUP

SERVES 4 TO 6

The addition of dried wild mushrooms in this recipe greatly enhances the soup's flavor. If you have access to fresh *Boletus edulis* by all means use them.

½ ounce dried wild mushrooms (Boletus edulis)
2 tablespoons butter
½ cup chopped onion
¼ teaspoon minced sage
2 tablespoons Tomato Sauce I (see recipe)
1 tablespoon flour
2½ cups hot milk
1½ pounds washed, trimmed, and thinly sliced fresh mushrooms
½ cup peeled and cubed potatoes

2 cups water or Vegetable Broth (see recipe)
½ cup thick cream
salt and freshly ground pepper to taste
1 tablespoon minced parsley
Croutons for Soup (see recipe) (optional)

Soak the dried mushrooms in 1 cup of warm water for 20 minutes and remove carefully from the water, reserving the soaking liquid. Rinse under cold water to remove grit and sand, drain, and chop fine. Strain the soaking liquid through thick cheesecloth or a coffee filter and set aside.

Heat the butter in a large saucepan, add the onion, and sauté over a low heat until transparent. It must not brown. Stir in the sage and the tomato sauce. Simmer, stirring constantly, for 2 minutes. While stirring, blend in the flour and cook for another minute or two. Still stirring, slowly add the milk in a thin stream. The mixture at this point should have the consistency of cream.

Blend in carefully all but ¼ cup of the thinly sliced fresh mushrooms and all the reconstituted dried ones. Add the potatoes, the water or vegetable broth, and the water in which the dried mushrooms were soaked, cover, and simmer for 30 minutes, stirring occasionally.

When cooked, remove ¾ cup of mushrooms from the broth with a slotted spoon, place in a mixing bowl, and set aside. Pour the rest of the soup into a blender or processor and blend until smooth. Return the purée to the saucepan, add the ¾ cup of unblended mushrooms and the cream, and heat through. Taste and adjust for salt and pepper.

Dot the surface with the uncooked fresh mushrooms and the minced parsley and serve immediately. You may wish to pass croutons with this soup.

♦ ♦ ♦ ♦ ♦

## Crema di Porri

CREAM
OF
LEEK
SOUP

SERVES 4 TO 6

A very popular soup in our family, this can be made with fewer potatoes. However, we find that this quantity provides just the right balance for the leeks.

3 cups peeled, diced potatoes
4 cups sliced leeks, the white and some of the green
1 cup sliced onions
3 cups water or Vegetable Broth (see recipe)
1 cup cream
7 tablespoons finely chopped chives
2 tablespoons finely chopped parsley
Croutons for Soup (see recipe) (optional)

Place the potatoes, leeks, onions, and water or broth in a large saucepan, bring to a boil, and simmer covered for 20 minutes, stirring occasionally, until the vegetables are tender.

Pour the soup into a blender or processor and purée. Return to the saucepan, add the cream and 4 tablespoons of chives, heat through (*do not boil*), and set aside.

When ready to serve, heat through once again without boiling. Combine the parsley and 3 tablespoons of chives and sprinkle over the top. Serve hot with or without croutons.

♦ ♦ ♦ ♦ ♦

## Crema di Castagne

### CREAM OF CHESTNUT SOUP

SERVES 4 TO 6

Chestnuts in Italy are used as vegetables, in desserts, and in soups. The season for chestnuts is late fall and winter, and this soup, a delicately flavored yet distinctive blend of chestnuts, cream, and rosemary, makes an ideal beginning for a dinner party on a chilly winter evening. Serve with a light dry red wine.

*1 pound fresh chestnuts*
*1 stalk celery*
*5 cups Vegetable Broth (see recipe)*
*1½ cups milk*
*1 cup thick cream*
*pinch of ground anise*
*salt and freshly ground pepper to taste*
*2 tablespoons butter*
*½ teaspoon dried rosemary, crushed*
*Croutons for Soup (see recipe) (optional)*

With a very sharp paring knife, cut an X in the flat side of the shell of the chestnuts. Bring 4 cups of salted water to a boil in a large saucepan, add the chestnuts, and boil, covered, for 20 minutes. Drain and when cool enough to handle, but still warm, remove both the outer shell and inner brown skin. Place the chestnuts in a saucepan, add the celery and the broth, and simmer for 20 to 30 minutes, until the chestnuts are tender.

Remove the celery and discard. Transfer the chestnuts with a slotted spoon to a blender or food processor, add ½ cup of broth, reserving the rest in the saucepan, and purée. Return the chestnut purée to the saucepan, stir in the milk, cream, and anise, and warm through. Taste and correct for salt and pepper and keep warm.

Melt the butter in a small saucepan, add the rosemary, and sauté for 1 minute. Blend the rosemary-butter mixture into the soup and serve hot. Pass croutons for those who want them.

♦ ♦ ♦ ♦ ♦

## *Zuppa di Lenticchie*

LENTIL
SOUP

SERVES 6

1½ cups lentils
1 bay leaf
2 tablespoons butter
3 tablespoons olive oil
1 medium onion, finely chopped
1 carrot, finely chopped
2 stalks celery, chopped
1 tablespoon fresh rosemary, or 1 teaspoon dried
3 cloves garlic, chopped
3 tablespoons chopped parsley
1 teaspoon seeded and finely chopped hot peppers
1 tablespoon capers, chopped
1½ cups peeled, seeded, and chopped tomatoes
salt and freshly ground pepper to taste
6 slices dried Italian bread, 3 inches square and ¼ inch
   thick
6 tablespoons freshly grated Parmesan

Soak the lentils in 4 cups of water for 8 hours or overnight. Rinse the lentils, place them in a saucepan with 7 cups of warm water, add the bay leaf, bring to a boil, and simmer over low heat until tender, about 20 to 25 minutes.

In the meantime, heat the butter and 2 tablespoons of olive oil in a large saucepan, add the onion, carrot, celery, and rosemary, and sauté over a medium heat for 10 minutes. Add the garlic, parsley, hot peppers, and capers, and sauté another 3 minutes. Add the tomatoes and simmer over a low heat for 20 minutes.

When cooked, drain the lentils but reserve the cooking liquid. Remove and discard the bay leaf. Add half the lentils to the tomato mixture and simmer for 5 minutes. Mash the other half of the lentils with a potato masher or purée in a blender or processor and add to the tomato mixture. Add the water in which the lentils were cooked, heat through, and keep warm. Taste and adjust for salt and pepper.

Heat the remaining tablespoon of olive oil in a frying pan, add the bread pieces, and fry, turning, until golden on both sides. Place a piece of bread in each soup bowl and sprinkle 1 tablespoon of Parmesan on each piece. Bring the soup to a boil, ladle it into the bowls, and serve immediately.

♦ ♦ ♦ ♦ ♦

## *Pasta e Fagioli alla Virginia*

VIRGINIA'S
PASTA
AND
BEAN
SOUP

SERVES 6

This classic bean soup is often prepared with *maltagliati* (literally, "badly cut"), those scraps of homemade pasta that remain after the lasagne or fettuccine are made. If you do have such leftovers by all means use them, but any kind of egg noodles will do. Serve with a light dry red wine.

1 cup dried red or white beans
1 tablespoon flour
3 tablespoons olive oil
1 cup chopped onions
4 garlic cloves, minced
1 stalk celery, with leaves, chopped
4 tablespoons chopped parsley
3 tablespoons chopped basil
1 cup canned Italian plum tomatoes, with juice
¼ teaspoon minced fresh or dried sage
¼ teaspoon seeded and finely chopped dried hot pepper
7 cups Vegetable Broth (see recipe)
salt and freshly ground pepper to taste
2 cups egg noodles cut in 2-inch lengths, small
    macaroni, or maltagliati
½ cup freshly grated Parmesan

Soak the beans overnight or for 8 hours with the flour in 3 cups of water. The flour softens the skin of the beans. When ready to use, rinse the beans and set aside.

Heat the oil in a large, heavy saucepan, add the onions, and sauté over medium heat until they begin to color. Add the garlic, celery, parsley, and basil, and cook for another minute. Stir in the tomatoes, sage, and hot pepper, and cook another 5 minutes. Add the vegetable broth and the beans. Bring to a boil, reduce the heat, and simmer covered until the beans are cooked, about 1 to 1½ hours, stirring occasionally. Taste and correct for salt and pepper.

Fifteen minutes prior to serving, bring the soup to a boil, add the pasta, and cook until al dente. Pass Parmesan for those who want it.

◆ ◆ ◆ ◆ ◆

*Minestra di*

*Ceci*

CHICK-PEA
SOUP

SERVES 6

This soup, made with chick-peas, pasta, herbs, and a little tomato sauce, improves with age. We often make double the amount indicated below and thus have enough to enjoy it on successive days. You can, if you wish, use 2 cups of canned chick-peas. They do not require cooking but should be rinsed before using. Discard the liquid.

1 cup chick-peas, dried
1 tablespoon flour
1 carrot, peeled
1 onion, cut in half
2 bay leaves
1 sprig parsley
¼ teaspoon salt
¼ teaspoon peppercorns
olive oil
4 garlic cloves, minced
2 leeks, thinly sliced
1 tomato, peeled, seeded, and chopped
2 tablespoons Tomato Sauce I (see recipe)
1 teaspoon dried rosemary
2 tablespoons chopped parsley or basil
⅓ pound short, stout pasta such as penne or elbow
    macaroni
salt and freshly ground pepper to taste

Soak the dried chick-peas for at least 8 hours, preferably overnight, in 3 cups of water with 1 tablespoon of flour. The flour softens the skin of the chick-peas. Drain and rinse them when ready to use, and place them in a saucepan with 8 cups of water. Add the carrot, onion, bay leaves, parsley, salt, and peppercorns. Bring to a boil, reduce heat, and simmer covered for 1½ to 2 hours. As an alternative, cook in a pressure cooker for 30 minutes.

Meanwhile, heat 3 tablespoons olive oil in a large saucepan, add the garlic and leeks, and sauté until the garlic begins to color. Add the tomato, the tomato sauce, and the rosemary. Simmer for 3 minutes, stirring constantly, then remove from the heat.

When the chick-peas are cooked, drain them, reserving the liquid, and discard the carrot, onion, bay leaves, and peppercorns. Blend the chick-peas into the tomato mixture in the large saucepan; add parsley or basil and the liquid in which the chick-peas were cooked. Bring to a rapid boil, add the pasta, and cook, uncovered, until the pasta is al dente. Adjust the seasoning and serve hot or at room temperature. Pass olive oil for those who wish to add a little to their soup. It enriches the flavor of the broth.

### VARIATION

Purée the chick-peas instead of adding them whole to the tomato mixture, and substitute rice for the pasta.

♦ ♦ ♦ ♦ ♦

## Intruglia

BEAN
SOUP
WITH
CORNMEAL

SERVES 6

The unlikely combination of cornmeal, beans, and vegetables actually makes a wonderfully textured, rich, and hearty minestrone. Served with slices of Fettunta (see recipe) and salad, it makes a light meal. *Intruglia* goes well with a light dry red wine.

*1 cup dried red or white beans*
*1 tablespoon flour*
*olive oil*
*¾ cup minced onions*
*¼ teaspoon minced sage*
*3 garlic cloves, minced*
*1 small carrot, minced*
*1 celery stalk, minced*
*3 tablespoons minced parsley*
*¼ cup Tomato Sauce I or II (see recipes)*
*1 to 2 cups Vegetable Broth (see recipe)*
*3 cups shredded cabbage*
*salt and freshly ground pepper to taste*
*¼ cup cornmeal*

Soak the beans for 8 hours or overnight with 1 tablespoon of flour in 3 cups of water. The flour softens the skin of the beans. When ready to use, rinse, drain, and cook beans covered in 4 cups of water until tender, about 1 to 1½ hours. As an alternative, cook in a pressure cooker for 25 minutes. Drain the beans and set aside. Reserve the liquid in which the beans were cooked.

Heat ¼ cup olive oil in a large, heavy saucepan and sauté the onions, sage, garlic, carrot, celery, and parsley for 3 minutes. Add the tomato sauce, combine well, and remove from the heat.

Purée 1 cup of the cooked beans in a blender or food processor and blend the purée with the sautéed vegetables and tomato sauce. Reserve the remaining whole beans to add later.

Add the water in which the beans were cooked and enough vegetable stock to make 6 cups of liquid in the large saucepan. Return to the heat, bring to a boil, stir in the cabbage, and simmer covered for 30 minutes, stirring occasionally.

When the cabbage is cooked, add the whole beans. Taste and correct for salt and pepper. Pour in the cornmeal slowly in a thin stream, stirring constantly to prevent it from lumping. Simmer covered for another 15 minutes and serve. Pass olive oil for those who want to add a teaspoon to their soup.

♦ ♦ ♦ ♦ ♦

## Pasta Ripiena in Brodo

STUFFED
PASTA
SOUP

SERVES 6

The flavor of this soup depends very much on the broth, so use a good, richly flavored homemade broth. You can use any of the stuffed pastas (ravioli, agnolotti, tortellini) for this dish. The stuffed pasta can be made especially for the soup or you can make extra when you're preparing stuffed pasta to be eaten with a sauce (*asciutta*) and keep the extra for soup. The soup is elegant and impressive, ideal for a dinner party.

8 to 10 cups Vegetable Broth (see recipe)
24 to 30 ravioli, agnolotti, or tortellini, p. 92, 4 to 5
    per person, depending on size
2 tablespoons chopped parsley
½ cup freshly grated Parmesan

Bring the broth to a boil in a large saucepan. If the pasta is uncooked, cook it for 5 to 15 minutes, depending on the thickness and freshness of the dough, until al dente. If the stuffed pastas have already been cooked, warm through. In either case, when ready, remove the pasta with a slotted spoon, place 4 or 5 in each of the soup bowls, add broth, sprinkle with parsley, and serve immediately. Pass the Parmesan for those who want it.

### VARIATIONS

This type of soup is also made with Potato Dumplings (see recipe) or with Florentine Dumplings (see recipe). Follow the procedure described above. If you use the spinach and ricotta dumplings, make them the size of large olives.

◆ ◆ ◆ ◆ ◆

## Stracciatella al Pomodoro

TOMATO
EGG-DROP
SOUP

SERVES 6 TO 8

1½ cups canned Italian plum tomatoes, drained and
finely chopped, or 5 tablespoons Tomato Sauce I or
II (see recipes)
3 garlic cloves, minced
1 bay leaf
4 extra-large eggs
3 tablespoons bread crumbs
pinch of nutmeg
5 tablespoons grated Parmesan
2 tablespoons finely chopped parsley
2 tablespoons finely chopped chives
8 or 9 cups Vegetable Broth (see recipe)
salt and freshly ground pepper to taste
Croutons for Soup (see recipe) (optional)

In a large saucepan combine the tomatoes, garlic, and bay leaf. Bring to a simmer and cook, stirring occasionally, for 5 minutes.

While the tomatoes cook, blend together in a mixing bowl the eggs, bread crumbs, nutmeg, Parmesan, parsley, and chives. Beat until frothy.

Discard the bay leaf and add the vegetable broth to the tomatoes. Bring the broth to a boil and, stirring constantly, pour the egg mixture in a thin stream into the broth. Reduce the heat and simmer for 5 minutes. Taste and correct for seasoning. Pass croutons for those who want to add them to their soup.

◆ ◆ ◆ ◆ ◆

## Minestra Celestina

CRÊPES
IN
BROTH

SERVES 6

This is an inspired combination of a light vegetable broth with sliced crêpes. It is elegant and delicately flavored, perfect for dinner parties.

Crêpes (see recipe) made with:
2 extra-large eggs
½ cup flour
1 cup milk
1 tablespoon melted butter
1 tablespoon Cognac or brandy
8 to 9 cups Vegetable Broth (see recipe)
2 tablespoons finely chopped chives
2 tablespoons finely chopped parsley
5 tablespoons freshly grated pecorino or Romano
¼ teaspoon freshly ground pepper

The crêpes can be made in advance if necessary. Roll each crêpe into a cylinder and cut into ¼-inch-thick slices with a sharp knife. You will obtain long strands that resemble fettuccine.

Distribute the crêpe strands evenly in the soup bowls. When ready to serve, bring the vegetable broth to a rapid boil and ladle it into the bowls. Add the remaining ingredients to the individual bowls and serve immediately.

♦ ♦ ♦ ♦ ♦

## Passatelli

BREAD
AND
CHEESE
STRANDS
IN
BROTH

SERVES 6

*Passatelli* are fine strands of bread crumbs and Parmesan cheese bound together and seasoned with nutmeg and pepper. They are cooked briefly in vegetable broth and served hot. This is a fast and easy soup to make.

*⅓ cup fine bread crumbs*
*⅓ cup plus ½ cup freshly grated Parmesan*
*pinch of nutmeg*
*¼ teaspoon freshly ground pepper*
*2 extra-large eggs, beaten*
*8 cups Vegetable Broth (see recipe)*
*salt to taste*
*2 tablespoons minced parsley*

Blend well in a mixing bowl the bread crumbs, ⅓ cup of Parmesan, nutmeg, and pepper. Stir in the eggs, a little at a time, beating vigorously to mix thoroughly. Set aside to rest for at least 30 minutes.

Place the vegetable broth in a large saucepan and bring to a simmer. Put the bread crumb–Parmesan mixture in a ricer or a food mill, using the disk with the largest holes and, holding the ricer or food mill directly over the saucepan, force the mixture through the holes, allowing the strands to fall directly into the broth. Taste and adjust for salt and pepper. Simmer gently for 5 minutes.

Remove from the heat and sprinkle with parsley. Pass Parmesan for those who want it.

# MAIN DISHES

All the recipes in this section are traditional Italian dishes. The range is large and varied. Some, such as tortes, flans, soufflés, and vegetable puddings, are drawn from the high art of Italian cooking and are somewhat elaborate and time-consuming to prepare. However, most of the steps can be done in advance. We reserve many of these dishes for dinner parties, since they are elegant and impressive.

The savory crêpes, many of the egg and fried dishes, the stuffed vegetables, and vegetables cooked with pasta are culled from the rich tradition of home cooking and tend to be quick and easy to prepare. They rely on simple, inexpensive ingredients and are ideal for modest meals with family and friends. These are, with only slight exaggeration, the unknown masterpieces of Italian cooking, inventive, simple, and superb.

# Fried Dishes

Italians are very fond of fried foods and, in moderation, they make excellent main dishes. We have included a few deep-fried dishes, the croquettes, and a few sandwiches that are pan-fried. We use a wok for deep frying as we explain in "Cooking Techniques" and a light seed oil such as safflower, sunflower, or corn oil. When deep frying, the oil must be hot so that it cooks the outside of the croquettes quickly, sealing in the flavors and sealing out the oil. However, do not make it so hot that the batter or bread crumbs burn instead of cooking.

Many of these dishes can also be served, in smaller portions, as appetizers, first courses, or snacks.

♦ ♦ ♦ ♦ ♦

## Suppli di Riso

### RICE CROQUETTES

SERVES 6

Rice croquettes are popular all over Italy, and, naturally enough, there are many different ways to make them. The recipe given here is made with a risotto base filled with mozzarella, tomato sauce, and parsley. These croquettes can be cooked up to 1 hour ahead of time and kept warm in a 250°F. oven.

One note of caution: Rice croquettes are so good that it is very easy to eat them nonstop. They are also heavy, so take care. This recipe is for 12 croquettes the size and shape of large eggs.

FOR THE RISOTTO:

3 tablespoons butter
½ cup chopped onion
1 cup Arborio rice
2 to 3 cups Vegetable Broth (see recipe)
¼ cup freshly grated Parmesan
salt and freshly ground pepper to taste

FOR THE CROQUETTES:

½ cup finely chopped or grated mozzarella
¼ cup freshly grated Parmesan
2 tablespoons finely chopped parsley
2 tablespoons Tomato Sauce I (see recipe)
2 extra-large eggs, beaten
1 cup bread crumbs
½ cup light seed oil

Make the risotto, cooking the rice 5 minutes longer than indicated on p. 105. Spread it on a plate to cool. It is important that the rice be well cooked and the risotto dry.

In a small mixing bowl, combine the mozzarella, Parmesan, parsley, and tomato sauce. When the rice is cool, combine it with the eggs in a mixing bowl. Sprinkle your hands lightly with the bread crumbs and scoop up 1 tablespoon of the risotto in your hand, shape into a flat oval, and make a depression in the center with your thumb. Place 1 teaspoon of the mozzarella mixture in the depression and cover the oval with another tablespoon of the risotto. Make sure that the mozzarella mixture is completely enclosed by the risotto.

Mold the rice into an egg shape 2 to 3 inches long, roll to coat in the bread crumbs, and set aside on a dry plate. Repeat until all the risotto is used.

Heat the oil in a pan suitable for deep frying and fry the croquettes, a few at a time, until golden on all sides. Remove from the oil with a slotted spoon, and drain on paper towels. Keep very warm until all are cooked. Serve hot.

♦ ♦ ♦ ♦ ♦

## Crocchette di Melanzane

### EGGPLANT CROQUETTES

SERVES 6

FOR THE CROQUETTES:

3 medium eggplants
⅔ cup bread crumbs
2 extra-large eggs
⅓ cup freshly grated Parmesan
1 tablespoon finely chopped basil
1 tablespoon finely chopped parsley
pinch of nutmeg
1 tablespoon chopped pine nuts
salt and freshly ground pepper to taste

FOR DREDGING, FRYING, AND SERVING:

3 tablespoons flour
2 extra-large eggs, beaten
¼ cup bread crumbs
½ cup light seed oil
1 lemon, cut into 6 pieces

Peel the eggplants, cut into small pieces, and steam until cooked but not mushy, about 15 minutes. Chop fine and place in a large mixing bowl. Add the bread crumbs, eggs, Parmesan, basil, parsley, nutmeg, pine nuts, salt, and pepper and combine thoroughly. The mixture should be dry enough to handle.

Form the croquette mixture into egg-shaped balls. Dredge lightly in the flour, dip into the eggs, and coat with bread crumbs. Place the croquettes on a large plate and set aside.

Heat the oil in a pan suitable for deep frying and, when hot, fry the croquettes, a few at a time, until golden on all sides. Remove from the oil with a slotted spoon, drain on paper towels, and keep warm until all are cooked. Serve hot with lemon wedges.

♦ ♦ ♦ ♦ ♦

## Crocchette di Formaggio

CHEESE
CROQUETTES

SERVES 4

We give two recipes for cheese croquettes: the first for fried mozzarella, a delicious dish prepared by Jewish restaurants in the old ghetto in Rome; the second, a more conventional croquette typical of the north. Both are good with a light dry red wine.

*1 pound mozzarella, cut into 1-inch cubes*
*milk to cover the mozzarella*
*2 extra-large eggs, separated*
*⅔ cup cream, milk, or a mixture*
*1 cup unbleached all-purpose flour*
*½ cup bread crumbs*
*¼ teaspoon salt*
*freshly ground pepper to taste*
*½ cup light seed oil*

Place the cheese in a mixing bowl, cover with milk, and soak for at least 1 hour. Meanwhile, place the 2 egg yolks in a mixing bowl, blend in the milk or cream, and add the flour a little at a time, beating vigorously to form a smooth, very dense batter. A dense batter is critical to protect the cheese from the hot oil. Set aside until ready to use.

When the cheese is ready, drain and set aside. Spread the bread crumbs on a plate or work surface. Season the crumbs with salt and pepper. Beat the egg whites until firm, then fold them into the batter.

In a pan suitable for deep frying, heat the oil over medium heat until very hot but not smoking. Roll the pieces of cheese in the bread crumbs until well coated, dip in the batter, making sure that the cheese is completely covered, then fry in the oil, a few pieces at a time, until golden brown. It is very important that the pieces of cheese be coated with the batter. If not, the cheese will run into the oil and you will lose most of your meal. Drain on paper towels and keep warm until all are cooked. Serve hot.

### VARIATION

*Béchamel Sauce (see recipe) made with:*
  *1¼ cups milk*
  *3 tablespoons butter*
  *3 tablespoons flour*
  *¼ teaspoon salt*
*freshly ground white pepper to taste*
*generous pinch of cayenne pepper*
*pinch of nutmeg*
*4 eggs plus 1 egg yolk*

*½ cup freshly grated Parmesan*
*1½ cups grated Gruyère*
*butter*
*½ cup light seed oil*
*¼ cup flour*
*½ cup bread crumbs*
*1 lemon, cut into wedges*
*sprigs of parsley*

Make the béchamel sauce, remove from the heat, add the white pepper, cayenne pepper, and nutmeg, and blend in 2 eggs and the egg yolk. Add the Parmesan and Gruyère, return to low heat, and cook, stirring constantly, until the cheese melts.

Generously butter a large platter and spread the cheese mixture on it. Spread a thin coat of butter on top and set aside until completely cooled.

When ready to cook, cut the cheese mixture into small squares or disks. Beat the remaining 2 eggs together in a small mixing bowl. Heat the oil in a pan suitable for deep frying. Sprinkle the cheese pieces with flour, dip in the eggs, roll in the bread crumbs to cover completely, and fry, a few at a time, in the oil until golden on all sides. Drain on paper towels and keep warm until all are cooked. Serve hot garnished with lemon wedges and sprigs of parsley.

♦ ♦ ♦ ♦ ♦

## Crocchette di Alberto

### ALBERTO'S CROQUETTES

SERVES 4

These most unusual, surprisingly light, and very tasty croquettes are composed of nothing more than bread crumbs, Parmesan cheese, and eggs. Serve with a light dry red wine.

1 cup bread crumbs
4 extra-large eggs, beaten
½ cup freshly grated Parmesan
2 tablespoons chopped parsley
2 tablespoons minced onion
pinch of nutmeg
½ teaspoon salt
abundant freshly ground pepper
⅓ cup milk
1 cup Tomato Sauce with Peppers or Tomato Sauce with Vinegar (see recipes)
½ cup light seed oil
1 lemon, cut into wedges

Thoroughly combine the bread crumbs, eggs, Parmesan, parsley, onion, nutmeg, salt, and pepper in a mixing bowl. Add the milk a little at a time, stirring constantly, until a fairly stiff but workable dough is formed. The dough can be made ahead of time and kept for a few hours in the refrigerator.

Prepare one of the two sauces and keep warm.

When ready to use, heat the oil until hot in a pan suitable for deep frying. Scoop up some of the batter with a tablespoon and, using your thumb, slide the batter off the spoon into the oil. Cook a few croquettes at a time until golden on all sides, remove from the oil, and drain on paper towels. Keep warm until all are cooked. Serve hot, garnished with lemon wedges, and pass the tomato sauce for those who want to add it.

♦ ♦ ♦ ♦ ♦

## *Mozzarella in Carrozza*

MOZZARELLA
IN
A
CARRIAGE

SERVES 6

The mozzarella is the passenger and the carriage is the bread in this most delectable of all fried cheese sandwiches, usually served in Italy with anchovy butter. We find that caper butter, described below, makes a very satisfactory substitute.

5 to 6 tablespoons butter, at room temperature

1 tablespoon capers, minced

12 slices mozzarella, about 3 inches square and ⅜ inch thick

24 slices Italian or whole wheat bread, 3 inches square, crust removed

3 tablespoons milk

¼ cup flour

2 eggs, beaten

½ teaspoon salt

Cream 2 tablespoons of butter together with the capers in a mixing bowl and set aside.

Heat 3 or 4 tablespoons of butter for frying in a large frying pan. Make sandwiches, placing the mozzarella in between the bread. Sprinkle with milk, dredge in the flour, shaking off any excess, coat thoroughly with the beaten eggs, and sprinkle with salt. Fry in the remaining butter until golden on both sides, turning over with a spatula. Drain on paper towels. Serve hot and pass the caper butter for those who wish to spread it on top of their sandwich.

♦ ♦ ♦ ♦ ♦

## *Tramezzino di Polenta*

FRIED
CORNMEAL
SANDWICHES

Although similar in preparation to Mozzarella in Carrozza (preceding recipe), polenta sandwiches are totally different in flavor and texture. Fried polenta is delicious on its own and exceptional when combined with cheese. The sandwiches must be eaten hot while the cheese is still soft and runny. They make a light but very satisfying main dish. Serve with a dry red wine.

SERVES 6

10 cups milk

2½ cups yellow or white coarse cornmeal

2 teaspoons salt

freshly ground pepper to taste

¾ pound Gruyère or fontina, thinly sliced

2 tablespoons capers, finely chopped (optional)

½ cup light seed oil

2 to 3 eggs, beaten

1 cup bread crumbs

Bring the milk to a boil in a large, heavy saucepan and pour in the cornmeal slowly in a thin stream, stirring constantly. Add salt and pepper, reduce the heat to low, and cook, stirring frequently, until the polenta is cooked, about 30 minutes.

While the polenta cooks, wet with water a large cutting board or the equivalent. Spread the cooked polenta evenly over the surface with a wet spatula to a thickness of a quarter inch. Set aside until completely cool.

Cut the polenta into 3-inch disks with a cookie cutter or the equivalent. You should have at least 24 disks. Any extra polenta can be fried on its own and served hot.

Place a slice of cheese on each of 12 disks and trim so that the cheese fits within the boundary of the disks. Spread a little of the chopped capers on the cheese, if you wish, and cover with another disk.

Heat the oil in a large frying pan. Dip the sandwiches first in the eggs, coat well, then cover thoroughly, even the edges, with bread crumbs. Fry the sandwiches, 6 at a time, if possible, until golden brown on both sides. Keep very warm until all are cooked and serve at once.

### VARIATION

Substitute Gorgonzola for fontina or Gruyère and omit the capers.

♦ ♦ ♦ ♦ ♦

*Tramezzino*

*di*

*Melanzane*

FRIED
EGGPLANT
SANDWICHES

SERVES 6

This dish is a delightful variation on the more traditional Mozzarella in Carrozza. The carriage in
this case is the eggplant. It is simple to prepare and
delicious. Serve with a chilled dry white wine.

*4 medium eggplants*
*1 tablespoon salt*
*½ to ¾ pound Gruyère*
*1 cup (approximately) bread crumbs*
*2 tablespoons flour*
*2 eggs, beaten*
*2 tablespoons finely chopped parsley*
*2 tablespoons finely chopped basil*
*salt and freshly ground pepper*
*2 tablespoons butter, at room temperature*
*½ cup seed oil*

Peel the eggplants and slice them lengthwise approximately ⅜ inch thick. Sprinkle the slices with the salt and place them in a colander to drain for 30 minutes.
Rinse with cold water and pat dry with paper towels. Cut the eggplants into 2½-
inch squares and set aside.

Cut the Gruyère into pieces approximately ¼ inch thick by 2½ inches square.
The Gruyère should be the same size as the eggplant squares. Set aside.

Sprinkle the bread crumbs on a work surface. Place the flour in a shallow dish
nearby and the beaten eggs in a mixing bowl also nearby. Place a piece of cheese
on a slice of eggplant, add a pinch of parsley and basil, salt and pepper to taste,
spread butter on another eggplant slice, and use it to form a sandwich. Dredge
the eggplant sandwich with flour, dip in the beaten eggs, and coat completely,
top, bottom, and edges, with the bread crumbs. Repeat until all the eggplant and
cheese is used.

Heat the oil in a pan suitable for deep frying. Fry the eggplant sandwiches, 1
or 2 at a time, turning with a spatula to cook on both sides, until golden. Remove
and drain on paper towels. Serve hot.

# Stuffed Vegetables

◆ ◆ ◆ ◆ ◆

## Zucchini Ripieni

STUFFED
ZUCCHINI

SERVES 6

Fresh, tender zucchini filled with a mixture of garlic, onions, Parmesan, and herbs are delicious as a light main course. This is an ideal midsummer dish when zucchini are at their best. We usually serve these with a light dry red wine.

This dish can be assembled ahead of time and baked before serving.

12 *medium zucchini*
3 *tablespoons olive oil*
1 *large onion, finely chopped*
3 *garlic cloves, finely chopped*
3 *tablespoons chopped basil*
3 *tablespoons chopped parsley*
3 *extra-large eggs, beaten*
1½ *cups freshly grated Parmesan*
¼ *cup bread crumbs*
1½ *teaspoons salt*
¼ *teaspoon freshly ground pepper*

Preheat the oven to 375°F. Generously oil a 9-by-12-inch baking dish.

Wash and scrub the zucchini, cut them in half lengthwise, and remove the pulp with a serrated spoon or paring knife. Chop the pulp fine and set aside.

Heat 2 tablespoons of olive oil in a saucepan, add the onion, and sauté over a medium heat until transparent. Add garlic, basil, and parsley, and sauté 1 more minute. Add the chopped pulp and cook another minute or two, until the pulp absorbs the flavor of the oil and herbs. Remove from the heat, blend in the eggs, Parmesan, 2 tablespoons of bread crumbs, ½ teaspoon of salt, and the pepper.

Parboil the zucchini shells for 5 minutes in water with 1 teaspoon of salt. Remove and drain well. Fill the zucchini shells with the stuffing, sprinkle the top of each with the remaining bread crumbs, and drizzle the tops with the remaining olive oil. Place the stuffed zucchini side by side in the prepared baking dish and bake in the preheated oven for 30 to 40 minutes, until the stuffing is golden on top and crisp. Serve hot in the baking dish.

◆ ◆ ◆ ◆ ◆

## Peperoni Ripieni con Lenticchie

PEPPERS
STUFFED
WITH
LENTILS

SERVES 6

Lentils make a delicious filling for peppers. Serve with a light dry red wine.

This entire dish can be prepared ahead of time and reheated before serving.

1 cup dried lentils
4 tablespoons butter
1 medium carrot, chopped
1 medium onion, chopped
½ cup dry white wine
½ teaspoon salt
freshly ground pepper to taste
1 tablespoon olive oil
2 garlic cloves, chopped
¼ cup fresh tomato pulp with skin and seeds removed,
    or ¼ cup canned Italian plum tomatoes, drained
    and chopped
½ teaspoon dried rosemary
¼ teaspoon cayenne pepper
2 tablespoons currants, soaked for 15 minutes in warm
    water to cover and drained
1 tablespoon pine nuts
3 to 4 tablespoons bread crumbs
6 large red or green bell peppers, cut in half lengthwise
    with seeds removed
¼ cup freshly grated Parmesan

Soak the lentils for 8 hours or overnight in 3 cups of water. Drain and rinse.

Heat 2 tablespoons butter in a large, heavy saucepan, add the carrot and onion, and sauté over a medium heat until they begin to brown. Blend in the lentils, add the wine, reduce the wine by half, add 3 cups of very hot water and salt and pepper. Reduce the heat and simmer covered, stirring occasionally, until cooked but still firm, about 20 to 25 minutes. Add more hot water if necessary during cooking. Drain the lentils, reserving any liquid for soup. Set the lentils aside.

In a large, low-sided saucepan or large frying pan, heat 1 tablespoon of butter and the olive oil, add the garlic, and sauté for 1 minute over medium heat. Stir in the tomato pulp or canned tomatoes, rosemary, and cayenne pepper. Cook, stirring, for 5 minutes. Add the lentils and cook another few minutes to combine well. Remove from the heat, and blend in the currants, pine nuts, and 1 to 2 tablespoons of bread crumbs—enough to absorb any excess liquid.

Preheat the oven to 375°F. Oil a 9-by-15-inch baking dish.

Stuff the pepper halves with the lentil mixture. Place the peppers in the prepared baking dish. Add enough water to the dish to bring it one-fourth of the way up the sides of the peppers. Combine the 2 tablespoons of bread crumbs with the Parmesan and sprinkle over the peppers. Dot the top of each pepper with the remaining tablespoon of butter and bake in the preheated oven until the peppers are tender, about 30 minutes. Transfer the peppers to a serving platter with a slotted spoon and serve hot or at room temperature.

◆ ◆ ◆ ◆ ◆

## Cavolo con Risotto

CABBAGE
LEAVES
STUFFED
WITH
RISOTTO

SERVES 6

A creamy, rich risotto baked in cabbage leaves makes an unforgettable dish. Serve with a chilled dry white wine. This dish can be prepared ahead of time and baked before serving.

6 large or 12 small cabbage leaves
4 tablespoons butter
½ medium onion, finely chopped
½ pound mushrooms, washed and thinly sliced
1½ cups Arborio rice
¼ cup dry white wine
¼ teaspoon salt
pinch of saffron, soaked in ¼ cup hot water
3 to 4 cups Vegetable Broth (see recipe)
¼ cup freshly grated Parmesan
½ pound fontina or Gruyère, thinly sliced
3 tablespoons Tomato Sauce I or II (see recipes), diluted
    with 1 cup water

Parboil the cabbage leaves whole in salted water. Drain and set aside. The cabbage leaves should be tender, but not fully cooked.

Heat 2 tablespoons of butter in a heavy saucepan, add the onion, and sauté until it begins to color. Stir in the mushrooms and rice, combine well with the butter and onion, and sauté for 2 or 3 minutes. Add the wine and cook, stirring, until the liquid evaporates. Add salt and the saffron and proceed to make a risotto with the vegetable broth. Cook for about 20 minutes; it should be slightly underdone. Add the Parmesan and 2 tablespoons of butter, and set aside.

Preheat the oven to 375°F. Butter a 9-by-12-inch baking dish.

Lay out the cabbage leaves on a work surface. Place equal amounts of the risotto on each of the leaves. Then place equal amounts of the fontina or Gruyère on the rice. Roll and fold the leaves to seal well, forming a pocket, pin them with a toothpick, and transfer them to the baking dish. Add the diluted tomato sauce and bake for 30 minutes, basting occasionally. Serve hot.

♦ ♦ ♦ ♦ ♦

## Cipolle Ripiene al Formaggio

### CHEESE-FILLED ONIONS

SERVES 6

Boiling the onions first tends to moderate their sharpness without repressing their flavor. The final result is a delightful and quite unusual dish. Serve with a light dry red wine.

6 large Spanish or red onions
2 tablespoons butter
1 cup cubed Gruyère or fontina, plus 6 thinly sliced
    pieces of the same cheese
½ cup coarsely chopped mushrooms
½ cup milk
2 eggs, beaten
salt and freshly ground pepper to taste
parsley sprigs

Preheat the oven to 350°F. Butter an attractive baking dish large enough to hold the 6 onions.

Peel the onions and boil them in water to cover for approximately 20 to 30 minutes. They should be cooked but firm. If they become too soft, they are difficult to handle. Drain and allow to cool. With a sharp paring knife cut off a third of the top of each onion, the part from which the shoots grow, leaving the root intact. Scoop out the inside of each onion, leaving 3 or 4 layers. Chop the onion pulp coarsely and sauté in a saucepan with butter for 5 minutes. Add the cubed cheese, mushrooms, and milk, and continue cooking over a medium heat until the cheese melts. Remove from the heat and let cool for a few minutes. Add the eggs and salt and pepper. Combine the ingredients thoroughly. Place the onions in the baking dish and fill each onion with the cheese mixture. Place any extra filling around the onions in the baking dish. On top of each onion place one slice of cheese. Put in the oven for 15 to 20 minutes, until the cheese begins to brown. Decorate with parsley and serve hot.

♦ ♦ ♦ ♦ ♦

## Pomodori al Formaggio

### TOMATOES STUFFED WITH CHEESE

Gruyère and mozzarella are combined with herbs in this dish and baked in tomatoes. Use firm, flavorful tomatoes. Serve with a chilled dry white wine.

You can prepare this dish ahead of time and bake before serving.

6 large firm tomatoes or 12 medium ones
1 teaspoon salt

SERVES 6

*1 cup small cubes of mozzarella*
*1 cup small cubes of Gruyère*
*1 cup diced celery*
*1 cup chopped scallions, white and green parts*
*⅓ cup chopped basil*
*3 tablespoons capers*
*pinch of dried oregano*
*2 tablespoons olive oil*
*freshly ground pepper to taste*
*lettuce and cucumber slices*

Preheat the oven to 375°F. Oil a baking dish large enough to hold the tomatoes side by side.

Cut the top quarter off each tomato, in a scalloped pattern if you like, with a sharp paring knife. Retain the tops. Scoop out the pulp from the inside of the tomatoes with a spoon. (The pulp is not used in this dish but can be reserved and used for sauce.) Sprinkle the interior of each tomato with salt, invert on a dish, and allow to drain for 30 minutes.

Meanwhile, combine the remaining ingredients (except lettuce and cucumbers) in a large mixing bowl and blend thoroughly. When ready, fill the tomatoes with the mixture, cover each tomato with its own top, and place them in the baking dish. Bake in the preheated oven for 20 to 30 minutes, until the tomatoes are cooked but still firm. Serve hot on a bed of fresh crisp lettuce surrounded by cucumber slices.

# Soufflés

Soufflés are essentially inflated egg dishes. In most cases, egg yolks are blended with a thick béchamel sauce and the main ingredient, such as cheese or spinach, to form a base. Egg whites are then beaten until very firm, combined with the base, and baked in a hot oven until the soufflé is cooked, brown and crusty on the outside and soft, light, and smooth on the inside. The trick to serving a soufflé is proper timing. It must be served at once, since it will "fall" a few minutes after being taken out of the oven.

A soufflé makes an excellent main dish. It is sure to impress, it is light and nutritious with a mild yet distinctive flavor, and, best of all, it is easy to make and

100 percent foolproof once you have the knack. The pointers that follow will speed you on your way to successful soufflés.

1. First have ready all the ingredients and essential utensils before you begin. The ingredients are specific to each recipe, but the utensils are the same for all. You will require a soufflé pan, a round, ovenproof dish usually made of glass or porcelain with straight sides about 3½ inches high. Butter the pan generously, sprinkle lightly with bread crumbs, and set aside. Although some cooks put collars around the pan to help the soufflé rise, this is unnecessary if the soufflé is made correctly.

   You will need a large wire whisk to beat the egg whites. An electric mixer can be used, but a whisk gives much more satisfactory results.

   In Italy and France, most cooks beat egg whites in an unlined copper mixing bowl. Acid from the copper helps the egg whites firm up and rise. If you do not have such a bowl, use any large mixing bowl and add a pinch of cream of tartar per egg white when they begin to foam.

   You will, finally, need a heavy saucepan for the béchamel sauce.

2. Always make the base before you beat the egg whites. In fact, in most cases the base can be made up to 24 hours in advance and kept until ready to use. If you do this, remember to spread a thin film of melted butter over the surface of the base while it is still hot to prevent a skin from forming. Cover, and keep in the refrigerator. The egg whites, however, must be beaten and combined with the base at the last moment.

3. It is important to get the most out of your egg whites, since it is the air trapped by the egg whites that expands as the soufflé cooks and causes it to rise. One usually uses 1½ times as many egg whites as yolks. The whites should be at room temperature and should contain no trace of yolk. Place them in the mixing bowl and begin beating slowly with the whisk, forming large circles by drawing the whisk up from the bottom of the bowl into the air above it to incorporate as much air as possible into the whites. Continue this process, beating more rapidly as the egg whites rise and stiffen, until stable peaks begin to form. Then place the whisk in the bottom of the bowl, and keeping it there, stir vigorously in a circle to firm up the egg whites. Continue until firm, but not dry.

4. The final step in the process is the combining of the base and egg whites. The base should be hot to the touch. If it was made ahead of time, remove from the refrigerator and heat it before mixing with the beaten egg whites. When ready, stir into the base a fourth of the egg whites. This will lighten the base and bring it closer in texture and density to the egg whites. Then pour the base into the egg whites and fold them together quickly and with a light touch, using a rubber spatula. The folding process is simple. Cut down the center of the mixture with the rubber spatula and slide it up along the side of the bowl

from the bottom, folding the bottom of the mixture over the top. Make a quarter turn of the bowl and repeat. Do not work at this process for more than a minute or two.

Transfer the mixture to the soufflé pan, even the top, and place it in the middle of a preheated oven.

5. A soufflé is cooked when the top is brown and crusty and it remains firm when the pan is shaken lightly. Some cooks recommend that you test it by inserting a skewer or trussing needle in the center—when it comes out clean the soufflé is ready.

As long as the soufflé is not exposed to a draft of cold air, the oven door can be opened and the soufflé checked during cooking. However, it is advisable not to open the oven door during the first 10 minutes of baking. When ready, serve immediately.

♦ ♦ ♦ ♦ ♦

## Soffiato di Formaggio

### CHEESE SOUFFLÉ

SERVES 4 TO 6

A cheese soufflé is light and rich with a distinct but subtle cheese flavor. Serve with a chilled dry white wine.

*Béchamel Sauce (see recipe) made with:*
  *2 cups milk*
  *5 tablespoons butter*
  *6 tablespoons flour*
  *½ teaspoon salt*
  *¼ teaspoon white pepper*
*4 extra-large egg yolks*
*½ cup freshly grated Parmesan*
*½ cup grated Gruyère*
*3 tablespoons bread crumbs*
*6 extra-large egg whites, at room temperature*

Preheat the oven to 400°F.

Make the béchamel sauce and, while hot, stir in the 4 egg yolks, one at a time, combining vigorously with a wooden spoon. Add the Parmesan and Gruyère, combine, and set aside. The sauce can be kept up to 24 hours before using. If you intend to keep it for any length of time, remember to coat the surface with melted butter and keep covered.

Butter generously and sprinkle with bread crumbs a 6-cup soufflé pan.

When ready to use, heat the sauce until hot to the touch, beat the 6 egg whites until firm, fold in the sauce, transfer the mixture to the prepared soufflé pan, and bake in the preheated oven for 15 to 20 minutes, until a crust forms and the soufflé is firm. Remove from the oven and serve immediately.

♦ ♦ ♦ ♦ ♦

*Soffiato di*

*Carciofi*

ARTICHOKE
SOUFFLÉ

SERVES 4 TO 6

This soufflé does not rise as much as a cheese soufflé, but it is still light, delicate, and delectable.

6 medium artichokes
2 tablespoons butter
2 garlic cloves, finely chopped
Béchamel Sauce (see recipe) made with:
   1⅓ cups milk
   3½ tablespoons butter
   4 tablespoons flour
   ½ teaspoon salt
   pinch of nutmeg
4 extra-large egg yolks
¼ cup freshly grated Parmesan
3 tablespoons bread crumbs
6 extra-large egg whites

Clean and trim the artichokes, remove the tough outer leaves, cut in half, and remove the chokes as explained on p. 215. Place them in acidulated water until ready to use. When ready, steam or boil the artichokes until tender, about 15 to 20 minutes. Drain well.

Heat a tablespoon of butter in a large frying pan, add the artichoke halves and garlic, and sauté for a minute or two, until the artichokes are thoroughly dry and well mixed with the butter. Remove from the pan and chop the artichokes very fine or purée in a blender, food processor, or food mill. Set aside.

Make the béchamel sauce and remove from the heat. Beat in the egg yolks and Parmesan, add the artichokes, and combine thoroughly. To this point, the soufflé can be made ahead of time. Remember to coat the surface of the béchamel mixture with butter if you wish to leave it for any length of time.

When ready, preheat oven to 400°F. Butter generously and sprinkle with bread crumbs the inside of a 6-cup soufflé pan.

Heat the béchamel mixture until it is hot to the touch.

Beat the egg whites until stiff and firm. Combine ¼ of the egg whites with the warm mixture, then add the mixture to the egg whites and fold in gently but quickly with a rubber spatula. Pour the soufflé mixture into the prepared soufflé pan and bake in the preheated oven until firm and browned on top, about 15 to 20 minutes. Serve immediately.

## VARIATIONS

This recipe works well with other vegetables such as spinach, mushrooms, and eggplant. You will need approximately 1 cup of cooked vegetable. If you want a richer soufflé, substitute heavy cream for milk. If you want a less rich one, reduce the number of egg yolks.

♦ ♦ ♦ ♦ ♦

## *Spuma di Cavolfiore*

CAULIFLOWER
SOUFFLÉ

SERVES 4 TO 6

This soufflé is made without béchamel sauce. It rises less than more conventional soufflés, since the egg whites have a less dense mixture to which they can adhere, but the flavor of the cauliflower is outstanding.

1 large cauliflower
3 tablespoons butter
1 garlic clove, chopped
1 teaspoon fresh or dried rosemary
4 slices stale Italian or good whole wheat bread soaked
    in milk to cover 15 minutes and squeezed dry
½ cup freshly grated Parmesan
4 extra-large egg yolks
salt and freshly ground pepper to taste
2 tablespoons bread crumbs
6 extra-large egg whites

Trim the cauliflower, cut into large pieces, and steam until very tender, 20 to 25 minutes. Drain well. Cut the cauliflower into small pieces and set aside.

Heat the butter in a large saucepan, add the garlic and rosemary, and sauté over medium heat for 1 minute. Stir in the cauliflower and cook, stirring frequently, for a few minutes until the cauliflower is well blended into the butter and dry.

Combine the bread with the cauliflower and purée the mixture in a blender, food processor, or food mill. Return the cauliflower purée to the stove, warm through, remove from the heat, add the Parmesan, and beat in the egg yolks one at a time. Season with salt and pepper. If you wish, the soufflé can be made ahead of time to this point and kept in the refrigerator until you are ready to use it.

When ready, preheat the oven to 400°F. Butter generously a 6-cup soufflé pan and sprinkle with bread crumbs.

Heat the purée until hot to the touch. Beat the egg whites until stiff and firm. Add one-fourth of the whites to the hot purée and combine well. Pour the purée onto the remaining egg whites and fold it in gently but quickly. Pour the soufflé mixture into the prepared pan and bake in the preheated oven until firm and browned on top, about 20 to 25 minutes. Serve immediately.

# Crêpes

◆ ◆ ◆ ◆ ◆

## Crespelle

MASTER
RECIPE
FOR
CRÊPES

MAKES 12 TO 15 CRÊPES

Both the French and the Italians use crêpes for desserts and for savory dishes. We give here our basic recipe for crêpes or *crespelle*. Some Italian recipes use more eggs and butter and less flour and milk, but we find these have just the right texture and flavor. Crêpes can be cooked up to a day ahead of time and kept in the refrigerator until needed. If making them more than an hour ahead of time, place pieces of paper between each crêpe, cover them all with wax paper or a dry dish towel, and place them in the refrigerator. If keeping for only a short while, cover with a dish towel and keep warm.

1 cup flour
pinch of salt
3 extra-large eggs, beaten
2 tablespoons plus 1 tablespoon butter, melted
1½ cups milk
1 teaspoon Cognac

Sift the flour and salt into a mixing bowl. Combine the eggs, 2 tablespoons of melted butter, milk, and Cognac in a mixing bowl and add the liquid ingredients slowly to the dry ones, beating constantly with a fork or whisk until thoroughly mixed. The batter should be smooth and free of lumps. Allow it to rest in a cool place for 2 hours before using.

When ready, stir the batter well. It should have the consistency of thick cream. If too dense, add a little milk. Heat a large frying pan or crêpe pan over a medium heat. Brush it lightly with some of the remaining melted butter and when hot (it should be just at smoking temperature) add about 2 tablespoons of the crêpe batter, turning the pan to distribute the batter evenly over the bottom in a thin layer. After about 1 minute, flip the crêpe and cook briefly on the other side. Transfer to a large plate and repeat until all the batter is used. If making them more than an hour ahead of time, layer with wax paper as explained above. It is not necessary to rebutter the pan after each crêpe. In most cases, the first crêpe will be unsatisfactory and should be discarded. It prepares the pan for all the perfect crêpes that will follow. The pan should not be too hot when cooking the crêpes. If it is, you will be unable to distribute the batter and your crêpes will be thick and rubbery.

### VARIATION

If you wish to change the flavor of the crêpes, eliminate the Cognac and substitute lemon zest or any other flavoring. If you are in a hurry and cannot allow the batter to rest for 2 hours, add an additional beaten egg.

♦ ♦ ♦ ♦ ♦

## *Crespelle di Funghi*

MUSHROOM
CRÊPES

SERVES 6

These delightful small crêpes stuffed with mushrooms and onions can be either fried or baked in a very hot oven. We give the recipe for baking but explain in a note at the end how to fry them. Serve with a light dry red wine.

*Crêpes (see recipe)*

FOR THE FILLING:

*2 tablespoons butter*
*1 medium onion, finely chopped*
*1 teaspoon fresh or dried rosemary*
*1 pound mushrooms, finely chopped*
*¼ cup dry red wine*
*1 egg, beaten*
*¼ cup freshly grated Parmesan*

FOR THE BAKING:

*¼ cup freshly grated Parmesan*
*2 tablespoons butter*

Make the batter and cook the crêpes according to the master recipe. For this recipe, make the crêpes with about 1 tablespoon of batter instead of two. You should have about 18 small crêpes. Store in the refrigerator or set aside until ready to use.

For the filling, heat the butter in a frying pan, add the onion and rosemary, and sauté over medium heat until the onion begins to color. Add the wine and let it evaporate. Turn the heat to high, stir in the mushrooms, and cook for 3 to 5 minutes, until the mushrooms begin to soften and extrude their liquid. Remove from the heat, blend in the egg and ¼ cup Parmesan, and set aside.

Preheat the oven to 450°F. Generously butter a 9-by-15-inch baking dish.

Place 1 tablespoon of the mushroom filling on one end of a crêpe and roll it up halfway. Fold in the two sides of the crêpe and roll up completely. Each crêpe should resemble a small package. Place in the baking dish and repeat until all the crêpes are filled. Sprinkle the crêpes with Parmesan, dot with butter, and bake in the preheated oven for about 15 minutes, until the crêpes are browned. Serve hot.

### VARIATION

As an alternative, the stuffed crêpes can be dipped in batter and fried. Make a light batter, beating together until smooth and setting aside to rest for 2 hours, ¾ cup flour, 1 egg yolk, 1 tablespoon melted butter, and ½ cup milk. When ready to use, beat until firm 2 egg whites and fold into the batter. Stuff the crêpes and secure them with toothpicks, dip them into the batter, and fry in hot light seed oil until golden. Drain on paper towels and serve hot.

♦ ♦ ♦ ♦/♦

## Crespelle di Ricotta

RICOTTA
AND
HERB
CRÊPES

SERVES 6

This is a very simple but elegant main course in which crêpes are filled with ricotta and herbs and baked in a béchamel sauce. Serve with a chilled dry white wine.

*Crêpes (see recipe)*

FOR THE FILLING AND THE SAUCE:

*2 cups fresh ricotta*
*3 tablespoons chopped basil*
*3 tablespoons chopped parsley*
*freshly ground pepper to taste*
*¾ cup freshly grated Parmesan*
*Béchamel Sauce (see recipe) made with:*
  *2½ cups milk*
  *6 tablespoons butter*
  *7 tablespoons flour*
  *1 teaspoon salt*

Make the crêpes, following the master recipe. When ready, preheat the oven to 400°F. Generously butter a 9-by-12-inch baking dish and set aside.

Combine the ricotta, herbs, pepper, and ½ cup of Parmesan in a mixing bowl.

Make the béchamel sauce and combine half of it with the ricotta and set aside. Reserve the other half of the béchamel for the sauce.

Spread 2 to 3 tablespoons of the ricotta mixture on each crêpe, roll them up, and transfer them to the buttered baking dish. Spread the remaining béchamel sauce lightly over the crêpes, sprinkle with the remaining ¼ cup of Parmesan, and bake in the preheated oven for about 20 minutes, until the crêpes begin to brown. Serve hot.

♦ ♦ ♦ ♦ ♦

## Crespelle alla Fonduta

CRÊPES
WITH
FONDUE

SERVES 6

Crêpes filled with cheese fondue and baked is a hearty dish from the Piedmont. These crêpes are excellent for a dinner party on a cold winter's evening. Serve with a full-bodied red wine.

*Crêpes (see recipe)*
*2 tablespoons butter*
*6 ounces fresh mushrooms, washed, trimmed, and*
    *thinly sliced*
*salt and freshly ground pepper to taste*
*⅔ cup milk*
*10 ounces fontina or Gruyère, cut into 1-inch cubes*
*2 egg yolks*
*¼ cup freshly grated Parmesan*

Make the crêpe batter according to the master recipe.

Preheat the oven to 425°F.

Heat 1 tablespoon of butter in a frying pan, add the mushrooms, salt, and pepper, and sauté over a high heat for 2 or 3 minutes, until the mushrooms begin to soften. Remove from the heat and set aside.

Generously butter a 9-by-12-inch baking dish and set aside.

Heat the milk in the top half of a double boiler, blend in the cheese, and continue cooking over a low heat, stirring constantly, until the cheese melts and combines with the milk. Add the egg yolks, one at a time, mixing constantly, and cook, stirring, for 3 or 4 minutes, until the mixture is smooth and silken. Blend in the sautéed mushrooms and remove from the heat. (This cheese fondue cannot be made ahead of time, as it does not reheat well.)

Spread about 2 tablespoons of the fondue on a crêpe, roll it up, and place it in the baking dish. Repeat with the other crêpes.

Dot the tops of the crêpes with the remaining butter, sprinkle with Parmesan, and bake in the preheated oven until the crêpes begin to brown on top, about 15 minutes. Serve hot.

♦ ♦ ♦ ♦ ♦

## Crespelle Soffiate al Formaggio

PUFFED
CRÊPES
WITH
CHEESE
SOUFFLÉ

SERVES 6

It is sometimes true in cooking—as in other activities—that the sum is greater than the parts. In this case, cheese soufflé combines with crêpes to make an outstanding dish: elegant, delicious, and surprisingly easy to prepare. Everything can be made ahead of time: the soufflé mixture, the crêpes, and the sauce. The only last-minute work is beating the egg whites, folding them in, and baking the crêpes filled with the soufflé. Serve with a chilled dry white wine.

Crêpes (see recipe)
Béchamel Sauce (see recipe) made with:
   1¼ cups milk
   3 tablespoons butter
   1 tablespoon grated onion
   4 tablespoons flour
   ½ teaspoon salt
   pinch of nutmeg
   freshly ground pepper to taste
2 egg yolks
¼ cup freshly grated Parmesan
¼ cup grated Gruyère or fontina
Mushroom Sauce (see recipe)
3 egg whites

First make the crêpes according to the master recipe.

Preheat the oven to 375°F. Butter a 9-by-15-inch baking dish.

Make the béchamel sauce, adding the grated onion to the butter and sautéing it for 5 minutes, until it just begins to color, before adding the flour, milk, salt, nutmeg, and pepper. Remove the béchamel sauce from the heat when cooked and beat in the 2 egg yolks and the cheeses. If you wish to make the mixture ahead of time, remember to coat the surface with melted butter to prevent a skin from forming. Keep in the refrigerator, covered, until ready to use.

Make the mushroom sauce and set aside.

When ready, heat the béchamel sauce until hot to the touch over low heat. Beat the egg whites and combine them with the soufflé batter as described in the master recipe for soufflé, p. 165.

Place 2 to 3 tablespoons of the soufflé mixture in the center of each crêpe, fold in half lightly, and place side by side in the baking dish. Bake in the preheated oven until the soufflé swells and the crêpes puff up.

While the crêpes bake, heat the mushroom sauce. When the crêpes are ready, serve immediately, passing the mushroom sauce separately.

♦ ♦ ♦ ♦ ♦

## *Fonduta Val d'Aostana*

FONDUE
FROM
THE
VAL
D'AOSTA

SERVES 4

As with all Italian fondues, this rich, mellow, and altogether satisfying dish is basically cheese, milk, and egg yolks. It is suitable as a light main dish or a substantial antipasto. While truffles are practically the raison d'être for this dish, mushrooms can be substituted. Serve with a full-bodied red wine.

*1 pound fontina, cut into 1-inch cubes*

*2 cups milk*

*3 egg yolks*

*a few slices of white truffle (if available) or 2 large fresh mushrooms, thinly sliced*

*12 pieces toast, 2 inches square*

Combine the fontina in a mixing bowl with 1 cup of milk and let soak for at least 1 hour.

When ready, heat the remaining cup of milk in the top half of a double boiler. Drain the cheese and add it to the double boiler. Cook over a low heat, stirring constantly, until the cheese melts and combines with the milk. Add the egg yolks one at a time, mixing constantly, and continue to cook until the mixture is smooth and silken, about 3 or 4 minutes.

Serve immediately in individual shallow bowls, decorating the top of each with slices of truffle or mushroom. Pass the toast separately.

# *Vegetable Puddings and Baked Vegetables au Gratin*

Vegetable puddings, *sformati*, are traditional Italian dishes and mainstays in our household. They take a little time to prepare, not because they are intrinsically complicated, but because the various parts have to be made separately. They are, however, well worth the effort, since they make elegant and delicious main courses. In this section, we include six baked vegetable recipes that contain eggs and/or béchamel sauce to give them substance and body and two that rely on cheese.

Once you get the knack, you can use any vegetable you want as the base of the pudding. Zucchini, artichokes, eggplant, and spinach are particularly good. You can add the yolks and the beaten whites separately as in the cheese pudding and obtain a light soufflé-type dish or you can add the eggs whole as in the cauliflower pudding and produce a denser, more down-to-earth dish. In all cases, the pudding is placed in a well-buttered, bread-crumb-coated mold—a loaf pan, ring mold, or the equivalent—and baked in the oven in a water bath until the eggs are firmly cooked. To prepare a water bath, place the mold pan in a baking dish large enough to accommodate it and add water until it comes halfway up the side of the mold.

*Sformato* in English means "unmolded." In Italy, the puddings are inverted on a serving platter and unmolded before being served. The operation can be tricky but not impossible to master. After cooking, remove the mold pan from the water bath and allow the pudding to cool for at least 15 minutes. As the pudding cools, it shrinks and pulls away from the sides of the pan. Slip a sharp knife along the sides of the pudding to detach it from the mold, place the serving platter on top, invert, tap gently, and hope for the best. If the pudding does not come away clean, do not despair. The top will be covered with a sauce, so no one will notice a few minor imperfections.

Puddings and other dishes in this section can be assembled ahead of time and baked just before serving. The puddings also can be reheated the next day.

♦ ♦ ♦ ♦ ♦

## Sformato di Cavolfiore

CAULIFLOWER
PUDDING

SERVES 4 TO 6

1 head cauliflower, about 2½ pounds
2 tablespoons butter
pinch of salt
freshly ground pepper to taste
6 extra-large eggs
Béchamel Sauce (see recipe) made with:
   1¼ cups milk
   3 tablespoons butter
   3 tablespoons flour
   ¼ teaspoon salt
¼ cup freshly grated Parmesan
3 tablespoons bread crumbs
1 cup Creamed Egg Sauce with Vinegar (see recipe)

Wash and trim the cauliflower, cut it into large pieces, and steam until tender, about 15 minutes. Remove from the heat, drain, and purée the cauliflower in a food processor, blender, or food mill.

Heat 2 tablespoons of butter in a large frying pan, add the puréed cauliflower, season with salt and pepper, and sauté over a low heat for a couple of minutes to dry the purée and combine it with the butter. Transfer the purée to a large mixing bowl and blend in the whole eggs one at a time. Make sure each egg is thoroughly incorporated before adding the next one.

Make the béchamel sauce. Stir in the Parmesan, then blend the sauce a little at a time into the purée.

Preheat the oven to 375°F. Generously butter and sprinkle with bread crumbs a loaf pan or mold. Invert to eliminate excess crumbs.

Pour the purée into the prepared pan or mold and bake in a water bath (p. 10), in the preheated oven for about 1 hour, until the pudding is firm.

While the pudding bakes, make the egg sauce and keep it warm. Remove the pudding from the oven and from the water bath and set aside to cool for at least 15 minutes. Unmold on a heated serving platter, coat with the sauce, and serve the pudding hot.

♦ ♦ ♦ ♦ ♦

## *Sformato a Tre Verdure*

### THREE-VEGETABLE PUDDING

SERVES 6

This pudding makes a light, delectable, and attractive main dish. You can alter the vegetables to suit the seasons, but choose a mixture with contrasting colors and flavors. Serve with a dry white wine.

2½ cups fresh or frozen peas
¾ pound carrots, peeled and roughly chopped
¾ pound fresh mushrooms, washed, trimmed, and
    roughly chopped
¼ cup dry white wine
pinch of nutmeg
1 tablespoon butter
3 tablespoons bread crumbs
Béchamel Sauce (see recipe) made with:
    ¾ cup milk
    2 tablespoons butter
    2 tablespoons flour
    ¼ teaspoon salt
¼ cup freshly grated Parmesan
4 extra-large eggs, beaten
freshly ground pepper to taste
½ cup Tomato Sauce I or II (see recipes)

Place the peas and carrots in separate saucepans, cover with water, season with salt, bring to a boil, reduce the heat, and simmer until tender. Drain well and purée separately in a blender, food processor, or food mill. Set aside.

Meanwhile, place the mushrooms in a small saucepan, add the wine, nutmeg, and ¼ cup of water, bring to a boil, and cook over a high heat until tender, about 10 minutes. Drain, purée as above, and set aside.

Heat 1 teaspoon of butter in a saucepan, add the mushroom purée, and cook over high heat for 1 minute to evaporate excess liquid. Transfer to a small mixing bowl. Repeat the process with the peas and the carrots.

Preheat the oven to 375°F. Generously butter a 9-by-5-inch loaf pan and cover completely with bread crumbs. Invert the pan to eliminate excess crumbs and set aside.

Make the béchamel sauce. Remove from the heat and blend in the Parmesan, eggs, and pepper while still hot. Divide the béchamel into 3 equal parts and combine each part separately with one of the vegetable purées. Mix well and spread the purées in the loaf pan in layers, beginning with the peas and ending with the carrots. Place the loaf pan in a water bath (p. 10), and bake in the preheated oven until the pudding is firm to the touch, 45 minutes to 1 hour.

Remove the pudding from the oven and allow to cool for at least 15 minutes. Unmold on a serving platter and spread the tomato sauce evenly over the top.

♦ ♦ ♦ ♦ ♦

## Sformato di Formaggio

### CHEESE PUDDING

SERVES 6

The first baking of this pudding can be done a few hours ahead of time. The second baking should be done just before serving.

*Béchamel Sauce (see recipe) made with:*
*2¼ cups milk*
*6 tablespoons butter*
*6 tablespoons flour*
*½ teaspoon salt*
*freshly ground white pepper to taste*
*pinch of nutmeg*
*¼ pound Gruyère or fontina, grated*
*½ cup freshly grated Parmesan*
*4 extra-large eggs, separated*
*3 tablespoons bread crumbs*
*2 cups fresh or frozen peas*
*1 tablespoon butter*
*1 garlic clove, minced*
*½ pound mushrooms, washed, trimmed, and thinly sliced*

Make the béchamel sauce. While on the heat add the cheeses and continue cooking, stirring constantly, until they melt. Remove from the heat and when the mixture has cooled slightly beat in the egg yolks one at a time. Keep warm.

Preheat the oven to 375°F. Generously butter and sprinkle with bread crumbs a 9-inch ring mold.

Beat the egg whites until firm. They need not be as stiff as they are for a soufflé, since the pudding will not rise as much. Mix one-fourth of the beaten whites with the pudding mixture, then pour the mixture into the egg whites, and fold in. Transfer the mixture to the prepared mold and bake in the preheated oven in a water bath (p. 10), until cooked, about 1 hour. The pudding is cooked when it is firm to the touch.

While the pudding bakes, cook the peas until just tender in salted water. Drain and set aside. Heat the butter in a frying pan, add the garlic and mushrooms, and sauté over high heat, stirring constantly, until the mushrooms are cooked, about 5 minutes. Combine with the peas and keep warm.

When cooked, remove the pudding from the oven. Allow the pudding to cool for at least 15 minutes.

Then heat the oven to 425°F, unmold the pudding onto an attractive ovenproof dish, and return to the oven for 15 to 20 minutes, until the pudding rises and the top browns. Remove from the oven, place the mushrooms and peas in the center, and serve immediately.

♦ ♦ ♦ ♦ ♦

## *Spinaci Gratinati*

SPINACH
AU
GRATIN

SERVES 4 TO 6

1½ pounds fresh or frozen spinach
¾ pound ricotta
1 cup heavy cream
4 extra-large eggs, beaten
salt and freshly ground pepper to taste
pinch of nutmeg
¼ pound butter, at room temperature
1½ cups unbleached all-purpose flour

Preheat the oven to 375°F. Generously butter an attractive 8-by-10-inch baking dish.

If using fresh spinach, trim and discard large tough stems, wash very well, and chop coarsely. If using frozen spinach, remove it from the freezer an hour or so in advance and allow it to thaw completely. Drain off any excess liquid and chop coarsely.

Combine in a large mixing bowl the ricotta, cream, eggs, salt, pepper, nutmeg, butter, and flour. Add the spinach and mix well until the ingredients are thoroughly blended.

Place the mixture in the prepared baking dish and bake in the preheated oven until a golden crust is formed, about 40 to 45 minutes. Serve hot.

♦ ♦ ♦ ♦ ♦

## Carciofi Gratinati

### ARTICHOKES AU GRATIN

SERVES 4

Artichokes baked in a rich cheese sauce make a very satisfactory light main dish. We indicate in the recipe that the artichokes should be halved, but you can also bake them whole with the cheese sauce poured into the centers and over the leaves. Be sure to remove the chokes. Serve with a light dry red wine.

juice of 2 lemons
8 medium artichokes
Béchamel Sauce (see recipe) made with:
  2¼ cups milk
  6 tablespoons butter
  6 tablespoons flour
  ¾ teaspoon salt
  pinch of nutmeg
1½ cups grated Gruyère or fontina
½ cup freshly grated Parmesan

Prepare acidulated water with half the lemon juice. Trim the artichokes, cut in half, and remove the chokes as explained on p. 216–17. Place in the acidulated water until ready to use.

Bring 2 cups of water to a boil in a large enameled or stainless steel saucepan, add the remaining lemon juice and the artichokes, and simmer over a low heat until tender, about 15 minutes. Drain well and set aside.

Preheat the oven to 350°F. Butter an 8-by-10-inch baking dish.

Make the béchamel sauce, add the cheeses, and, stirring constantly, cook over a low heat until the cheeses melt and combine with the sauce.

Place the artichokes in the baking dish, with centers facing down. Pour the sauce over the artichokes and bake in the preheated oven until golden, about 40 minutes.

♦ ♦ ♦ ♦ ♦

*Melanzane*

*alla*

*Parmigiana*

ALBERTO'S
EGGPLANT
PARMESAN

SERVES 4 TO 6

There are many recipes for this dish but none as light and delectable as this one. The eggplants are broiled, not fried, garlic and parsley are added raw, and tomato sauce is used sparingly, to flavor, not overwhelm, the dish. This dish can be assembled ahead of time and baked before serving.

*3 medium eggplants, approximately 3 pounds*
*2 to 3 tablespoons olive oil*
*4 garlic cloves, minced*
*5 tablespoons minced parsley*
*1 cup Tomato Sauce I (see recipe)*
*1 cup freshly grated Parmesan*
*salt and freshly ground pepper to taste*

Peel the eggplants and cut them into disks ¼ inch thick. Broil them on both sides until browned.

Preheat the oven to 350°F. Oil generously a 9-by-15-inch baking dish.

Place a layer of the eggplant slices in the baking dish. Drizzle with 1 tablespoon of olive oil, or more if you wish. Combine the garlic and parsley and sprinkle half the mixture over the eggplant. Spread a thin layer of tomato sauce evenly over the eggplant and sprinkle on top ½ cup of Parmesan. Season with salt and pepper. Repeat the process, ending with the Parmesan. Bake in the oven for 20 to 25 minutes, until the Parmesan begins to brown. Allow to cool for 5 minutes, then serve from the baking dish.

VARIATION

Make the dish exactly as described but add a layer of hard-boiled eggs before the tomato sauce. The results are spectacularly good.

♦ ♦ ♦ ♦ ♦

*Polenta a*

*Sorpresa*

CORNMEAL
MOLDS

In this hearty main dish, cooked cornmeal is filled with cheese, egg yolks, and mushrooms and baked until golden. We bake the cornmeal in individual molds and unmold it before serving. The results are both attractive and delicious. Serve with a full-bodied red wine.

The dish can be prepared and assembled a few hours ahead of time and baked when ready to serve.

SERVES 6

4 cups Vegetable Broth (see recipe)
1 cup cornmeal
2 to 3 tablespoons bread crumbs
3 tablespoons butter
⅓ cup freshly grated Parmesan
½ teaspoon salt
freshly ground pepper to taste
½ pound Gruyère, grated
6 egg yolks
6 small mushrooms, washed, trimmed, and thinly sliced
parsley sprigs

Bring the broth to a boil and add the cornmeal a little at a time in a thin stream, stirring constantly to prevent the cornmeal from forming lumps. Reduce the heat to low and cook, stirring frequently, for at least 30 minutes. Remove from the heat and set aside.

Preheat the oven to 400°F. Generously butter and sprinkle with bread crumbs 6 individual baking dishes about 4 inches in diameter by 2 inches deep.

When the cornmeal is cooked, add the butter and Parmesan, combine well, and adjust for salt and pepper. Line each mold with 2 tablespoons of the cooked cornmeal, sprinkle on top 1 teaspoon of Gruyère, place an egg yolk on the Gruyère, and cover the yolk with another teaspoon of Gruyère, add some pepper, and top the mold with a layer of cornmeal.

Bake the polenta in the preheated oven for 15 minutes. Remove from the oven, allow to cool for 5 minutes, then unmold on individual plates or a large serving platter. Garnish with parsley and serve.

♦ ♦ ♦ ♦ ♦

## Torta di Carciofi Sarda

SARDINIAN
ARTICHOKE
PIE

SERVES 6

This dish has a number of very appealing features. The taste and texture are marvelous—the cheeses, olives, artichokes, and tomatoes are the very essence of Mediterranean cuisine. The ingredients can be assembled beforehand and baked at the last minute. The dish is elegant and impressive, thus suitable for dinner parties. And last, but certainly not least, it is very easy to prepare. Serve with a chilled dry white wine.

two 14-ounce cans artichoke hearts, thinly sliced, or the
    hearts and tender leaves of 12 medium artichokes,
    prepared as explained on p. 215

¾ *cup bread crumbs*

½ *cup freshly grated Parmesan*

½ *cup freshly grated sharp Romano*

3 *tablespoons capers, rinsed, drained, and chopped*

1 *heaping cup black olives, rinsed well if salty, pitted, and cut in half*

5 *medium tomatoes, peeled and thinly sliced, or 2 cups canned Italian plum tomatoes, well drained and chopped*

10 *ounces Gruyère or fontina, thinly sliced*

3 *tablespoons olive oil*

*parsley sprigs*

If using fresh artichokes, clean and boil them until tender, and slice thin. Set aside until ready to use.

Preheat the oven to 350°F.

Butter well and coat with ¼ cup of bread crumbs a 10-inch springform pan and set aside. Combine the Parmesan, Romano, and ½ cup of bread crumbs in a mixing bowl. Prepare the remaining ingredients.

Alternate layers in the pan in the following order: first artichokes, followed by capers and olives, then tomatoes, Gruyère or fontina, and the bread crumb–cheese mixture. Drizzle 1 tablespoon of olive oil on top. Press down after each layer is formed. You should have enough ingredients to make 3 layers.

Bake in the oven for 25 minutes. Remove and let cool for 10 minutes. Unmold and serve garnished with parsley on a heated serving platter.

# Flans and Tortes

We distinguish in this section between flans and tortes. Both are made with fillings cooked in a pastry shell: in the former, the filling is cooked without a top in a prebaked shell; in the latter the filling is completely enclosed by a light flaky dough and the filling and pastry are cooked together. The tortes, in particular, require more time and effort to prepare than other dishes, but they do make impressive main courses. And since most of the preparation can be done ahead of time, they are ideally suited for dinner parties.

The shells for the flans can be baked in a pie or flan pan. The latter has the advantage that the side rim can be removed, but the dough must be strong enough to support the contents of the flan. If you intend to remove the sides, you may wish to roll the dough out a little thicker than ⅛ inch. Most of the flans must be baked slowly to cook the eggs thoroughly without making them rubbery. Allow at least 30 minutes cooking time.

We usually make the tortes in a springform pan. This makes it easy to unmold them and reveals the torte in all its glory. The tops of the tortes can be decorated with the excess dough that remains after the pan has been lined and the filling covered. The tortes take longer to cook, since both the dough and filling must bake.

There are many types of dough suitable for flans and tortes. We give a recipe for a traditional and relatively easy-to-prepare pastry dough that is suitable for all except the Easter Torte, which is made with a pasta-type dough. You can substitute another savory dough if you wish—a puff pastry is particularly good for the tortes.

♦ ♦ ♦ ♦ ♦

## Pasta per Crostate e Torte

PASTRY
DOUGH
FOR
FLANS
AND
TORTES

This dough is suitable for the flan and torte recipes that follow. We give quantities to make a 9- to 10-inch pastry shell rolled out ⅛ inch thick for a flan. If you are making a torte double the recipe.

*2 cups unbleached all-purpose flour*
*¼ teaspoon salt*
*1 egg yolk*
*¼ pound butter*
*5 tablespoons cold water*

Place the flour in a large mixing bowl, and add the salt, egg yolk, and butter cut into small pieces. Combine with your fingers or with a pastry cutter, breaking the butter into very small pieces, until the dough has the texture of coarse oatmeal. Add the water, a little at a time, again combining with your fingers.

Place the dough on a lightly floured work surface and knead it quickly away from you a little at a time with the heel of your hand. The objective is to blend the butter and flour with a minimum of handling. Roll the dough into a ball, wrap in wax paper or a dry dish towel, and store in the refrigerator for at least 2 hours. The dough will keep for a few days in the refrigerator and indefinitely in the freezer. It will actually improve if allowed to rest for 24 hours before using.

The shell for the flans must be precooked. Preheat the oven to 400°F. Generously butter a 9- to 10-inch pie pan.

Place the dough on a lightly floured work surface and roll approximately ⅛ inch thick, using a floured rolling pin with or without a pastry cloth cover. Always roll from the center to the edge, giving the dough a quarter turn after each roll. Transfer the dough to the pan, allowing any extra to drape over the edge. Press firmly into the pan and prick the bottom with the tines of a fork to prevent the dough from rising. Trim the edges. Butter a piece of aluminum foil and place it over the dough. Put dried beans or pastry weights on the foil and bake in the preheated oven for 8 to 10 minutes, until the dough is set and lightly browned. Remove the weights and the foil and return to the oven for another 3 to 5 minutes. The shell, at this point, is partially baked and suitable for all the flans that follow.

The shell can be partially baked up to a day ahead of time.

♦ ♦ ♦ ♦ ♦

## Crostata di Asparagi

ASPARAGUS
FLAN

SERVES 4 TO 6

Everything for this flan can be prepared up to a day ahead of time, although the egg whites must be beaten and incorporated at the last minute. You can also mix the whole eggs into the béchamel sauce instead of separating them and beating the egg whites.

Pastry Dough (preceding recipe)
2 pounds asparagus, tough parts of the stems removed
3 tablespoons butter
Béchamel Sauce (see recipe) made with:
    1¼ cups milk
    3 tablespoons butter
    3½ tablespoons flour
    ½ teaspoon salt
pinch of nutmeg
4 tablespoons freshly grated Parmesan
2 tablespoons thick cream
3 extra-large eggs, separated

Make the dough and bake the pastry shell as described in the master recipe, and set aside until needed.

Steam the asparagus until cooked but still firm and drain well. Heat the butter in a large frying pan, add the asparagus, and sauté over a low heat for 5 minutes, mixing carefully to incorporate the butter with the asparagus. Set aside.

Make the béchamel sauce, remove from the heat, and let cool a few minutes before blending in the nutmeg, 2 tablespoons of Parmesan, the cream, and the egg yolks. Keep hot to the touch over a double boiler or very low flame.

Preheat the oven to 350°F.

Distribute the asparagus on the bottom of the pastry shell in a shape resembling the spokes of a wheel with the tops facing outward. Beat the egg whites until stiff and firm, stir one-fourth of them into the béchamel sauce, then fold the sauce into the remaining egg whites. Pour the sauce over the asparagus, sprinkle the top with the remaining Parmesan, and bake in the preheated oven until golden brown, about 25 to 30 minutes. Serve hot or at room temperature. If the flan is allowed to cool, the egg whites will deflate, but some of the lightness will remain.

◆ ◆ ◆ ◆ ◆

## Crostata di Cipolle

ONION
FLAN

SERVES 4 TO 6

Pastry Dough (see recipe)
1½ pounds red or white onions, thinly sliced
4 tablespoons butter
6 extra-large eggs, beaten
1 cup heavy cream
½ cup milk
pinch of nutmeg
2 tablespoons freshly grated Parmesan
salt and freshly ground pepper to taste
1 tablespoon minced parsley
1 teaspoon fresh or dried rosemary
1 medium tomato, peeled, seeded, and cut into strips

Make the dough and bake the pastry shell according to the master recipe, and set aside until needed.

Meanwhile, soak the onions in cold water to cover for 30 minutes. Drain and pat dry.

Heat the butter in a medium saucepan, add the onions, and cook slowly over a low heat until the onions are tender, but not brown, about 20 minutes.

Preheat the oven to 350°F.

In a large mixing bowl, combine the eggs, cream, milk, nutmeg, Parmesan, salt, and pepper. Spread the onions evenly over the bottom of the pastry shell, cover with the egg mixture, and sprinkle parsley and rosemary on top. Decorate the surface with the strips of tomato and bake in the preheated oven for 40 to 50 minutes, until firm and browned on top. Serve hot or at room temperature.

◆ ◆ ◆ ◆ ◆

## Crostata di Erbette

**BASIL-PARSLEY
FLAN**

SERVES 4 TO 6

The success of this dish depends entirely on the quality of the herbs used. Fresh parsley is available year round, but basil is a summer herb. You can, however, use frozen or salted basil (see p. 2); dried basil lacks flavor and is unacceptable. Serve with a chilled dry white wine.

*Pastry Dough (see recipe)*
*5 extra-large eggs*
*1 cup heavy cream*
*4 tablespoons milk*
*4 tablespoons freshly grated Romano cheese*
*¼ cup finely chopped basil*
*¼ cup finely chopped parsley*
*salt and freshly ground pepper to taste*
*2 tablespoons roughly chopped walnuts*

Make the dough and bake the pastry shell according to the master recipe and set aside until needed.

Preheat the oven to 300°F.

In a large mixing bowl, beat the eggs with a wire whisk until light and frothy. Add the cream and the milk a little at a time, beating constantly, then continue to beat for a minute more. Blend in the Romano, herbs, salt, pepper, and walnuts and pour the mixture into the pastry shell. Bake in the preheated oven 40 to 50 minutes, until the top browns. Serve hot or at room temperature.

◆ ◆ ◆ ◆ ◆

## Crostata di Ricotta e Zafferano

**RICOTTA
AND
SAFFRON
FLAN**

SERVES 4 TO 6

A little saffron does wonders for this ricotta flan, imparting to it a golden hue and a rich, warm flavor. Serve with a chilled dry white wine.

*Pastry Dough (see recipe)*
*generous pinch of saffron*
*¼ cup dry white wine*
*2 extra-large eggs*
*1 pound fresh ricotta*
*4 tablespoons freshly grated Parmesan*
*¼ cup butter, melted*
*1 tablespoon finely chopped basil*
*½ teaspoon salt*
*freshly ground pepper to taste*

Make the dough and bake the pie shell according to the master recipe and set aside until needed.

Soak the saffron in the wine for 30 minutes.

Preheat the oven to 350°F.

In a large mixing bowl, beat the eggs and blend in the ricotta, Parmesan, butter, basil, salt, pepper, wine, and saffron. Mix thoroughly. Pour the mixture into the pie shell and bake for 30 minutes, until golden. Serve hot or at room temperature.

♦ ♦ ♦ ♦ ♦

## Torta di Bietola

SWISS
CHARD
TORTE

SERVES 6

The yellow and white of the hard-boiled eggs contrast beautifully with the green of the chard, creating a dish that is as pleasing to look at as it is to eat. Serve with a light dry red wine.

*Pastry Dough (see recipe), double the amount*
*3 pounds Swiss chard, washed well*
*3 tablespoons butter*
*pinch of nutmeg*
*salt and freshly ground pepper to taste*
*1 medium onion, thinly sliced*
*Béchamel Sauce (see recipe) made with:*
 *2¼ cups milk*
 *6 tablespoons butter*
 *6 tablespoons flour*
 *¾ teaspoon salt*
*½ cup freshly grated Parmesan*
*¼ cup freshly grated Romano*
*6 hard-boiled eggs, cut in half*
*1 egg, beaten*

Make the pastry dough and set it aside to rest.

Separate the stems from the leaves of the Swiss chard, set the leaves aside, and cut the stems into small pieces. Heat 2 tablespoons of butter in a large saucepan, add the stems, and sauté over a medium heat for 10 minutes. Meanwhile chop the leaves roughly and when ready add them to the stems along with the nutmeg, salt, and pepper. Continue cooking, stirring occasionally, until the leaves are tender, about 15 minutes. If necessary, add only enough water to prevent the leaves from sticking to the pan. If, when cooked, any liquid remains, drain the chard thoroughly. Set aside.

Heat 1 tablespoon of butter in a small frying pan, add the onion, and sauté over a low heat until soft and transparent, about 10 to 15 minutes. Mix with the chard.

Preheat the oven to 375°F. Generously butter a 9-inch springform pan.

Roll out two-thirds of the dough, ⅛ inch thick. Snugly line the bottom and sides of the springform, allowing any excess dough to hang over the edges.

Make the béchamel sauce, remove from the heat, and blend in the cheeses.

Spread the chard on the dough, place the hard-boiled eggs on top of the chard with the cut part of the eggs resting on the vegetable, then pour the béchamel sauce over the eggs and the chard.

Roll out the remaining third of the dough ⅛ inch thick and place it over the springform. Trim off excess pastry and reserve, allowing ½ inch all around to overlap. Join the top with the sides well, using water as a sealer, pinching the dough with your fingers. Press firmly all around the edge with the tines of a fork. Trim any excess pastry and reserve.

Roll out the excess dough and use it to make decorations, if you like. Brush the top and decorations with the beaten egg. Bake in the preheated oven for 45 minutes to 1 hour, until the pastry is golden brown and firm. Remove from the oven and allow to cool for 15 minutes before removing the sides of the springform. Serve hot or at room temperature.

♦ ♦ ♦ ♦ ♦

## Torta di Carciofi

### ARTICHOKE TORTE

SERVES 6 TO 8

Artichokes make an excellent filling for pie crusts. Choose young tender artichokes, or make sure that you remove all tough parts. Serve with a full-bodied dry red wine.

*Pastry Dough (see recipe), double the amount*
*12 medium artichokes, trimmed, chokes removed, and*
    *cut into wedges ¼ inch thick (p. 215)*
*Béchamel Sauce (see recipe) made with:*
    *2¼ cups milk*
    *6 tablespoons butter*
    *6 tablespoons flour*
    *¾ teaspoon salt*
*pinch of nutmeg*
*2 egg yolks*
*6 tablespoons freshly grated Parmesan*
*3 tablespoons olive oil*
*3 garlic cloves, finely chopped*
*5 extra-large eggs*
*2 tablespoons butter*

Make the pastry dough and set it aside to rest.

Prepare the artichokes and place them in water acidulated with the juice of 1 lemon until ready to use. When ready, drain the artichokes and boil them in salted water to cover until cooked but still firm, about 15 minutes. Drain and set aside.

Make the béchamel sauce, add the nutmeg, mix, and allow to cool slightly. Stir in the egg yolks and 3 tablespoons of Parmesan. Place in a large mixing bowl.

Heat the oil in a large saucepan, add the garlic and artichokes, and sauté over medium heat for a few minutes to dry the artichokes and flavor them with the garlic and oil. Combine the artichokes with the béchamel sauce, taking care not to break them.

Beat 4 eggs together in a mixing bowl and stir in the remaining 3 tablespoons of Parmesan. Heat 1 tablespoon of butter in a frying pan not more than 9 inches in diameter and make a flat Italian omelet, p. 200, with half the eggs. Place the omelet on a plate and make another with the remaining tablespoon of butter and the beaten eggs. Place the second omelet on a plate and set aside.

Preheat the oven to 375°F.

Generously butter a 9-inch springform pan. Roll out two-thirds of the dough about ⅛ inch thick on a floured board and use it to line snugly the bottom and sides of the springform. Allow any excess dough to hang over the edges.

Distribute a third of the artichoke-béchamel mixture on the pastry. Place an omelet on this mixture, cover the omelet with another third of the mixture, then cover with the remaining omelet. Spread the remaining third of the mixture on the omelet.

Roll out the remaining third of the dough ⅛ inch thick and place it on top of the springform. Trim excess pastry and reserve, leaving ½ inch all around to overlap. Join the top with the sides, using water as a sealer, pinching with your fingers. Press the borders together firmly with the tines of a fork. Trim away all excess dough.

Roll out the excess dough until thin and use it to make decorations for the top of the torte, if you wish. Beat the remaining egg and brush it over the top and the decorations. Bake in the preheated oven for 45 minutes to 1 hour, until the dough is golden brown and firm. Remove and let stand at room temperature for 15 minutes before removing the sides of the springform. Serve hot or at room temperature.

♦ ♦ ♦ ♦ ♦

*Torta di*
*Melanzane*

EGGPLANT
TORTE

SERVES 6 TO 8

The eggplant in this torte is broiled and then placed in the pie crust together with mushrooms, tomatoes, and cheese. As the pie cooks, the ingredients blend to form a light, delicious mixture. Serve with a chilled dry white wine.

*Pastry Dough (see recipe), double the amount*
*4 medium eggplants, approximately 3 to 3½ pounds,*
    *peeled and sliced ½ inch thick*
*1 tablespoon salt*
*¾ ounce dried wild mushrooms (Boletus edulis)*
*2 tablespoons butter*
*1 cup finely chopped onions*
*2 garlic cloves, finely chopped*
*2 tablespoons olive oil*
*1 cup thinly sliced mozzarella*
*1 cup peeled, seeded, and sliced fresh ripe tomatoes, or 1*
    *cup canned Italian plum tomatoes, drained and*
    *chopped*
*2 tablespoons chopped parsley*
*1 teaspoon oregano*
*4 extra-large eggs*
*¼ cup freshly grated Parmesan*
*salt to taste*
*freshly ground pepper to taste*

Make the pastry dough and set it aside to rest.

Sprinkle the eggplant with 1 tablespoon salt and place in a colander to drain for 1 hour. Rinse with cold water and pat dry.

Meanwhile, soak the dried mushrooms in 1 cup of warm water for 20 minutes, remove carefully from the water, and rinse under cold water to remove grit and sand. Drain, chop, and set aside.

Brown the eggplant slices on both sides under a broiler and set aside.

Heat the butter in a small frying pan, and add the onions, garlic, and mushrooms. Sauté over medium heat for 2 to 3 minutes. Remove from the heat and set aside.

Preheat the oven to 375°F. Generously butter a 9-inch springform pan.

Roll out two-thirds of the dough, ⅛ inch thick, on a floured board and use it to line snugly the bottom and sides of the springform. Allow excess dough to hang over the edges. Distribute the eggplant in the springform, packing them tightly into the form. You may want to cut some slices in half. Sprinkle them with olive oil. Spread the mushrooms, onions, and garlic over the eggplant, cover that layer with the mozzarella, and on top of that place the layer of tomatoes. Sprinkle with parsley and oregano.

Beat 3 eggs together in a small mixing bowl, pour them over the filling, and sprinkle with Parmesan. Add salt and pepper to taste.

Roll out the remaining third of the dough and place it on top of the springform. Trim excess dough, allowing ½ inch for overlap. Join the top with the sides, using water as a sealer, and pinching the dough with your fingers. Press firmly all around the edge with the tines of a fork. This will reinforce the seal and also give an attractive pattern to the border.

Roll out the excess dough and use it to make shapes (braids, leaves, etc.) to decorate the top. Beat the remaining egg and use it to brush the top and the decorations.

Bake in the preheated oven for 45 minutes to 1 hour, until the pastry is golden brown and firm. Remove and let stand at room temperature for 15 minutes before removing the sides of the springform. Serve hot or at room temperature.

♦ ♦ ♦ ♦ ♦

## *Torta Pasqualina*

### EASTER TORTE

SERVES 6 TO 8

This elaborate, impressive torte from Genoa is eaten during the Easter season. It was made originally with thirty-three layers of dough, a symbol of the years of Christ's life, but is today usually made with ten. The torte takes time and effort to prepare, but is really quite extraordinary. Serve with a chilled dry white wine.

FOR THE DOUGH:

*2 pounds (8 cups) unbleached all-purpose flour*
*2 tablespoons olive oil*
*½ cup water*
*1 teaspoon salt*

FOR THE FILLING:

*2 pounds spinach, washed well*
*1 tablespoon butter*
*1 small onion, chopped*
*2 garlic cloves, finely chopped*
*½ cup freshly grated Parmesan*
*2 tablespoons finely chopped parsley*
*1 pound fresh ricotta*
*3 tablespoons flour*
*½ cup heavy cream*

*¼ teaspoon salt*
*¼ cup butter, melted*
*6 extra-large eggs*
*freshly ground pepper to taste*

FOR GLAZING THE SURFACE:

*1 whole egg, beaten*

First make the dough. Place the 2 pounds of flour in a mound on a work surface and form a large well in the center. Place the oil, water, and salt in the well and, drawing flour into the liquid from the inner wall of the well with your fingers or a fork, proceed to combine the flour with the liquid. The dough should be fairly soft but not wet. You may have to add water, but do so a little at a time. When the ingredients are combined, knead for at least 10 minutes, then divide the dough into 10 equal parts, shape into balls, place on a lightly floured dish towel or work surface, cover with a damp dish towel, and set aside to rest for 30 minutes.

Meanwhile, make the filling. Place the spinach, with some water still clinging to its leaves, in a saucepan without adding water, bring to a boil, and simmer gently until cooked, about 5 minutes. Drain the spinach very well by squeezing out excess water with your hands or by pressing the spinach against the sides of a colander. Place on a cutting board and chop roughly.

Heat 1 tablespoon of butter in a frying pan, add the onion, and sauté over medium heat until the onion is transparent. Stir in the garlic, sauté another ½ minute, then add the spinach. Sauté, stirring constantly, over a medium heat for 3 or 4 minutes. Remove from the stove, sprinkle with 2 tablespoons of Parmesan and the parsley, combine, and set aside.

Combine the ricotta with the 3 tablespoons of flour, cream, and salt in a mixing bowl, and set aside.

Preheat the oven to 350°F. and generously butter a 9-inch springform pan.

Roll out 5 balls of the dough on a floured work surface until very thin, almost transparent. Line the bottom and sides of the pan with the sheets of dough, brushing melted butter on each layer before adding the next. Do not butter the final layer. Allow any excess dough to drape over the sides of the pan.

Spread the spinach mixture evenly over the top layer and on top of that spread the ricotta. Make 6 indentations in the ricotta to contain the eggs. Carefully break the eggs one at a time and deposit them whole in the indentations. Grind pepper over each egg and sprinkle with the remaining Parmesan.

Roll out the remaining 5 balls of dough into very thin sheets. Place a sheet of dough over the springform, brush with melted butter, and place the second layer over the first. Press along the edges to seal the dough. It is absolutely essential to trap air between the sheets of dough, otherwise, they will not cook. If in doubt about the amount of trapped air, you can insert a straw from the side and blow air between the layers. Repeat the layering process until the 5 sheets are in place. Do not butter the top layer. Cut off excess dough from the edges and reserve. Make sure the edges are well sealed.

Roll out the excess dough and use it to decorate the top, if you like. We usually place strips of dough on the top, radiating from the center, dividing the torte into 6 sections. If serving 6 people, these divisions indicate where to cut so that everyone gets a whole egg. Brush the surface with a beaten egg and prick the top layer extensively with the tines of a fork. Bake in the preheated oven for 1 hour, until the crust is golden brown. Remove and allow to sit for 15 minutes before removing the sides of the springform. Serve warm or at room temperature.

# Baked Vegetables with Pasta

All the dishes in this section are made with vegetables that are first cooked, then baked together with other ingredients such as eggs or cheese. They are usually served in Italy as a first course but are quite substantial and thus ideal as a main course.

The pasta dishes use pasta that is cooked first, then baked. All the dishes in this section are relatively easy to make and suitable for either dinner parties or family meals.

♦ ♦ ♦ ♦ ♦

## Pasticcio di Spaghettini

In this delicious *pasticcio*, thin spaghetti forms a crisp crust for a filling of mushrooms and peas. Serve as a main dish with a vegetable antipasto or a light soup and a salad. Serve with a light dry red wine.

SPAGHETTINI
BAKED
IN A
MOLD

1 pound spaghettini
½ ounce dried wild mushrooms (Boletus edulis)
4 extra-large eggs
2 cups Tomato Sauce I (see recipe)
½ cup freshly grated Parmesan

SERVES 6 TO 8

*⅓ cup grated Romano*
*1 cup grated Gruyère or fontina*
*½ teaspoon salt*
*4 tablespoons butter*
*1 small onion, finely chopped*
*1 pound fresh mushrooms, washed, trimmed, and thinly*
   *sliced*
*pinch of rosemary*
*1 cup fresh or frozen peas*
*¼ cup bread crumbs*

Bring 4 quarts salted water to a rapid boil and add the spaghettini. Cook, stirring occasionally, until almost al dente, and drain. The pasta should be undercooked. Run cold water over the pasta to stop the cooking and set aside.

Soak the dried mushrooms in 1 cup of warm water for 20 minutes, remove carefully from the water, and rinse under cold water to remove grit and sand. Drain, chop fine, and set aside.

In a large mixing bowl, beat the eggs, then combine with the tomato sauce, Parmesan, Romano, and ¾ cup of the Gruyère or fontina. Add the pasta and salt and blend thoroughly. Set aside.

Melt 2 tablespoons of butter in a frying pan and sauté the onion over medium heat until transparent. Add the fresh and dried mushrooms and rosemary, and sauté, stirring constantly over high heat, until the mushrooms are brown. Add the peas and cook over medium heat, if they are fresh, until done, or if frozen, until they are thawed. Remove from the heat and blend in ¼ cup of Gruyère or fontina.

Preheat the oven to 375°F.

Generously butter a 9-inch springform pan and sprinkle it with 3 tablespoons of bread crumbs. Place half the spaghettini mixture on the bottom of the pan, making a slight depression in the center. Place the mushroom-and-pea mixture in the depression, making sure that the mixture stays in the center. Cover with the rest of the spaghettini and press down gently to make the surface even. Sprinkle the top with the remaining bread crumbs and dot with the remaining butter. Place in the oven for 35 to 40 minutes, until the top is brown and crisp. Remove from the oven. Let stand for 5 minutes, then open the springform, slipping a knife around the edge if necessary. Serve hot on a serving dish.

♦ ♦ ♦ ♦ ♦

*Pasta con Melanzane al Forno*

BAKED
EGGPLANT
AND
PASTA

SERVES 4

In this hearty mixture the eggplants are first crisply broiled, then combined and baked with pasta, tomatoes, and a sharp southern Italian cheese. Serve with a light dry red wine.

This dish can be assembled a few hours ahead of time and baked when needed. If necessary, it can even be baked ahead of time and reheated just before serving.

3 medium eggplants, approximately 2½ to 3 pounds
1 tablespoon salt
1 teaspoon olive oil
½ pound rigatoni, penne, or some other short, stout pasta
1½ cups Tomato Sauce I (see recipe)
2 tablespoons chopped basil
10 almonds, blanched, peeled, and chopped
½ cup freshly grated Parmesan
salt and freshly ground pepper to taste
½ pound caciocavallo or sharp provolone cheese, thinly sliced

Peel the eggplants, slice lengthwise approximately ¼ to ½ inch thick, sprinkle all over with salt, and place in a colander to drain for 30 minutes.

Rinse all the salt off the eggplant slices, pat them dry between paper towels, and broil them until browned on both sides.

Preheat the oven to 375°F. Generously oil a 9-inch square baking dish.

Cut the eggplants into pieces roughly the size of the pasta you intend to use and set aside.

Bring 4 quarts of salted water to a rapid boil, stir in the pasta, and cook until almost al dente. The pasta should be underdone. Drain thoroughly and transfer to a large mixing bowl. Combine the tomato sauce with the basil. Add to the pasta half the eggplant pieces, half the chopped almonds, half the tomato sauce, ¼ cup of Parmesan, salt, and pepper and combine well. Place the mixture in the prepared baking dish and press down firmly.

On top of the mixture first spread the remaining eggplant, then the almonds, and finally the tomato sauce. Cover with the thinly sliced *caciocavallo* or provolone, sprinkle the remaining Parmesan on top, cover with foil, and bake in the preheated oven until the cheese melts. Remove the foil and bake for another 5 or 10 minutes to brown. Remove from the oven and allow it to rest for 5 minutes, then serve.

♦ ♦ ♦ ♦ ♦

*Pasta*

*Gratinata*

*con Peperoni*

BAKED
PEPPERS
AND
PASTA

SERVES 4

This dish can be assembled a few hours ahead of time and baked when needed. If necessary, it can even be baked ahead of time and reheated.

1 tablespoon olive oil

1 large onion, thinly sliced

3 large red or green bell peppers, approximately 1½ pounds, peeled (p. 257), seeded, and cut lengthwise into ¼-inch-wide strips

4 large ripe tomatoes, peeled, seeded, and chopped, or 1½ cups canned Italian plum tomatoes, drained and chopped

2 tablespoons chopped parsley

salt and freshly ground pepper to taste

2 tablespoons pine nuts

½ pound rigatoni, penne, or some other short, stout pasta

2 tablespoons butter

¼ cup plus 2 tablespoons freshly grated Parmesan

pinch of nutmeg

½ pound fontina or Gruyère, thinly sliced

1 egg white

Heat the oil in a large frying pan or low-sided saucepan, add the onion, and sauté over medium heat until transparent. Add the pepper strips, tomatoes, parsley, salt, and pepper. Mix well and continue cooking, partly covered, stirring occasionally, until the peppers are cooked but still firm, about 15 minutes. Remove the top completely during the last 10 minutes of cooking to evaporate excess liquid. The sauce should be dense. Add the pine nuts and set aside.

Preheat the oven to 350°F. and butter a 9-inch square baking dish, approximately 3 inches deep.

Bring 4 quarts of salted water to a rapid boil, add the pasta, and cook until almost al dente. The pasta should be undercooked. Drain thoroughly, add butter, ¼ cup of Parmesan, and a pinch of nutmeg.

Place half the pasta in the bottom of the prepared baking dish and pat down with a wooden spoon. Spread half the fontina or Gruyère over the pasta, and spread half the pepper-tomato mixture on top. Repeat the layering with the remaining ingredients, ending with the pepper-tomato mixture. Combine 2 tablespoons of Parmesan with the egg white and spread it evenly over the top. Bake in the preheated oven for 30 to 40 minutes, until the top begins to brown. Allow to rest for 5 minutes, then serve in the baking dish.

♦ ♦ ♦ ♦ ♦

## Pasticcio Verde alla Mozzarella

PASTA
MOLD
WITH
SPINACH
AND
MOZZARELLA

SERVES 6

The ingredients for this mold can all be prepared ahead of time and assembled and baked before serving. If necessary, it can even be baked, unmolded, and reheated before serving.

*1 pound short, stout pasta such as small macaroni*
*2 pounds spinach, washed well and trimmed*
*¼ cup bread crumbs*
*Béchamel Sauce (see recipe) made with:*
    *2 cups milk*
    *4 tablespoons butter*
    *5 tablespoons flour*
    *½ teaspoon salt*
*freshly ground pepper to taste*
*pinch of nutmeg*
*1 cup grated mozzarella*
*⅔ cup freshly grated Parmesan*
*⅓ cup freshly grated Romano or sharp pecorino*
*5 extra-large eggs*
*1 cup Tomato Sauce I or II (see recipes)*

Cook the pasta in 4 quarts rapidly boiling salted water until almost al dente. The pasta should be a little undercooked. Drain in a colander, run under cold water, and set aside.

Cook the spinach in a saucepan without adding water until tender, 5 to 10 minutes. Drain well and squeeze all the water out either with your hands or by pressing the spinach against the sides of a colander. Chop the spinach fine and set aside in a mixing bowl.

Preheat the oven to 300°F. Generously butter an 8-cup soufflé pan or 9-inch springform and sprinkle well with bread crumbs. Invert to eliminate excess crumbs.

Make the béchamel sauce and add it to the chopped spinach. Add pepper and nutmeg, blend in the cheeses, combine well, and set aside.

Beat the eggs in a large mixing bowl, add the pasta, and mix thoroughly. Place 1 cup of the pasta-egg combination in the bottom of the prepared baking dish. Combine the remaining pasta with the béchamel-spinach mixture and pour it into the baking dish. Bake in the preheated oven until the eggs are set, about 1 hour. Remove from the oven and allow to sit for 15 minutes. Unmold on a heated serving platter and serve, passing the tomato sauce separately.

♦ ♦ ♦ ♦ ♦

*Rotolo Verde*

PASTA
ROLL
STUFFED
WITH
SPINACH
AND
RICOTTA

SERVES 4 TO 6

In this delicious variation on a traditional theme, a single sheet of hand-rolled pasta is coated with a layer of spinach and ricotta, rolled up, wrapped in cheesecloth, and boiled until cooked. We find it ideal as a main dish for a luncheon or light supper. Serve with a chilled dry white wine.

FOR THE FILLING:

*2 pounds spinach*
*½ teaspoon salt*
*2 egg yolks*
*1 cup ricotta, drained*
*⅓ cup freshly grated Parmesan*

FOR THE PASTA:

*2 cups unbleached all-purpose flour*
*2 extra-large eggs*
*2 teaspoons olive oil*
*pinch of salt*

FOR THE SAUCE:

*1 cup Tomato Sauce I (see recipe)*
*¾ cup freshly grated Parmesan*

Make the filling first. Wash and trim the spinach. Place in a pan with the salt and cook over medium heat for 10 minutes. Let the spinach cool, then thoroughly drain its water by squeezing it between your hands or pressing it against the sides of a colander. When well drained, chop the spinach fine. Place it in a mixing bowl and add the egg yolks, ricotta, and ⅓ cup Parmesan. Combine thoroughly and set aside until ready to use.

To make the pasta, place the flour in a mound on a work surface and hollow out a large well in the center. Put the eggs, oil, and salt in the well, and stir briefly until combined. Carefully draw the flour from the inside of the well with your fingers or a fork and combine with the liquid in the center. Continue until a soft dough is formed. Add the remaining flour and knead for a few minutes until the ingredients are thoroughly mixed. The dough should be fairly stiff. If it is too dry, add water and knead until it is incorporated; if too wet, add a little flour. When you have achieved the correct consistency, knead the dough until it is smooth, homogeneous, and elastic, 5 to 10 minutes. Shape into a ball, cover with a dry dish towel, and let rest for 20 minutes.

The dough can also be made in a food processor. Insert the metal blade in the processor, add the flour and salt to the bowl and, with the machine running, pour in the olive oil through the feed tube, then the eggs, one at a time, and continue processing until the dough clears the sides of the bowl, about 1 minute. If the dough is too dry to form into a ball, add, one at a time, 1 or 2 tablespoons of water through the feed tube. Set aside to rest as explained above.

Sprinkle the work surface with a little flour, flatten the ball with your hand, and begin rolling the dough with a rolling pin, starting from the center and rolling to the edge. After each roll give the dough a quarter turn. After a complete revolution turn the dough over and roll on the other side. Continue this process, rolling, turning, inverting, until a large, almost transparent sheet of pasta is obtained. Make sure that at all times the work surface is lightly floured— the dough must not be allowed to stick. You will be surprised how elastic the pasta dough is and how easy it is to roll out thin without tearing. It is important to roll it thin; otherwise the inner layers will not cook.

When the dough is rolled out, spread the filling in a thin layer over the entire surface of the pasta, leaving a 1-inch border. Very carefully roll the pasta into a long, thick, sausage-shaped roll. Wrap in a large piece of cheesecloth and tie the ends securely. Bring 4 to 5 quarts of salted water to a boil in a pot large enough to accommodate the roll horizontally. We use a fish poacher, but any type pot will do. If you lack a pot long enough to hold the pasta roll, you can make two shorter ones and package them separately in cheesecloth.

Cook for 20 minutes. If the pasta is not tissue-paper thin, cook longer. Remove carefully from the water and place on a heated serving platter. Remove and discard the cheesecloth, cut into slices across the roll, and arrange the slices on the platter so they overlap. Spread half the tomato sauce on top, sprinkle with ¼ cup of Parmesan, and serve immediately. Pass the remaining tomato sauce and Parmesan for those who wish to add them.

NOTE: The *rotolo* can be prepared and cooked up to an hour ahead of time and heated in a hot oven for 10 minutes before serving. If you do this, do not slice the roll until you are ready to bake it. When ready, slice across the roll but keep the pieces together, coat with half the tomato sauce, sprinkle with ¼ cup of Parmesan, dot with butter, and bake for 5 to 10 minutes, until warmed through.

♦ ♦ ♦ ♦ ♦

## *Riso al Forno*

Don't be fooled by the simplicity of this dish. It is elegant, nourishing, and delicious. Serve with a chilled dry white wine.

BAKED
RISOTTO
WITH
CHEESE

*Risotto alla Milanese (see recipe), made with 3 cups Arborio rice*

*4 extra-large eggs, beaten*

*1¼ pounds fontina or Gruyère, freshly grated*

SERVES 6

Preheat the oven to 400°F.

Cook the risotto al dente, remove from the heat, and let cool for 5 minutes. Add the eggs and combine well with a wooden spoon.

Butter a baking dish approximately 8 by 11 inches and spread half of the risotto on the bottom. Sprinkle the cheese over the rice. Spread the remaining risotto over the cheese. Place in the oven and bake 25 minutes, until a crust begins to form. Serve hot.

# *Eggs*

In Italy, egg dishes in the past were served as *tramezzi*, that is, dishes squeezed between the first and the main course. Today, they are served most often as light main dishes, exactly as we use them here. This section is subdivided into hard-boiled eggs, poached and baked eggs, and Italian omelets (frittate). Many of the recipes are given for six extra-large eggs, one per serving. Adjust quantities to meet your requirements. Since there are some tricks to cooking eggs correctly, we first describe cooking techniques and then present the recipes.

## *How to Hard-Boil Eggs*

Nothing is easier than boiling an egg. Hard-boiled eggs, however, are often over-cooked and consequently indigestible. A properly cooked hard-boiled egg should have right at the center of the hard-cooked yolk a drop of yolk that is still runny. And hard-boiled eggs, like other eggs, should not cook too quickly. We find that the best method is to place the eggs in a saucepan, add tepid water to cover, bring the water to a boil, allow it to boil for about 4 minutes, then remove the pan from the heat and allow the eggs to sit in the water until it has once again cooled to tepid. Then run the eggs under cold water and peel them.

## How to Poach and Bake Eggs

In Italy, eggs are poached by breaking them directly into boiling water and cooking them until done. The technique is simple, and the eggs are lighter and more digestible than eggs poached in a North American poacher.

To poach 6 eggs, bring 1 quart of water to a rolling boil, add 4 tablespoons of vinegar, and, one at a time, break the eggs directly over the pan, dropping them into the boiling water. Reduce the heat immediately to low and cook them for 3 minutes just below a simmer. The eggs are cooked when the whites are firm but the yolks still soft. Remove from the water with a slotted spoon when done and use them as directed. You can, if you wish, trim the ragged edges of the whites to make the eggs more attractive.

You should use eggs as fresh as possible for poaching. The fresher the egg, the more the white adheres to the yolk when dropped into the boiling water and the more appetizing the final results.

In baking eggs the only trick is to cook them at a temperature low enough to prevent them from scorching. We simply bake them at a low temperature. An alternative method is to bake them in a water bath, p. 10, at a temperature of 375°F. Either technique is perfectly adequate.

## How to Cook Italian Omelets

Italian omelets, frittate, are flat and thick, somewhat similar in shape to a shallow cake or *torta*. In fact, some omelets, such as those made with artichokes, are commonly referred to as *tortini*. The technique for making a flat omelet is simple.

In most cases, the vegetable or other flavoring is first cooked, then combined with the beaten eggs and returned to the pan to cook. In some cases, the vegetables are cooked in the omelet pan and the eggs are simply poured over them and cooked. In either case, the pan must be hot when the eggs are added. When the eggs are set, the omelet is inverted, cooked briefly on the other side, and served warm or at room temperature. The easiest way to turn the omelet is to place a plate over the pan, invert it so that the omelet drops onto the plate, and then slide the omelet back into the pan, uncooked side down, to cook another minute or two until brown. It is then transferred to a serving platter.

You should use a heavy cast-iron or stainless steel pan for cooking the omelet, preferably one that has been prepared for omelets and used only for them. To prepare the pan, add a layer of oil to the pan with some coarse salt, bake it for a couple of hours in a medium oven, pour off the oil and salt, and wipe dry. The pan from this point need not be washed; it can simply be wiped clean after each use.

♦ ♦ ♦ ♦ ♦

## *Uova con Melanzane*

EGGS
IN
EGGPLANT
NEST

SERVES 6

It may come as a surprise to some, but eggs and eggplant go very well together, as you will discover when you try this recipe. The eggs are semi-hard-boiled, then baked in an eggplant nest with mushrooms and béchamel sauce. Serve with a chilled dry white wine.

3 medium eggplants, cut in half lengthwise
1 tablespoon salt
1 tablespoon butter
½ pound mushrooms, washed, trimmed, and thinly
    sliced
Béchamel Sauce (see recipe) made with:
    2¼ cups milk
    5 tablespoons butter
    6 tablespoons flour
    pinch of salt
3 tablespoons freshly grated Parmesan
½ cup cream
½ teaspoon dry mustard
6 eggs, cooked for 5 minutes in boiling water and peeled
freshly ground pepper to taste

Make long slits in the flesh of the eggplants, sprinkle with salt, and place in a colander to drain for 30 minutes.

Meanwhile, heat the tablespoon of butter in a frying pan, add the mushrooms, and sauté over high heat for 3 to 5 minutes, until the mushrooms begin to wilt. Remove from the heat and set aside.

Make the béchamel sauce, remove from the heat, and blend in the Parmesan, cream, and mustard.

Preheat the oven to 375°F. Butter an 8-by-12-inch baking dish, large enough to hold all the eggplant halves.

Rinse the salt from the eggplants and pat dry with paper towels. Scoop two-thirds of the pulp out of the eggplants with a serrated spoon or sharp knife without damaging the skin. Discard the pulp. Place 1 tablespoon béchamel sauce in each eggplant half, place an egg on the béchamel sauce, season with pepper, and transfer the eggplants to the prepared baking dish.

Drain any liquid from the mushrooms and combine with the remaining béchamel. Pour the sauce over the eggs and place in the preheated oven for 15 to 20 minutes, until a golden crust is formed. Serve hot.

♦ ♦ ♦ ♦ ♦

## Uova alla

## Crema

EGGS IN
CREAM
SAUCE

SERVES 6

½ cup Vegetable Broth (see recipe)
2 tablespoons butter
¾ cup finely chopped onions
2 tablespoons flour
1 cup heavy cream, hot
6 hard-boiled eggs, cut in half lengthwise
2 extra-large eggs, beaten
¼ cup freshly grated Parmesan
salt and freshly ground pepper to taste
1 tablespoon finely chopped parsley

Reduce ½ cup vegetable broth to ¼ cup by boiling uncovered in a small saucepan. Set aside.

In a large, low-sided saucepan melt the butter, add the onions, and sauté over medium heat until light gold in color. Add the flour, cook for 1 minute, then pour in the hot cream a little at a time, stirring constantly, to make a light béchamel sauce. Place the hard-boiled eggs, cut side down, in the sauce and keep warm.

In a mixing bowl combine the beaten eggs, broth, and Parmesan. Pour over the eggs and simmer over low heat, covered, for 5 minutes. Add salt and pepper, sprinkle with parsley, and serve hot, directly from the pan.

♦ ♦ ♦ ♦ ♦

## Uova alla

## Fiesolana

EGGS, FIESOLE
STYLE

At our farm near Fiesole it is not at all uncommon for surprise guests to appear around lunchtime. Fortunately, with fresh vegetables, fresh eggs, a little butter, and Parmesan, an outstanding dish can be prepared in no time at all. We give the recipe using asparagus, but green leafy vegetables such as spinach or Swiss chard are also good. Serve with a light dry red wine.

SERVES 6

2 pounds asparagus, washed, trimmed, and prepared
for steaming (p. 222)
2 tablespoons butter
6 extra-large eggs
4 tablespoons vinegar
½ cup freshly grated Parmesan
salt and freshly ground pepper to taste

Steam the asparagus, drain it, and place it on a heated serving platter with the tips all facing the same way. Dot with butter and keep warm.

Poach the eggs in water with the vinegar added as explained on p. 200. When cooked, remove from the water with a slotted spoon and place on the asparagus. Sprinkle with the Parmesan, season with salt and pepper, and serve immediately.

♦ ♦ ♦ ♦ ♦

*Uova
"Il Poggio"*

DEVILED
EGGS
"IL POGGIO"

SERVES 6

Hard-boiled eggs are not usually considered a glamorous dish, but in this recipe they are. The eggs are first hard-boiled, then baked with a delectable stuffing of the yolks, ricotta, Parmesan, and beaten egg whites, and placed on a bed of creamed spinach. Serve with a chilled dry white wine.

6 hard-boiled eggs
2 tablespoons butter, at room temperature
1 cup fresh ricotta
¼ cup freshly grated Parmesan
salt and freshly ground pepper to taste
pinch of dry mustard
4 eggs, separated
1 pound fresh or frozen spinach
Béchamel Sauce (see recipe) made with:
   1¼ cups cream
   3 tablespoons butter
   3 tablespoons flour
   ¼ teaspoon salt

Preheat the oven to 375°F. Generously butter an 8-by-10-inch baking dish, or one large enough to hold 12 hard-boiled egg halves snugly.

Peel the hard-boiled eggs, cut them in half lengthwise, and carefully remove the yolks. Mash the yolks in a mixing bowl. Then combine with the butter, ricotta, Parmesan, salt, pepper, mustard, and the 4 separated egg yolks. Set aside.

Place the spinach in a saucepan and cook, without adding water, until tender, about 5 to 10 minutes.

Drain very well, squeezing out excess water with your hands or by pressing the spinach against the sides of a colander. Chop fine and set aside.

Make the béchamel sauce. Set aside ¼ cup of the sauce and blend the rest with the spinach. Spread the spinach-béchamel mixture in the bottom of the prepared baking dish.

Combine the remaining ¼ cup of béchamel with the egg yolk–ricotta mixture. Beat the egg whites until firm and stiff. Mix a fourth of the egg whites with the ricotta-yolk mixture, then fold in the remaining egg whites. Use the mixture to stuff the empty hard-boiled egg whites and place them on the bed of béchamel and spinach. Spread any leftover mixture over the eggs.

Bake in the preheated oven for 15 minutes, until the stuffing is puffed and begins to brown. Serve hot.

♦ ♦ ♦ ♦ ♦

## Uova al Forno

**BAKED EGGS WITH CHEESE**

SERVES 6

This scrumptious dish could not be easier to prepare. It is nothing more than eggs baked with mozzarella, garlic, basil, and tomatoes—an ideal quick feast for family and friends. Serve with a chilled dry white wine.

*12 eggs*
*1 pound mozzarella, cut in slices and soaked in milk to cover for 1 hour*
*2 garlic cloves, chopped*
*3 tablespoons chopped basil*
*2 large firm tomatoes, cut into 12 slices*
*salt and freshly ground pepper*
*½ cup freshly grated Parmesan*
*6 slices toasted Italian or whole wheat bread*

Heat the oven to 325°F. Generously butter 6 attractive baking dishes about 6 to 8 inches in diameter, or large enough to hold 2 sunny-side-up eggs.

Break 2 eggs into each baking dish. Drain the mozzarella, pat dry, and place a layer of the cheese over the eggs. Sprinkle with garlic and basil, cover with a layer of tomato slices, add salt and pepper to taste, and top with Parmesan. Bake in the preheated oven for approximately 20 minutes, until the egg whites set. The yolks should be soft and runny. Serve hot with toast on the side.

♦ ♦ ♦ ♦ ♦

*Uova*

*Affogate in*

*Sugo di*

*Pomodoro*

EGGS
POACHED IN
TOMATO
SAUCE

SERVES 6

There is more than one way to poach an egg, as this recipe so admirably demonstrates. The eggs are poached in tomato sauce.

2 cups Tomato Sauce I (see recipe)
4 garlic cloves, chopped
6 eggs
salt and freshly ground pepper to taste
6 slices good Italian or whole wheat bread, rubbed with
    garlic

Heat the tomato sauce to boiling in a large frying pan. Add the garlic and cook for 1 or 2 minutes.

Break the eggs into the sauce, cover the frying pan, and simmer over a low heat until the eggs are poached, 3 to 5 minutes. The eggs can be served on toast with the tomato sauce spread on top or served in the tomato sauce with the toast on the side.

♦ ♦ ♦ ♦ ♦

*Uova al*

*Vino*

EGGS IN
WINE
SAUCE

SERVES 6

In this recipe, the eggs are poached in a wine sauce and served on toast. Serve with the same wine used to make the sauce.

1 cup dry red wine
1 cup Vegetable Broth (see recipe)
1 medium onion, peeled and stuck with 2 cloves
10 sprigs parsley
1 stalk celery with leaves
1 bay leaf
6 slices good Italian or whole wheat bread
1 garlic clove, peeled
6 eggs
4 tablespoons butter
1 tablespoon flour
salt and freshly ground pepper to taste

Preheat the oven to 200°F.

In a large saucepan combine the wine, broth, onion, parsley, celery, and bay leaf, bring to a boil, and simmer gently for 10 minutes. Remove and discard the herbs and the onion and set the sauce aside.

Toast the bread lightly, rub the slices with the garlic clove, and place them on a shallow, attractive baking dish, approximately 9 by 15 inches. They should all fit in a single layer.

Bring the sauce to a boil, add the eggs, and cook them, covered, over a low heat until poached, about 3 minutes. When cooked, remove the eggs with a slotted spoon, place them on the slices of bread, and place the dish in the preheated oven to keep warm.

Bring the sauce to a boil, add the butter, stir in the flour, and when thickened remove from the heat. Take the eggs out of the oven, pour the sauce over them, and serve immediately.

♦ ♦ ♦ ♦ ♦

## Uova Affogate al Insalata

POACHED
EGGS
IN SALAD

SERVES 6

Poached eggs are generally eaten hot, but they are also good cold. In this dish, the poached eggs are placed on a bed of boiled potatoes, seasoned with homemade mayonnaise, and served inside scooped-out tomatoes. It is an excellent dish for a summer buffet or dinner party.

*6 large firm tomatoes*

*3 cups peeled potatoes, cut into ½-inch cubes*

*1 cup Mayonnaise (see recipe)*

*4 tablespoons vinegar*

*6 eggs*

*parsley sprigs and cucumber rounds for garnishing*

Cut off the top quarter of the tomatoes, scoop out the pulp with a spoon and set the tomatoes aside. Discard the tops and pulp.

Steam or boil the potatoes until cooked but still firm. Drain well and allow them to cool. When cool, combine with ½ cup of mayonnaise in a mixing bowl and set aside.

Poach the eggs in water with the vinegar added as explained on p. 200. Remove with a slotted spoon and place them on a platter to cool.

To assemble, place the tomatoes on a serving platter. Distribute the potato mixture evenly around the tomatoes, place a poached egg in each tomato, and cover with the remaining mayonnaise. Garnish with the parsley and cucumbers and chill in the refrigerator for at least 30 minutes before serving.

♦ ♦ ♦ ♦ ♦

*Uova in*

*Crostata*

EGGS
IN
PIE
SHELLS

SERVES 6

In this pleasing dish, poached eggs are served in a pastry shell with mushrooms and an egg vinegar sauce. It is perfect for a luncheon or the main course for a light dinner. Serve with a chilled dry white wine.

All the ingredients for this dish can be prepared ahead of time, including the poached eggs. It is best, however, to assemble them just before serving.

*Pastry Dough (see recipe), double the recipe*
*Creamed Egg Sauce with Vinegar (see recipe), double the recipe*
*3 tablespoons butter*
*¾ pound fresh mushrooms, washed, trimmed, and thinly sliced*
*3 tablespoons finely chopped parsley*
*pinch of salt*
*freshly ground pepper to taste*
*6 eggs*
*4 tablespoons vinegar*

Preheat the oven to 400°F. Generously butter 6 individual baking molds approximately 4 inches in diameter by 2 inches deep. Roll the dough out between ⅛ inch and ¼ inch thick and use it to line the molds. Bake as directed in the master recipe for pastry shells, until fully baked and brown. Remove from the oven and, when cool, unmold and set aside.

Make the creamed egg sauce and set aside. Adjust the amount of vinegar to taste.

Heat the butter in a frying pan, add the mushrooms, and sauté over a high heat until the mushrooms are tender and slightly browned, about 5 minutes. Stir in the parsley, salt, and pepper to taste, remove from the heat, and set aside.

Poach the eggs in water with vinegar added as explained on p. 200. Drain, trim them, and set aside. You are now ready to assemble the ingredients.

Combine the mushrooms with the sauce, reserving about 6 tablespoons of the sauce. Spoon the mushroom mixture into the individual pastry shells, leaving enough room for the eggs. Deposit an egg in each of the pastry shells, cover with the remaining sauce, and serve warm or at room temperature.

♦ ♦ ♦ ♦ ♦

## Tortino di Carciofi

### ARTICHOKE OMELET

SERVES 6 TO 8

This is the best Italian omelet there is—at least, from our point of view. The artichokes, cut into wedges and fried until golden, are perfect complements to the eggs. This particular frittata is typically Tuscan, and, when the artichokes are in season, you can find it in almost every restaurant in the region, from modest trattorie to grand ristorante. Serve with a light dry red wine.

6 to 8 medium artichokes
⅓ cup light seed oil
4 tablespoons flour
2 tablespoons butter
2 tablespoons olive oil
8 extra-large eggs
½ teaspoon salt
freshly ground pepper to taste

Wash, trim, and remove the chokes from the artichokes, cut into wedges about ⅛ inch thick, and place in water acidulated with the juice of 1 lemon. Keep the prepared artichokes in the acidulated water until ready to use.

Drain the artichokes well and pat them dry. Heat the light seed oil until almost smoking in a pan suitable for deep frying, dredge the artichokes in the flour, and fry them, a few at a time, until crisp and golden. Remove from the oil and drain on paper towels. Continue until all the artichokes are fried.

Turn on the broiler.

Heat the butter and olive oil in a large frying pan over medium heat. Beat the eggs in a mixing bowl until light and frothy and season with salt and pepper. Spread the artichokes evenly on the bottom of the pan and add the eggs. Reduce the heat to low, and continue to cook until the bottom of the omelet begins to brown.

Place the pan under the broiler for a couple of minutes to brown the top and set the eggs. Serve hot or at room temperature. You can also follow the more traditional method and flip the omelet in the pan as explained on p. 200.

### VARIATION

Place the fried artichokes and the beaten eggs in a buttered 10-inch round baking dish and bake in a 325°F. oven until firm.

## ◆ ◆ ◆ ◆ ◆

# Frittata alla Fiesolana

OMELET,
FIESOLE
STYLE

SERVES 6 TO 8

In this recipe, the eggs are beaten very little before being added to the pan. They float on top of the vegetables and are actually steamed, not fried. The result is superb: light, digestible, and attractive. An omelet made in this way is particularly suitable for green leafy vegetables, zucchini, and leftover spaghetti. We give the recipe for Swiss chard. Serve with a light dry red wine.

*2 tablespoons butter*
*1 tablespoon olive oil*
*2 garlic cloves, chopped*
*approximately 1 pound Swiss chard, washed, stems*
*    removed, and roughly chopped (2 cups)*
*9 extra-large eggs*
*salt and freshly ground pepper to taste*

Heat the butter and oil in a large frying pan, add the garlic, and sauté over a medium heat for 1 minute. Add the chard, mix well, and cook until tender, about 10 to 15 minutes. Do not add water.

When the chard is tender, distribute it evenly to cover the bottom of the pan. Beat the eggs very briefly, just enough to break the yolks and partly combine them with the whites. Pour the eggs on top of the chard. Do not mix the two together. Season with salt and pepper, reduce the heat to low, and cover the frying pan. Cook for 5 minutes, then remove from the heat, keeping the top on the pan until the eggs are firm, about 15 minutes. The eggs should be cooked but not hard and dry. Serve hot or at room temperature.

NOTE: Vegetables and leftover spaghetti can be seasoned any way you wish. It is important, however, not to have them too moist. Otherwise, the eggs won't set properly and the full flavor of the dish will not develop.

## ◆ ◆ ◆ ◆ ◆

# Pila di Frittatine

OMELET
FLAN

In this hearty dish, Italian herb omelets are layered with tomato sauce and cheeses and baked. We often serve this as part of a buffet or for a large dinner party. Serve with a chilled dry white wine.

This dish lends itself to variations. You can vary the ingredients in the omelets, you can substitute béchamel or some other sauce for tomato, and you can vary the cheeses.

SERVES 6 TO 8

All the ingredients can be prepared ahead of time and assembled and baked before serving.

*8 extra-large eggs*
*2 tablespoons flour*
*¼ cup milk*
*½ teaspoon salt*
*freshly ground pepper to taste*
*2 tablespoons each chopped parsley, basil, and chives*
*2 tablespoons butter*
*1 cup grated Gruyère or fontina*
*½ cup freshly grated Parmesan*
*1½ cups Tomato Sauce I (see recipe)*
*1 tomato, sliced*
*parsley sprigs*

Beat the eggs, flour, milk, salt, and pepper together in a mixing bowl until the eggs are light and frothy. Add the chopped herbs, mix well, and set aside.

Heat 1 teaspoon of butter in an 8- or 9-inch frying pan. Add ¼ cup of the egg batter, tip the pan to distribute, and cook over low heat until browned on the bottom. Then turn the omelet and brown the other side. Transfer the omelet to a plate and continue until all the omelets are prepared, adding butter to the pan as necessary.

Preheat the oven to 350°F.

To assemble the stack, butter a baking dish slightly larger in diameter than the diameter of the omelets. Combine the Gruyère or fontina and Parmesan in a mixing bowl. Place an omelet in the bottom of the dish; cover with 2 tablespoons of tomato sauce and 2 tablespoons of the cheese mixture. Repeat until all the ingredients are used. Cover the top omelet with the remaining tomato sauce and then the cheeses, allowing the sauce to spill over the sides.

Bake in the preheated oven for 15 minutes, until the cheese is melted and begins to brown. Remove from the oven and transfer to a heated serving platter. Garnish with tomato slices and parsley sprigs. Serve hot, cutting the stack in wedges like a cake.

◆ ◆ ◆ ◆ ◆

*Frittatine
Ripiene di
Ricotta e
Funghi*

BAKED
OMELETS
WITH
RICOTTA
AND
MUSHROOMS

SERVES 6

In this dish thin frittate, used like crêpes, are stuffed and baked in the oven with a light béchamel sauce. It is a delicious and substantial variation on the crêpes theme. Serve with chilled dry white wine.

FOR THE OMELETS:

*8 extra-large eggs*
*¼ cup milk*
*2 tablespoons flour*
*½ teaspoon salt*
*freshly ground pepper to taste*
*3 tablespoons butter*

FOR THE FILLING:

*2 tablespoons butter*
*¾ pound mushrooms, washed, trimmed, and thinly
    sliced*
*2 garlic cloves, finely chopped*
*¾ pound ricotta*
*3 tablespoons freshly grated Parmesan*
*pinch of nutmeg*

FOR THE TOPPING:

*Béchamel Sauce (see recipe) made with:*
    *1½ cups milk*
    *3 tablespoons butter*
    *3 tablespoons flour*
    *pinch of salt*
*¼ cup freshly grated Parmesan*

Beat the eggs in a mixing bowl together with the milk and flour until light and frothy and season with salt and pepper. Heat 1 teaspoon of butter in an 8-inch frying pan, add ¼ cup of the egg mixture, and cook as you would crêpes. Tip the pan to distribute the eggs evenly over the bottom and turn the omelet when browned on one side to cook on the other. Transfer the cooked omelet to a plate and repeat, adding butter to the pan as necessary, until all the eggs are cooked. You will end up with 12 omelets. Set aside.

To make the filling, heat the butter in a saucepan, add the mushrooms and the garlic, and sauté over a high heat until the mushrooms begin to brown, about 5 minutes. Remove from the heat and set aside.

Butter an 8-by-12-inch baking dish.

Combine the ricotta and 3 tablespoons of Parmesan in a mixing bowl, add the nutmeg and the mushrooms, and combine thoroughly. Place about 2 table-spoons of the filling on each of the omelets, roll them up, and place them in the buttered baking dish.

Preheat the oven to 350°F.

Make the béchamel sauce and distribute it evenly over the omelets. Sprinkle with the Parmesan and bake in the preheated oven for 20 minutes, until the top begins to brown. Serve hot from the baking dish.

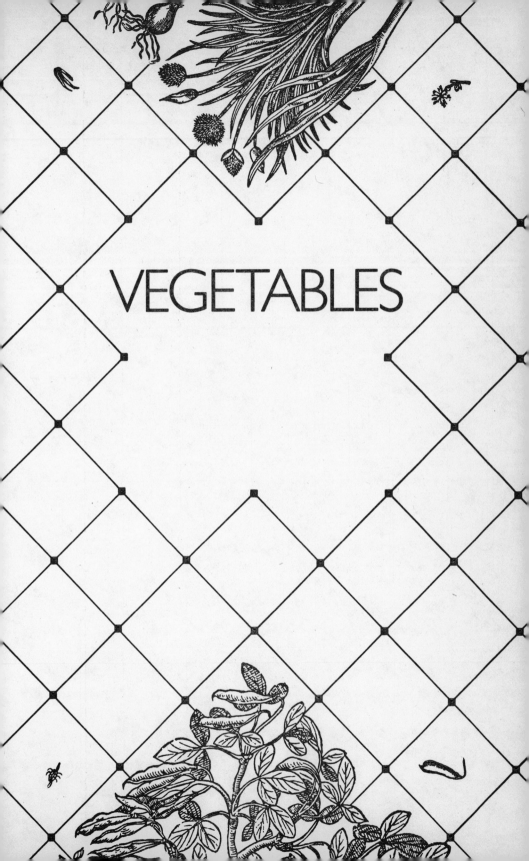

# VEGETABLES

Vegetable cooking is one of the glories of Italian cuisine. Italy produces an enormous variety of vegetables, and Italian cooks over the centuries have developed a vast and impressive range of vegetable dishes. Vegetables are not treated as an afterthought, as an appendage to a regimen of meat and potatoes, but are instead principal parts of an Italian meal.

Every section of an Italian city has its market, and every market is dominated by stalls loaded with a dazzling array of fresh, young, and tender vegetables. Most cooks still shop daily at these local markets, purchasing vegetables to be cooked and eaten the same day. If you wish to see just how seriously Italians regard their vegetables, visit one of these markets in the early morning and observe the care with which shoppers inspect the vegetables to make sure they get only the best.

Markets, of course, are only as good as the products, and Italian vegetables are very good indeed. In Italy, even the largest metropolitan areas are ringed by green belts of small market gardens that provide the cities with fresh produce on a daily basis. Thus, the vegetables that one buys in Italian markets are mostly vine ripened and bursting with sun-sweetened flavor.

For the most part, Italian vegetable cooking relies very little on sauces or elaborate preparation. Vegetables are cooked quickly and simply in very little water, with perhaps the addition of an herb, thus retaining the nutrients and fresh flavor.

A vegetable is served as *contorno*, that is, it surrounds the main dish, sometimes literally, and complements it. Thus, when planning a meal, make sure that the vegetable dish and the main course are good companions. For more on how to use the vegetable recipes in conjunction with other dishes, see the sample menus at the end of the book.

We have attempted to include in this section recipes for a wide variety of vegetables. Some of the vegetables, such as celery, carrots, and cabbage, are so commonplace that they are often overlooked. These recipes, we hope, will help you to appreciate their possibilities. Others, such as artichokes, fennel, and escarole, are much less common in North American kitchens, an unfortunate and, we think, easily altered state of affairs.

# ARTICHOKES

The artichoke, native to North Africa and southern Europe, has been cultivated in Italy since Roman times and highly esteemed since the Renaissance. Artichokes, it is said, were a great favorite of Catherine de Medici, who on at least one occasion indulged her passion almost to the point of bursting.

In Italy, artichokes are braised, stewed, stuffed, broiled, fried, grilled, used as a sauce for pasta and rice, made into omelets, cooked with peas, mushrooms, potatoes, tomatoes, onion, garlic, mint, and cheese. The recipes included here and elsewhere in the book will give you some inkling of what Italian cooks can do with this thistle bud.

Three principal varieties of artichokes are cultivated in Italy, but the recipes included in this book are perfectly suitable for the single variety available in North American markets.

## *How to Prepare Artichokes*

Choose artichokes that are firm and heavy for their size with tightly packed, unblemished leaves. To prepare artichokes for cooking, first fill a large mixing bowl two-thirds full with cold water and add the juice of 1 lemon, reserving the squeezed lemon halves for use later. The acidulated water is used to prevent the artichokes from discoloring.

With a sharp paring knife, trim off all but 1 inch of the stem of the artichoke. Break off and discard the small leaves at the base and one to three rows of the large, dark green outer leaves until you begin to uncover the leaves that are pale green at the base. Hold the artichoke in one hand and with the other bend each leaf back, snapping off and discarding the dark green top and leaving the light-colored, tender, and edible portion. Continue this process, turning and snapping, until the edible portion of the leaves extends two-thirds up the artichoke. At this point, cut off and discard the top third of the remaining inner leaves. The entire process of eliminating the inedible parts of the leaves can also be done with a sharp pair of scissors, turning and cutting instead of turning and snapping. Rub the sides and top of the artichoke with the reserved lemon.

Return now to the base of the artichoke and trim away with a sharp paring knife any dark green parts that remain, exposing the pale white flesh underneath. Rub immediately with the reserved lemon and place the artichoke in the acidulated water.

It is now necessary to remove some of the pointed inner leaves and the choke or fuzz. The method depends on how the artichokes will be used. If the recipe calls for artichokes in halves or quarters, the process is simple. Cut the artichoke in half and remove the choke and spiky inner leaves with a sharp paring knife as you would core half an apple. Rub with the lemon and return the artichoke to the acidulated water.

If the recipe calls for whole artichokes, usually to be stuffed, spread the outer leaves apart and expose the center. With a sharp-edged metal spoon cut away the spiky inner leaves, then scrape out the choke. Rinse the artichoke and return it to the acidulated water. The artichokes can be prepared up to this point a few hours before you need them.

Always cook artichokes in an enameled, stainless steel, copper, or earthenware pan. Do not use aluminum or cast iron because they may adversely affect both the flavor and the color of the artichokes.

◆ ◆ ◆ ◆ ◆

## *Carciofi con Funghi*

### ARTICHOKES WITH MUSHROOMS

SERVES 6

The addition of wild mushrooms to the sauce, although not absolutely necessary, does wonders for the flavor of this dish.

½ ounce dried wild mushrooms (Boletus edulis)
8 medium artichokes
2 tablespoons olive oil
1 cup dry white wine
2 tablespoons butter
½ pound fresh mushrooms
½ cup finely chopped onion
pinch of thyme
1 bay leaf
2 tablespoons finely chopped parsley
1 garlic clove, finely chopped
salt and freshly ground pepper

Soak the dried mushrooms in 1 cup of warm water for 20 minutes and when ready remove carefully from the water. Rinse under cold running water to remove grit and sand. Drain, chop fine, and set aside.

Trim, clean, and remove the choke from the artichokes as explained above. Cut each into 8 wedges and place them in water acidulated with the juice of 1 lemon until ready to use. When ready, drain, place in the saucepan, add the oil and ½ cup of wine, and cook, covered, over a medium heat, stirring occasionally with a wooden spoon until tender, about 20 minutes. Add water, if necessary, 1 tablespoon at a time. The artichokes, when cooked, should be dry.

In a separate saucepan, melt the butter, add the mushrooms and onion, and sauté over high heat for 3 minutes, until the mushrooms begin to soften. Reduce the heat to low; add the remaining wine, the thyme, bay leaf, parsley, garlic, and salt and pepper to taste. Cover and simmer, stirring occasionally, for 10 minutes.

Arrange the artichokes on the heated serving platter, cover them with the mushroom sauce, and serve.

◆ ◆ ◆ ◆ ◆

## Carciofi alla Piemontese

ARTICHOKES
WITH EGGS
AND CAPERS

SERVES 6

8 medium artichokes
2 tablespoons olive oil
2 tablespoons butter
2 garlic cloves, roughly chopped
½ cup dry white wine
salt and freshly ground pepper
2 eggs, hard-boiled
3 tablespoons chopped parsley
1½ tablespoons capers, chopped
4 tablespoons freshly grated Parmesan

Trim, clean, and remove the choke from each artichoke as explained on p. 215. Cut the artichokes into 8 wedges and place them in water acidulated with the juice of 1 lemon until ready to use. Heat 1 tablespoon each of oil and butter in a large saucepan, add the garlic, and sauté for 2 minutes. Add the artichoke wedges and sauté for a few minutes. Add the wine and salt and pepper to taste. Simmer, covered, until tender, about 15 minutes. Add water to the artichokes, 1 tablespoon at a time, to prevent sticking.

Preheat the oven to 400°F.

Peel and finely chop the 2 hard-boiled eggs. Combine with the parsley and capers. Heat the remaining oil and butter in a small saucepan and add the egg-parsley mixture. Combine well, remove from the heat, but keep warm.

Butter an 8-by-10-inch baking dish, add the artichokes in a single layer, sprinkle with Parmesan, and bake for 8 minutes. Remove from the oven, spread the egg-parsley sauce over the artichokes, return to the oven for 2 minutes to heat through, and serve immediately.

◆ ◆ ◆ ◆ ◆

## Carciofi Gratinati

ARTICHOKES
AU
GRATIN

SERVES 6

The slow baking of the artichokes with garlic, parsley, and Parmesan brings out their wonderful flavor.

9 medium artichokes
3 garlic cloves, chopped
3 tablespoons chopped parsley
½ teaspoon salt
freshly ground pepper to taste
2 tablespoons olive oil
4 tablespoons freshly grated Parmesan

Preheat the oven to 350°F. and generously oil a 10-inch pie pan.

Trim the artichokes, cut them into wedges ¼ inch thick, and remove the chokes as explained on p. 215. Place them in water acidulated with the juice of 1 lemon until ready to use.

Drain the artichokes and pat them dry. Line the pie pan with the artichoke wedges, overlapping them so that they all fit in a single layer. Spread the garlic and parsley evenly over the artichokes, add the salt and pepper, drizzle with the oil, and finally sprinkle the Parmesan on top.

Bake in the preheated oven for 30 to 35 minutes, until tender. Serve hot.

◆ ◆ ◆ ◆ ◆

## *Carciofi al Boscaiolo*

ARTICHOKES
FORESTER'S
STYLE

SERVES 6

As you will discover in this dish, artichokes and mushrooms make a wonderful combination of textures and flavors. Do not overcook the artichokes, since it is through their texture that they maintain their personality. This dish can be cooked ahead of time and reheated just before you are ready to serve it.

8 artichokes
1 tablespoon olive oil
1 tablespoon butter
3 garlic cloves, chopped
½ cup Tomato Sauce I (see recipe), or 1 cup canned
    Italian plum tomatoes, drained
½ pound fresh mushrooms, cleaned and sliced
⅓ cup dry white wine
pinch of salt
freshly ground pepper to taste
2 tablespoons chopped basil
2 tablespoons chopped parsley

Trim, clean, quarter the artichokes, and remove the chokes as explained on p. 215. Place them in water acidulated with the juice of 1 lemon until ready to use. Heat the oil and butter in a saucepan, add the garlic, and sauté 1 minute. Drain the artichokes, add them to the garlic, and sauté for 3 to 4 minutes. Add the tomato sauce or tomatoes, the mushrooms, ⅓ cup of water, wine, salt, and pepper. Combine thoroughly and simmer, partly covered, stirring occasionally, for 20 to 25 minutes, until the artichokes are cooked but still firm. Add the basil and parsley, adjust for seasoning, and serve.

♦ ♦ ♦ ♦ ♦

## Carciofi con Piselli

ARTICHOKES
AND
PEAS

SERVES 6

Artichokes and peas make a marvelous pair, elegant and richly flavored. Use fresh or frozen peas.

6 medium artichokes
3 tablespoons butter
2 cups fresh or frozen peas
2 tablespoons chopped parsley
1 tablespoon chopped onion
2 egg yolks
3 tablespoons lemon juice
½ cup Croutons for Soup (see recipe)

Clean and trim the artichokes, remove the chokes, cut into thin wedges as explained on p. 215, and place in water acidulated by the juice of 1 lemon.

Heat the butter in a large saucepan, drain the artichokes, add them to the saucepan, and simmer, covered, over low heat, stirring frequently, until half cooked, about 10 minutes. If using frozen peas, cook the artichokes until almost done. You will probably have to add water, but add only enough to keep the artichokes from sticking to the pan.

Add the peas, parsley, and onion, sauté a couple of minutes, add ¼ cup of water, and simmer covered, stirring frequently, until the vegetables are cooked but still firm.

While the vegetables cook, combine the egg yolks and lemon juice in a small mixing bowl. When the vegetables are cooked, add the egg-lemon mixture, combine gently, and serve topped with the croutons.

♦ ♦ ♦ ♦ ♦

## Carciofi Ripieni alla Virginia

STUFFED
ARTICHOKES,
VIRGINIA
STYLE

SERVES 6

12 medium artichokes
2 tablespoons butter
1 pound mushrooms, washed, trimmed, and finely
    chopped
4 garlic cloves, finely chopped
1 teaspoon chopped fresh rosemary, or ½ teaspoon dried
4 tablespoons chopped parsley
freshly ground pepper to taste
¾ teaspoon salt
3 tablespoons bread crumbs
3 tablespoons olive oil

Trim, clean, and prepare the artichokes for stuffing as explained on p. 215. Place them in water acidulated with the juice of 1 lemon until ready to use. Heat the butter in a frying pan. Add the mushrooms, garlic, rosemary, parsley, and pepper and sauté over high heat for 3 or 4 minutes, until the mushrooms give up their liquid. Remove from the heat. Stir in ½ teaspoon of salt and the bread crumbs.

Stuff the artichokes with the mushroom mixture, pressing as much stuffing as possible into each artichoke center. Place the artichokes upright in a saucepan large enough to hold them snugly. Drizzle the artichokes inside and out with 2 tablespoons of olive oil, sprinkle with the remaining salt, and pour the remaining olive oil along with 2 cups of water into the pan. Cover and simmer over a low heat for 45 minutes, until the artichokes are cooked but still firm. Serve hot or at room temperature.

♦ ♦ ♦ ♦ ♦

## *Carciofi alla Romana*

ARTICHOKES,
ROMAN
STYLE

SERVES 6

These delicious artichokes, stuffed and baked with garlic and mint, are found in Roman trattorie throughout the winter season. They can be served hot or at room temperature, and can be eaten as either a vegetable or an antipasto. Use tender young artichokes.

*6 large or 12 small artichokes*
*1½ tablespoons finely chopped mint*
*4 garlic cloves, finely chopped*
*4 tablespoons bread crumbs*
*½ teaspoon salt*
*¼ teaspoon pepper*
*¼ cup olive oil*

Clean, trim the artichokes, and prepare them for stuffing as explained on p. 215. Place them in water acidulated with the juice of 1 lemon until ready to use. In a small mixing bowl combine the mint, garlic, bread crumbs, salt, and pepper with 2 tablespoons of olive oil.

Preheat the oven to 350°F.

Drain the artichokes. Spread the leaves. Place a little of the stuffing between them and put some in the center of each artichoke. Place the artichokes standing up side by side in an ovenproof casserole in which they fit snugly. Add the remaining oil to the casserole and enough water to come halfway up the sides of the artichokes. Cover with aluminum foil and bake in the preheated oven for 30 minutes. Remove the foil and continue baking until the artichokes are tender, about 30 minutes, basting occasionally with the liquid in the pan. Test for doneness by inserting the tines of a long-handled fork or skewer into the flesh of the artichoke heart. The artichokes are cooked when the fork or skewer meets some resistance but enters with relative ease.

Remove from the oven and transfer to a serving dish. Reduce the cooking liquid over a medium heat to ½ cup. Pour over the artichokes and serve either warm or at room temperature.

♦ ♦ ♦ ♦ ♦

## Carciofi Fritti

FRIED
ARTICHOKES

SERVES 6

Artichokes prepared and fried in this way capture the essence of this marvelous vegetable. If you are partial to artichokes and you like fried vegetables, you will find this dish irresistible.

*8 medium artichokes*
*¾ cup all-purpose flour*
*salt*
*abundant freshly ground pepper*
*½ to 1 cup seed oil*
*3 extra-large eggs, beaten*
*lemon wedges*

Trim, clean, and remove the chokes as explained on p. 215. Cut into ⅛-inch-thick wedges and place in water acidulated with the juice of 1 lemon until ready to fry.

Combine the flour, ¼ teaspoon salt, and pepper, and place on a large plate. Put the oil in a pan suitable for deep frying and heat to a moderate temperature. There should be enough oil to completely cover the artichoke wedges. Add more if necessary.

Drain the artichokes and pat them dry between paper towels. Dredge with flour, dip in the beaten eggs, and fry in batches, turning if necessary until golden and tender, about 3 minutes. Remove from the oil with a slotted spoon and drain on paper towels. Sprinkle with salt to taste and serve hot with lemon wedges.

## ASPARAGUS

Nothing compares with the first fresh asparagus of spring. This pleasure has been enjoyed since at least the time of the ancient Egyptians, who immortalized the vegetable in bas-relief. The Greeks were fond of the delectable green spears, and so were the Romans, as the testimony of Cato, Pliny, and Martial indicates. Asparagus is grown today in all parts of Italy, although connoisseurs contend that the best still come from Ravenna as they did in Pliny's day and from Bassano del Grappa in the Veneto, after which one of the main varieties is named.

## How to Select and Prepare Asparagus

Fresh asparagus spears have closed, firm tips and firm but tender stalks. They may be kept for a few days in the refrigerator, but are best eaten right away.

Asparagus is grown in sandy soil, and some sand always clings to the tops as they push up through the earth. Wash asparagus well in cold water to eliminate all traces of sand. To cook, break or cut off and discard the coarse, woody part at the bottom. Peel the lower section of what remains until you arrive at tender, edible flesh.

Asparagus should be steamed, not boiled, and there are two ways to go about steaming it. One is simply to devise or purchase a vegetable steamer and steam the spears, covered, until tender. Since many vegetables are best if cooked by steam, a steamer is a good investment. The other, more traditional method of cooking asparagus in Italy and France is to tie the asparagus into sheaths, stand them in a tall pot with a couple of inches of water in the bottom, and cook them, covered, until tender. In this way, the tougher bottoms boil and the tender tips steam.

Do not overcook asparagus. It should be tender but firm—al dente is perhaps the best way to describe it. Test for doneness by inserting a fork into the stem—it should enter but meet with some resistance. Asparagus takes from 5 to 10 minutes to cook, depending on size and freshness. Remove from the pot immediately, by using tongs or sliding two forks under the asparagus, drain well, and proceed according to the recipe.

♦ ♦ ♦ ♦ ♦

## Asparagi al Limone

ASPARAGUS
WITH
LEMON
AND
OIL

SERVES 6

There could be nothing simpler than this recipe for asparagus and, perhaps, nothing better.

2 pounds asparagus
1 lemon
3 tablespoons olive oil
salt and freshly ground pepper
3 tablespoons freshly grated Parmesan

Trim the asparagus and cook the spears according to directions, p. 222. Drain and place them on a heated serving platter. Squeeze over them the juice of the lemon, drizzle with olive oil, add salt and pepper to taste, sprinkle with Parmesan, and serve hot.

◆ ◆ ◆ ◆ ◆

## Asparagi all'Aglio

ASPARAGUS
WITH GARLIC
SAUCE

SERVES 6

This formidable-sounding sauce is really quite delicate and exceedingly good with asparagus.

2 pounds asparagus
5 tablespoons butter
5 garlic cloves, minced
2 tablespoons finely chopped parsley
¼ teaspoon salt
freshly ground pepper to taste

Prepare the asparagus and cook according to directions on p. 222.

While the asparagus cooks, prepare the following sauce. Heat the butter in a small saucepan or frying pan, add the garlic, and sauté until the garlic just begins to color, about 1 minute. Remove from the heat, allow to cool for a few minutes, then blend in the parsley, salt, and pepper.

When cooked, drain the asparagus, place it on a heated serving platter, pour the sauce over it, and serve.

◆ ◆ ◆ ◆ ◆

## Crespelle agli Asparagi

ASPARAGUS
ROLLED
IN
CRÊPES

SERVES 6 TO 8

A simple, impressive way to serve asparagus, this dish can also be used as the main course for a luncheon or light supper. The crêpes can be made ahead of time.

Crêpes (see recipe)
2 pounds asparagus
salt and freshly ground pepper to taste
½ cup grated Gruyère or fontina
3 tablespoons butter
about 24 strands chives
2 tablespoons bread crumbs
3 tablespoons freshly grated Parmesan

Make 12 crêpes as explained in the recipe, and set aside until ready to use. If you wish to keep them for more than a few hours before using, interleave buttered wax paper between each crêpe and store in the refrigerator.

Preheat the oven to 375°F. Butter a baking dish large enough to hold 12 rolled crêpes in a single layer.

Cook the asparagus according to directions, p. 222, drain, and divide into 12 equal bunches. Place one bunch on each of the 12 crêpes. Sprinkle with salt and pepper and the grated Gruyère or fontina and place on each a dot of butter, using in all 1 tablespoon. Add 2 chive strands to each bunch, roll the crêpes, and place them in the buttered baking dish. Combine the Parmesan and bread crumbs in a small mixing bowl and sprinkle the mixture over the crêpes. Dot with remaining butter and bake in the preheated oven for 20 minutes, until a golden crust forms. Serve hot.

♦ ♦ ♦ ♦ ♦

## *Asparagi ai Funghi*

ASPARAGUS
WITH
MUSHROOM
SAUCE

SERVES 6

Hard-boiled eggs are used to garnish the asparagus here. The color combination is delightful, and the flavor of asparagus and creamy wild mushroom sauce is superb. If you want to make the dish more substantial and turn it into a light main course, simply increase the number of eggs.

*½ ounce dried wild mushrooms (Boletus edulis)*
*2 tablespoons butter*
*3 tablespoons finely chopped parsley*
*½ cup finely chopped onion*
*1 cup thick cream*
*pinch of nutmeg*
*1 egg yolk*
*¼ teaspoon salt*
*freshly ground pepper to taste*
*2 tablespoons lemon juice*
*2 pounds asparagus*
*2 hard-boiled eggs*

Soak the wild mushrooms in 1 cup of warm water for 20 minutes, remove carefully from the water, and rinse well under cold water to remove grit and sand. Drain, finely chop, and set aside.

Make the sauce. Heat the butter in a saucepan, add the parsley and onion, and sauté over a medium heat for 1 minute. Add the dried mushrooms and sauté another minute. Then stir in the cream, nutmeg, and the egg yolk. Continue cooking, stirring constantly, until the sauce thickens, about 3 minutes. Add salt and pepper and lemon juice and set aside.

Cook the asparagus according to directions on p. 222. Drain it well and arrange on a heated serving dish. Warm the sauce through and pour over the asparagus. Garnish with quartered hard-boiled eggs. Serve hot.

# BEANS

One wonders how Italians, especially Florentines, managed before kidney beans, often called "poor man's meat," were introduced into Italy from the Americas at the beginning of the sixteenth century. Their diet must have been sadly inferior without the nutritious, sturdy legume that figures in so many dishes today.

There are numerous varieties of kidney beans grown commercially in Italy, but the two most common are the white *cannellino* and the red-and-white streaked cranberry bean. They are available dried, canned, and, in the late summer when they mature, fresh. Most of the recipes below call for dried beans, although in some, as we indicate, canned beans can be substituted. If fresh beans are available, by all means use them. They are far superior to dried or canned ones. They are cooked in exactly the same way as the dried beans, but require no soaking and a shorter cooking time. Italians add flour to the water in which the dried beans are soaked to soften the skin of the beans. We recommend that you do the same.

♦ ♦ ♦ ♦ ♦

## *Fagioli all'Uccelletto*

BEANS
WITH
TOMATO
SAUCE

SERVES 6 TO 8

This may be the best known of all the Tuscan bean dishes, a delicious blend of white beans, garlic, sage, and tomatoes. It is especially good prepared with fresh beans that do not require any soaking.

1½ cups dried white beans
1 tablespoon flour
3 tablespoons olive oil
3 garlic cloves, chopped
3 or 4 sage leaves
¼ teaspoon freshly ground pepper
¼ teaspoon salt
4 tablespoons Tomato Sauce I (see recipe), or ½ cup
    canned Italian plum tomatoes, drained and
    chopped

Soak the beans for 8 hours or overnight in 4 cups of water with 1 tablespoon of flour. The flour softens the skin of the beans. Drain and rinse the beans. Place them in a large saucepan with water to cover and simmer, covered, for 1 hour, until the beans are just tender. Do not allow them to overcook. As an alternative, cook in a pressure cooker for 20 minutes.

Drain the beans well, reserving the liquid for use in soup. Heat the oil in a frying pan, add the garlic, sage, pepper, and salt, and sauté for 30 seconds. Blend in the beans, simmer for a few minutes to amalgamate the flavors, then add the tomato sauce or the tomatoes and cook over a low heat, stirring frequently, until the liquid from the tomatoes evaporates. Serve hot.

♦ ♦ ♦ ♦ ♦

*Fagioli con Peperoni*

BEANS
WITH
PEPPERS
AND
HERBS

SERVES 6

It is possible in this recipe to use either dried or canned Italian white beans. We've tried both and find them equally good. This particular combination of herbs and peppers brings out all the natural sweetness of the beans. It is a simple but very satisfying dish.

*1 cup dried white beans, or 2 cups canned Italian white beans*
*1 tablespoon flour (optional)*
*2 tablespoons olive oil*
*1 medium onion, finely chopped*
*1 medium carrot, finely chopped*
*1 stalk celery, finely chopped*
*1 hot pepper, fresh or dried, seeded and chopped*
*1 teaspoon crushed dried sage*
*2 tablespoons finely chopped parsley*
*1 large red or green bell pepper, seeded and diced*
*¼ teaspoon salt*
*freshly ground pepper to taste*

Soak the dried beans for 8 hours or overnight in 3 cups of water with 1 tablespoon of flour. The flour softens the skin of the beans. Drain, rinse, and cook in 4 cups of water until tender, about 1 hour. Drain and set aside. As an alternative, cook in a pressure cooker for 25 minutes, drain, and set aside. If canned beans are used, omit soaking with water and flour and simply drain before assembling the rest of the dish.

Heat the olive oil in a large saucepan or frying pan, add the onion, carrot, and celery, and sauté over a medium heat, stirring, for 5 minutes. Stir in the hot pepper, sage, parsley, and bell pepper and continue to sauté for another 5 to 7 minutes, until the pepper is tender. Add 2 cups of the cooked beans, salt, and pepper. Combine well, reduce the heat to low, and cook, stirring frequently, for another 5 minutes. Serve hot.

◆ ◆ ◆ ◆ ◆

## Fagioli al Fiasco

BAKED
BEANS
IN A
FLASK

SERVES 6 TO 8

When I was a child bread was baked once a week at the villa. Since the brick oven was large, it took time and lots of wood to heat it, so that it was practical to bake other foods at the same time. One of the real treats was beans baked in a flask, Fagioli al Fiasco. Beans were placed in a large chianti flask from which the straw wrapping had been removed, and water, oil, garlic, and sage were added. Fresh sage leaves were placed on top of the beans in the neck of the flask to seal in some of the vapors. The flask was deposited in the oven on the smoldering embers and left for a few hours. When retrieved, the water was absorbed, the beans cooked, and the flask intact. We would eat the beans cold with lemon juice, olive oil, salt, and pepper. Beans cooked in this simple manner were light, tender, and richly flavored. We have found that exactly the same results can be achieved in any modern kitchen.

It is important to cover the beans only partially. Vapor must be allowed to escape during cooking, otherwise there's danger of the jar or bottle exploding.

2 cups dried white kidney beans
1 tablespoon flour
3 sage leaves
2 garlic cloves, roughly chopped
1 tablespoon olive oil
salt and freshly ground pepper to taste
1 lemon, cut in wedges
olive oil for serving with the beans

Soak the beans for 8 hours or overnight in 5 cups of water with 1 tablespoon of flour.

When ready to cook, preheat the oven to 325°F.

Drain and rinse the beans, combine them with the sage and garlic, and pour them into a 1-quart Mason jar. Add the olive oil and enough hot water to come approximately ¾ inch above the top of the beans. Place the flask or jar in the rear of the oven, partially cover the top of the jar with aluminum foil, and bake until the beans are tender, about 2 hours. The beans should cook at a slow simmer. Adjust the oven temperature if necessary. Transfer the beans to a terra cotta bowl, season with salt and pepper, and serve warm or at room temperature with lemon wedges. Pass olive oil for those who want to add it.

♦ ♦ ♦ ♦ ♦

*Broccoli*

*Stufati*

BROCCOLI
SMOTHERED
IN
WINE

SERVES 6

When choosing broccoli, select a bunch with glossy, firm stems and dark green compact flowerets. Fresh broccoli is now available all year round.

*1½ pounds broccoli*
*2 tablespoons olive oil*
*1 cup thinly sliced onions*
*2 tablespoons capers, chopped*
*freshly ground pepper to taste*
*½ pound provolone, thinly sliced*
*½ cup dry red wine*
*juice of ½ lemon*

Wash the broccoli in cold water. Trim away the dark green inedible outer skin of the stems, exposing the tender, pale green inner flesh. If the stems are very thick, cut them into ½-inch slices. Otherwise cut the broccoli lengthwise into ½-inch strips, keeping the flowerets intact.

The ideal pan in which to cook the broccoli is a large saucepan or casserole with low sides that can hold the broccoli in two layers. Add the olive oil to the pan, evenly spread half the onions in the bottom of the pan, and cover with half the broccoli and half the capers. Sprinkle with pepper and distribute on top half the provolone slices. Repeat the layering process, ending with the cheese. Pour in the red wine, cover, and simmer over low heat until the broccoli is cooked but still firm, about 20 minutes. Do not stir the broccoli while it cooks. Add the lemon juice just prior to serving.

♦ ♦ ♦ ♦ ♦

*Cavolo*

*Strascicato*

SAUTÉED
CABBAGE

SERVES 4 TO 6

Cabbage is available when many other vegetables are not. It has a high mineral and vitamin content and, if properly prepared, is very tasty. This is one of the simplest and best ways to prepare cabbage.

3 tablespoons olive oil or butter
4 garlic cloves, chopped
1 small leek, thinly sliced (approximately ½ cup)
1 small cabbage, preferably Savoy, shredded
¼ teaspoon minced hot red pepper
salt and freshly ground pepper

In a large frying pan, heat the oil or butter, add the garlic, and sauté until golden over medium heat. Add the leek and sauté for 3 minutes. Add the cabbage and continue cooking until the cabbage wilts. Add the red pepper and cook over a low heat until the cabbage is tender, stirring occasionally, about 15 to 20 minutes. If the cabbage sticks to the pan, add a few tablespoons of water. When cooked, add salt and pepper to taste and serve.

♦ ♦ ♦ ♦ ♦

*Cavolo*

*Agrodolce*

SWEET-AND-
SOUR
CABBAGE

SERVES 6 TO 8

Sweet-and-sour cabbage, a dish from northern Italy, reflects the German influence on Italian food. This recipe can also be prepared with red cabbage, which is usually tougher than the common white or Savoy and will therefore take a little longer to cook.

1 medium cabbage, coarsely chopped
3 tablespoons olive oil
2 cups thinly sliced onions
3 garlic cloves, chopped
4 to 5 tablespoons wine vinegar
4 tablespoons sugar
½ teaspoon salt
freshly ground pepper to taste

Rinse the cabbage in cold water and drain thoroughly. Heat the oil in a large saucepan, add the onions, and sauté until translucent, about 5 minutes. Add the garlic and cook, another minute or two, until the onions begin to brown. Add the cabbage and continue to cook, stirring, until the ingredients are thoroughly combined, about 4 minutes. Blend in 4 tablespoons of vinegar, the sugar, salt, and pepper. Reduce the heat to low and cook the cabbage, covered, stirring occasionally, until tender, about 25 minutes. If you want a sharper flavor, add 1 tablespoon of vinegar 10 minutes before the cabbage is cooked. Serve hot.

♦ ♦ ♦ ♦ ♦

*Cavolo Stufato al Vino*

BRAISED
CABBAGE
IN
WINE

SERVES 6 TO 8

Since it is the wine that flavors the cabbage, use a good-quality Italian dry white wine such as Soave or Pinot Grigio.

2 tablespoons olive oil
1 large onion, thinly sliced
½ teaspoon dried rosemary, or 1 teaspoon fresh
1 medium head cabbage, coarsely shredded
1 tablespoon Tomato Sauce I (see recipe)
1 cup dry white wine
salt and freshly ground pepper

Heat the oil in a large saucepan, add the onion and rosemary, and sauté over a medium heat until the onion becomes translucent. Add the cabbage and cook, stirring, for 5 minutes until the cabbage begins to wilt. Add the tomato sauce, the white wine, and salt and pepper to taste, cover, and cook slowly over a low heat for about 25 minutes until the cabbage is tender. Serve hot.

♦ ♦ ♦ ♦ ♦

*Cavolo Nero con Bruschetta*

SIMMERED
CABBAGE
ON
GARLIC
TOAST

It is amazing how localized some foods are. *Cavolo nero* or black cabbage, a kind of cabbage that does not form a head, is immensely popular in central Italy, especially in Tuscany, but is hardly ever eaten elsewhere in the country. It has a marvelous flavor, less pungent than the common cabbage, but unmistakably of the same family. Although it is impossible to find black cabbage in North America, we have discovered two very good substitutes, collard greens and kale. The former is somewhat bitter with a robust taste, while the latter is quite mild and sweet.

SERVES 4

1 pound kale or collard greens
6 slices hearty Italian bread, homemade Tuscan White
   or Whole Wheat Bread if possible (see recipes)
1 garlic clove, peeled
salt and freshly ground pepper
2 or 3 tablespoons olive oil

Wash the greens thoroughly in cold water. Cut away and discard the tough stems. Place about ½ inch of water in the bottom of a large saucepan, bring it to a boil, add the greens, and cook for about 10 to 15 minutes, until tender.

Meanwhile, toast the bread and rub each slice vigorously with the garlic clove.

When the greens are cooked, drain them well in a colander, squeeze out as much water as possible, and chop them coarsely. Sprinkle with salt and pepper to taste.

Place the slices of toast on a serving platter, cover abundantly with the chopped greens, drizzle generously with olive oil, and serve.

♦ ♦ ♦ ♦ ♦

*Carote*

*Marinate*

MARINATED
CARROTS

SERVES 6

These carrots can be served as a vegetable accompaniment to a main dish, as an antipasto, or as a salad.

2 pounds young, tender carrots, peeled and cut into
   pieces 2 inches long by ¼ inch thick
¼ cup olive oil
3 tablespoons lemon juice
2 tablespoons chopped parsley
2 tablespoons chopped basil
½ teaspoon salt
freshly ground pepper

Steam the carrots until tender but still firm, about 10 to 15 minutes.

Place the carrots in a mixing bowl.

Combine the remaining ingredients in a small bowl, pour the dressing over the carrots while they are still hot, toss to mix, and chill in the refrigerator before serving.

♦ ♦ ♦ ♦ ♦

## *Carote alla Virginia*

CARROTS
VIRGINIA

SERVES 4 TO 6

Ever since Virginia introduced this dish to us a few years ago, a scrumptious combination of parboiled carrots, garlic, and onions baked in a light béchamel sauce, it has become a staple with us. Try to find young, tender carrots that have not developed a coarse, woody center.

*1½ pounds carrots, peeled and cut lengthwise in thin strips*
*1 garlic clove, thinly sliced*
*1 teaspoon sugar*
*1 medium red onion, thinly sliced*
*Béchamel Sauce (see recipe) made with:*
 *1¾ cups milk*
 *4 tablespoons butter*
 *4 tablespoons all-purpose flour*
 *¼ teaspoon salt*

Place the carrots, garlic, sugar, and onion in the saucepan, add water to cover, bring to a boil, and simmer until the carrots are just tender, about 10 minutes. Do not overcook. Drain and set aside.

Preheat the oven to 350°F.

Butter an 8-by-10-inch baking dish and distribute the carrots, onion, and garlic evenly in the dish. Make the béchamel sauce and pour it over the carrots. Most of the sauce will remain on top, but some should penetrate between the carrots. Bake in the preheated oven for 20 minutes. Serve hot.

♦ ♦ ♦ ♦ ♦

## *Cavolfiore ai Capperi*

CAULIFLOWER
WITH
CAPERS

SERVES 4 TO 6

Cauliflower, a member of the cabbage family, is now usually available fresh all year round. Choose cauliflowers that are stark white and heavy for their size, with tightly packed, unblemished flowerets. To cook, trim and discard the outer leaves and the hard woody part of the stem. We recommend that you steam, not boil, cauliflower. The former cooking method seals in flavor and nutrients and produces a much finer-textured vegetable.

In this recipe, a sauce of capers, garlic, and vinegar adds real zest to a steamed cauliflower.

1 medium cauliflower
½ teaspoon salt
freshly ground pepper to taste
3 tablespoons olive oil
2 cloves garlic, minced
2 tablespoons capers, finely chopped
3 tablespoons wine vinegar
parsley sprigs (optional)

Wash and trim the cauliflower, retaining the outer leaves, if available, for garnish. Season with salt and pepper, and steam whole in a large saucepan until just cooked, but still firm, about 15 to 20 minutes.

While the cauliflower cooks, prepare the sauce. Heat the olive oil in a small saucepan, add the garlic, and sauté for 1 minute. Add the capers and vinegar, heat through, and keep warm.

When the cauliflower is cooked, transfer it whole to a large, heated serving platter garnished with the cauliflower leaves or parsley sprigs, pour on the sauce, and serve.

♦ ♦ ♦ ♦ ♦

## *Cavolfiore Siciliano*

CAULIFLOWER,
SICILIAN
STYLE

SERVES 6

4 tablespoons olive oil
½ cup thinly sliced leeks (white parts only) or onions
3 garlic cloves, thinly sliced
1 medium cauliflower, washed, trimmed, and cut into
    small flowerets
1 medium tomato, thinly sliced
1 green or red bell pepper, seeded and thinly sliced
½ cup dry white wine
freshly ground pepper to taste
¼ teaspoon chopped oregano
1 tablespoon chopped parsley
1 tablespoon chopped basil
2 tablespoons capers
2 tablespoons Italian black olives, pitted, rinsed if very
    salty, and chopped
1 lemon, cut into 6 wedges
salt (optional)

Heat the olive oil in a large low-sided saucepan, add the leeks or onions, and sauté until they begin to color, about 5 minutes. Add the garlic, sauté another minute, stir in the cauliflower, and cook over a medium heat, stirring constantly for 3 minutes to combine the ingredients. Reduce the heat and cook covered for 5 minutes.

Remove the cover, add the tomato, bell pepper, white wine, and pepper. Combine and simmer covered for another 5 minutes. Blend in the oregano, parsley, basil, and 1 tablespoon each of capers and olives; heat through, and place the cauliflower in a heated serving bowl. Sprinkle the remaining olives and capers on top, surround with the lemon wedges, and serve. If salt is needed, add just before serving.

♦ ♦ ♦ ♦ ♦

*Cavolfiore*

*Mimosa*

CAULIFLOWER
MIMOSA

SERVES 6

Cauliflower coated with a sauce of eggs, butter, lemon, and parsley recalls the delicate yellow flower, mimosa.

*1 medium cauliflower*
*2 hard-boiled eggs*
*3 tablespoons chopped parsley*
*¼ cup butter, heated until lightly browned*
*juice of ½ lemon*
*½ teaspoon salt*
*freshly ground pepper to taste*
*1 hard-boiled egg, sliced*
*1 lemon, cut in wedges*
*parsley sprigs*

Trim and wash the cauliflower. Place in a large saucepan and steam whole until just tender, about 15 to 20 minutes.

While the cauliflower steams, prepare the following sauce. Peel and finely chop the 2 hard-boiled eggs and combine with the parsley in a small bowl. In a separate bowl, mix the butter and lemon juice.

When ready to serve place the whole cauliflower on a serving platter, pour over it the lemon-butter mixture, sprinkle the eggs and parsley on top, add the salt and pepper, and serve garnished with a sliced hard-boiled egg, lemon wedges, and parsley sprigs.

♦ ♦ ♦ ♦ ♦

*Cavolfiore al*

*Forno*

BAKED
CAULIFLOWER
WITH
BÉCHAMEL
SAUCE

SERVES 6

This is, for us, cauliflower at its best. The béchamel sauce highlights the delicate taste of the cauliflower while the baking brings out its full flavor.

1 medium cauliflower, washed, trimmed, and cut into
     flowerets
1 tablespoon butter
pinch of salt
Béchamel Sauce (see recipe) made with:
     1¾ cups milk
     4 tablespoons butter
     4 tablespoons flour
     ¼ teaspoon salt
1 egg yolk
2 tablespoons freshly grated Parmesan

Preheat the oven to 375°F. Butter well a 9-by-12-inch baking dish.

Steam the cauliflower until just cooked but still firm, about 15 minutes. Drain well. Heat the tablespoon of butter in a saucepan, add the cauliflower and salt, and sauté for 2 or 3 minutes to dry the cauliflower thoroughly. Remove from the heat and distribute evenly in the buttered baking dish.

Make the béchamel sauce, remove from the heat, beat in the egg yolk, add the Parmesan, and combine. Pour the sauce over the cauliflower and bake in the preheated oven until the top browns, about 25 to 30 minutes.

♦ ♦ ♦ ♦ ♦

*Cavolfiore*

*Strascicato*

SAUTÉED
CAULIFLOWER

SERVES 4 TO 6

1 medium cauliflower
4 tablespoons butter
4 garlic cloves, finely chopped
½ teaspoon salt
freshly ground pepper
2 tablespoons finely chopped parsley

Wash, trim, and separate the cauliflower into flowerets. Steam for 5 to 10 minutes, until partly cooked but still very firm.

Heat the butter in a large frying pan and add the garlic. Sauté over medium heat for 1 minute. Add the cauliflower and cook, stirring frequently and scraping the bottom of the pan, for 10 minutes. The cauliflower should brown lightly. Add salt and pepper, remove from the heat, and sprinkle with parsley.

♦ ♦ ♦ ♦ ♦

## *Sedano alla Crema*

CELERY
WITH
CREAM
SAUCE

SERVES 6

A light lemon and cream sauce transforms ordinary celery into a gourmet's delight.

3 tablespoons butter
½ cup minced carrots
½ cup minced onions
½ cup Vegetable Broth (see recipe)
6 celery hearts, approximately 6 inches long
1 tablespoon flour
1 egg yolk
1 cup thick cream
¼ cup lemon juice
salt and freshly ground pepper to taste

In a large frying pan, melt the butter, add the carrots and onions, and sauté, stirring frequently, for 3 to 4 minutes, until lightly browned. Add the broth, combine, and set aside.

Boil the celery hearts in water to cover for 10 to 15 minutes, until half cooked. If you are unable to find packaged celery hearts, buy 6 bunches of celery, remove the outer stalks until you arrive at the tender pale green inner stalks, and cut each bunch to a length of 6 inches. Trim the bottoms to eliminate the brown, woody parts. When half-cooked, drain the hearts and place them in the frying pan with the onions, carrots, and stock. Return the pan to a low heat and cook, covered, until the celery is tender, about 10 to 15 minutes. Do not overcook the celery— it should be firm.

While the celery cooks, combine the flour, egg yolk, cream, lemon juice, salt, and pepper in a small mixing bowl.

When ready to serve, carefully remove the celery from the frying pan to a heated serving platter. Add the lemon-cream sauce to the frying pan a little at a time, stirring constantly with a whisk or wooden spoon. Simmer over a low heat until the sauce begins to thicken. Pour the sauce, piping hot, over the celery and serve at once.

♦ ♦ ♦ ♦ ♦

## *Sedano Rifatto*

SAUTÉED
CELERY

SERVES 4 TO 6

2 bunches celery, leaves and tough outer stalks removed
3 tablespoons olive oil
5 garlic cloves, minced
2 tablespoons chopped parsley
1 cup peeled, seeded, and chopped fresh tomatoes, or 1
    cup canned Italian plum tomatoes, drained and
    chopped
½ teaspoon salt
freshly ground pepper to taste

Wash the celery, cut the stalks into 1-inch-long segments, and steam until almost tender, but still firm, about 5 to 7 minutes. Remove from the heat and drain.

Heat the olive oil in a large frying pan, add the garlic, and sauté for 1 minute. Blend in the parsley and tomatoes, add the steamed celery, and cook over medium heat, stirring frequently, until the liquid evaporates and the sauce becomes dense, about 10 minutes. Add the salt and pepper and serve hot.

♦ ♦ ♦ ♦ ♦

## *Radice di Sedano alla Piemontese*

CELERY
ROOT,
PIEDMONT
STYLE

SERVES 4

Although available all year round, celery roots—also known in the United States as celeriac—are best in the fall and early part of the winter. In this recipe the celery root is simmered in broth and white wine—a simple but excellent way to bring out the delicate, earthy taste of this vegetable.

1 medium celery root
4 tablespoons butter
¼ cup finely chopped onion
2 tablespoons flour
1 cup Vegetable Broth (see recipe)
½ cup dry white wine
½ teaspoon salt
freshly ground pepper to taste
6 slices toasted Tuscan White or Whole Wheat Bread
    (see recipes)
2 tablespoons chopped scallions (white and green parts)
    or chives

Peel and rinse the celery root, cut it into thick slices, and place in water acidulated with the juice of 1 lemon to cover. When ready to cook, drain, and steam for 10 minutes, until cooked but still quite firm. Do not overcook. Drain and keep warm.

While the celery root cooks, make the sauce. Melt the butter in a saucepan, add the onion, and sauté over a medium heat until the onion is translucent. Add the flour and cook for 1 minute, stirring constantly. Add the broth slowly in a thin stream, stirring constantly, then add the wine in the same manner. Reduce the heat to low and simmer for 10 minutes, until the sauce is velvety and begins to thicken. Taste and adjust for salt and pepper.

Place the slices of toast on a heated serving platter, distribute the celery evenly over the toast, and just before serving pour the sauce piping hot over the celery root. Sprinkle with scallions or chives and serve immediately.

♦ ♦ ♦ ♦ ♦

## Ceci alla Romana

CHICK-PEAS,
ROMAN
STYLE

SERVES 6

Chick-peas are a nourishing, starchy legume with a long history of cultivation in the Mediterranean and Middle East. They are grown mostly in the south of Italy but are popular all over the country. You can, if you wish, substitute canned chick-peas.

1½ cups dried chick-peas or 2½ to 3 cups canned
1 tablespoon flour, if dried chick-peas are used
1 teaspoon salt for cooking dried chick-peas
2 tablespoons olive oil
2 teaspoons fresh rosemary or 1 teaspoon dried
3 garlic cloves, chopped
½ hot pepper, seeded and chopped
2 tablespoons chopped parsley
3 medium tomatoes, peeled, seeded, and chopped, or 1
    cup canned Italian plum tomatoes, drained and
    chopped
½ teaspoon salt
freshly ground pepper

Soak the dried chick-peas for 8 hours or overnight in 4 cups of water with 1 tablespoon of flour. Rinse, place the chick-peas in a large saucepan with 6 cups of water and 1 teaspoon of salt, and cook until tender, about 1½ hours. As an alternative, cook in a pressure cooker for 30 minutes. When cooked, drain and set aside. The cooking liquid can be reserved and used for soup.

While the chick-peas are cooking, prepare the sauce. Heat the olive oil in a saucepan, add the rosemary, garlic, and hot pepper, and sauté for 1 to 2 minutes over a medium heat, until the garlic begins to color. Add the parsley, tomatoes, salt, and pepper and simmer over a low heat for 15 to 20 minutes, until you have a fairly thick tomato sauce. Add the cooked or canned chick-peas, cook for 5 to 10 minutes, stirring occasionally, to amalgamate the flavors, and serve.

# EGGPLANT

Eggplant was introduced into Italy from the Middle East at the end of the fourteenth century. Today it is an essential ingredient in southern Italian cuisine.

## *How to Choose and Prepare Eggplant*

Eggplants come in a wide variety of shapes and sizes, from long and thin to plump and round, and in a range of colors from dark purple to white. Be sure to choose small ones that are glossy with smooth unblemished skins.

Eggplants must be cooked—they should not be eaten raw. In most cases, the eggplant is first peeled and cut up, sprinkled with salt, and placed in a colander to drain for 30 minutes. This causes the eggplant to expel some of its bitter juices and gives it a milder, sweeter taste. It is then rinsed to remove the salt and patted dry with paper towels.

♦ ♦ ♦ ♦ ♦

## *Melanzane al Forno*

BAKED
EGGPLANT

SERVES 6

This dish may seem too simple to be good, but it is even better than that—it is truly outstanding. The tomato sauce, oregano, and garlic draw out the eggplant's unique taste. For those who like eggplant, there may be no better way to prepare it.

6 small, young eggplants, washed and cut in half
    lengthwise
2 garlic cloves, finely chopped
½ cup Tomato Sauce I (see recipe)
1 teaspoon oregano
½ teaspoon salt
freshly ground pepper to taste
3 tablespoons olive oil

Preheat oven to 375°F.

Cut cross hatches ½ inch apart about ¼ inch deep on the skin of the eggplants. Place the eggplants, skin side up, in an oiled baking dish large enough for them to fit side by side. Rub the garlic into the slits. Spread about 1 tablespoon of tomato sauce on each eggplant half, sprinkle with oregano, salt, and pepper, and drizzle with the olive oil. Bake in the preheated oven for 35 to 40 minutes, until the eggplants are tender and cooked through. To test, plunge a cake tester or toothpick into the center of an eggplant. If cooked, the tester will slide in easily. Remove from the oven and serve hot.

◆ ◆ ◆ ◆ ◆

## *Melanzane con Cipolle e Pomodori*

### EGGPLANT WITH ONIONS AND TOMATO

SERVES 4 TO 6

2 medium eggplants, approximately 1½ pounds

3 firm medium tomatoes

3 medium onions, peeled

3 tablespoons olive oil

1 garlic clove, peeled and crushed

½ teaspoon salt

freshly ground pepper to taste

½ cup freshly grated pecorino or Romano

2 tablespoons chopped basil

½ hot pepper, seeded and chopped (optional)

Wash and cut the eggplants into ½-inch-thick disks. If they are small and tender do not peel them. Sprinkle with salt and place in a colander to drain for half an hour. Cut the tomatoes in half and remove the seeds. Place the tomatoes on a platter cut side down and let drain for 30 minutes. Slice the onions ½ inch thick.

Heat 1 tablespoon of olive oil in a large frying pan, add the garlic clove, and sauté for 1 minute over a medium heat. Discard the garlic. Brown the onion slices on both sides, taking care to prevent them from falling apart. Remove from the pan with a slotted spoon, drain on paper towels, and place in a 9-by-12-inch baking dish.

Rinse the salt off the eggplants and dry between paper towels. In the same frying pan, brown the eggplant slices on both sides. Add more oil as needed, but use as little as possible—eggplants tend to absorb oil. Drain on paper towels and distribute the eggplants over the onions.

Preheat the oven to 300°F.

Cut the tomato halves into ½-inch horizontal slices. Sauté briefly in the same pan and place on top of the eggplants. Do not overcook the tomatoes.

Correct for seasoning. Sprinkle the top with the grated pecorino or Romano, the basil, and the hot pepper. Bake in the preheated oven for 10 minutes, to warm through and melt the cheese. Serve hot.

♦ ♦ ♦ ♦ ♦

## Melanzane al Funghetto

This is one of the simplest and most traditional ways to prepare eggplant. The Italian name means "eggplant mushroom style," and indeed, the preparation is almost identical to Funghi al Funghetto (see recipe).

EGGPLANT
SAUTÉED
WITH
GARLIC

SERVES 6 TO 8

*salt*

*4 medium eggplants, approximately 3 to 3½ pounds,*
*    peeled and quartered*

*3 tablespoons olive oil*

*2 garlic cloves, chopped*

*2 tablespoons chopped parsley*

*1 teaspoon chopped mint leaves*

*1 teaspoon freshly ground pepper*

*1 lemon, cut into wedges*

Sprinkle 1 tablespoon of salt on the eggplants, and place in a colander to drain for 30 minutes. When ready, rinse off the salt, pat dry, and cut into 1-inch cubes.

Heat the oil in a large frying pan. Add the garlic and the eggplants and sauté over medium heat, stirring frequently, until almost cooked, about 10 minutes. Add the parsley, mint, pepper, and salt to taste and continue cooking for another few minutes.

Serve hot, passing lemon wedges to squeeze over the eggplants.

♦ ♦ ♦ ♦ ♦

## Indivia alla Romana

BRAISED
ENDIVE

SERVES 6

Curly endive is a member of the chicory family. Like other members, it is slightly bitter, rich in vitamins and minerals, and available in the fall and winter when many other leafy vegetables are out of season. Curly endive is hardly ever served as a cooked vegetable in North America—we presume because people don't know how good it is. Try this recipe and become, along with us, a fan of cooked endive. Escarole, a close relative of curly endive, can also be cooked in this way.

*1 large head fresh curly endive*

*3 tablespoons olive oil*

*4 garlic cloves, finely chopped*

*½ cup Tomato Sauce I (see recipe), or 1 cup canned*
*    Italian plum tomatoes, drained and chopped*

1 teaspoon minced mint leaves
1 tablespoon capers, chopped
¼ hot pepper, seeded and chopped
¼ teaspoon salt
freshly ground pepper to taste

Discard the tough outer leaves of the endive and rinse well in abundant cold water. Place the endive in a large saucepan with water to cover, bring to a boil, reduce the heat, and simmer until tender, about 10 minutes. As an alternative, steam the endive until tender. Drain well, squeezing out excess water, chop roughly, and set aside.

In a large frying pan, heat the olive oil, add the garlic, and sauté over medium heat for 1 minute. Stir in the tomato sauce or tomatoes, mint, capers, and hot pepper and cook, stirring frequently, 5 to 10 minutes, until the sauce begins to thicken. Add the endive, salt, and pepper, and simmer over a low heat for 5 minutes, until the mixture is thoroughly amalgamated. The endive can be served at once or reheated.

◆ ◆ ◆ ◆ ◆

*Escarola
all'Alberto*

ESCAROLE
ALBERTO

SERVES 6

Escarole, a member of the chicory family, is, like other members, a slightly bitter vegetable, rich in vitamins and minerals. It is, in fact, almost identical to curly endive, except for the shape of the leaves. The use of currants and carrots in this recipe moderates the bitterness of the escarole and highlights its sweeter, more delicate characteristics. Curly endive can also be cooked in this way.

3 tablespoons olive oil
4 small carrots, peeled and thinly sliced
2 garlic cloves, chopped
1 large or 2 small heads of escarole, washed well, tough
    outer leaves removed, drained, and roughly
    chopped
2 tablespoons Italian black olives, pitted, rinsed in cold
    water if very salty, and chopped
1 tablespoon pine nuts
2 tablespoons currants, soaked for 10 minutes in water
    to cover and drained
freshly ground pepper to taste

Heat the oil in a large frying pan, add the carrots, and sauté over medium heat for 10 minutes. Add the garlic, cook another minute, stir in the escarole, reduce the heat to low, and cook covered for 5 minutes. Remove the cover and sauté over medium heat, stirring constantly, until the water evaporates, about 3 to 5 minutes. Add the remaining ingredients. Taste and add salt if necessary.

# FENNEL

Once, many years ago, we visited Calabria in February. One damp, chilly, overcast day we stopped at a small trattoria in Cosenza for lunch. After the meal, a large bowl of fruit was placed on the table and there in the center of the bowl were two huge, stark white fennel bulbs. We couldn't believe it. For us, fennel was a vegetable served raw in salads or cooked as a *contorno* for a main dish. The Calabrese, as it turned out, knew exactly what they were doing. The fennel, crisper, fresher, juicier, and sweeter then any we had ever tasted, brightened the day and brought the meal to a perfect end.

Fennel, a member of the parsley family, grows wild throughout the countries that surround the Mediterranean and has been used since ancient times as an herb and medicine. It has been cultivated in Italy since the sixteenth century as a vegetable. Fennel is a winter vegetable and is so delicious that it almost compensates for short days and cold weather.

## How to Choose and Prepare Fennel

Select firm, tightly packed bulbs. The feathery tops should be vivid green and the bulb white with a tinge of green. Do not be put off if the outer layers of the bulb are cracked and battered. They will be discarded and give no indication of the quality of the bulb. Fennel comes in two shapes, one stout and bulbous, the other flatter and elongated. We reserve the bulbous ones for use raw in salads and the elongated ones for cooking.

To prepare fennel, cut away the feathery tops to the point where the bulb begins to swell and remove the outer layer, as it is usually tough and stringy. If the next layer is also a bit stringy, it can be trimmed with a sharp paring knife. Trim the base of the bulb, cutting away any woody, dark parts. Proceed according to the recipe.

♦ ♦ ♦ ♦ ♦

## Finocchio Fritto

FRIED
FENNEL

SERVES 4 TO 6

6 small fennel bulbs, trimmed, p. 244, and cut into
 wedges 1 inch thick
½ teaspoon salt
½ cup flour
½ cup light seed oil
½ cup Tomato Sauce I (see recipe)
freshly ground pepper to taste

Fill a large saucepan half full of water, add the salt, and bring to a boil. Add the fennel bulbs and boil for 3 minutes to blanch. Drain the bulbs well, being careful to keep the wedges intact. Dredge them in the flour, coating all sides, shake to remove excess flour, and set aside.

Heat the oil in a frying pan until almost smoking. Add the floured fennel wedges and fry until golden on all sides. Drain on paper towels and serve, flavored with the light tomato sauce and freshly ground pepper.

♦ ♦ ♦ ♦ ♦

## Finocchio al Pomodoro

FENNEL
WITH
TOMATO
SAUCE

SERVES 4 TO 6

3 tablespoons butter
1 leek, green leaves included, washed well, and sliced in
 thin rounds
3 garlic cloves, minced
4 large fennel bulbs or 6 small ones, trimmed, p. 244,
 and cut into wedges 1 inch thick
3 tablespoons Tomato Sauce I (see recipe)
¾ cup water
½ teaspoon salt
freshly ground pepper to taste
1 tablespoon finely chopped parsley

Melt the butter in a large saucepan, add the leek, and sauté over medium heat, stirring frequently, until lightly browned, about 3 minutes. Add the garlic, cook 1 minute more, then add the fennel wedges and sauté for 2 minutes, turning the wedges to coat them with the butter.

Combine the tomato sauce with ¾ cup of water and pour the mixture over the fennel. Add salt and pepper, cover, reduce heat to low, and simmer, stirring occasionally, for 10 to 15 minutes, until the fennel is cooked through but still firm. Transfer to a heated serving platter, sprinkle with parsley, and serve hot.

♦ ♦ ♦ ♦ ♦

*Finocchio*
*al*
*Forno*

BRAISED
FENNEL

SERVES 4 TO 6

The slow oven cooking of fennel brings out the full sweet flavor of this vegetable.

*6 medium-size fennel bulbs, trimmed, p. 244, and cut*
  *in half lengthwise*
*juice of ½ lemon*
*½ teaspoon salt*
*⅓ cup butter, melted*
*freshly ground pepper to taste*
*2 tablespoons freshly grated Parmesan*
*3 tablespoons finely chopped parsley*

Steam the fennel for about 15 minutes, until half cooked. You should meet with resistance when piercing the bulbs with the tines of a fork.

Preheat the oven to 275°F.

Drain the fennel bulbs, taking care to keep them intact. Place them side by side in a buttered baking dish and sprinkle them with the lemon juice, salt, melted butter, a generous grind of pepper, and the Parmesan. Bake them in the oven, basting often with the juices. Test for doneness after 30 to 40 minutes by piercing with a fork. They are ready when the fork enters without resistance. The fennel bulbs should not brown. Sprinkle with parsley and serve warm.

♦ ♦ ♦ ♦ ♦

*Finocchio*
*alla*
*Besciamella*

FENNEL
WITH
BÉCHAMEL
SAUCE

SERVES 6

Fennel baked with béchamel sauce is a blend of subtle flavors and contrasting textures, elegant enough for dinner parties but too good to restrict to special occasions.

*6 small fennel bulbs, trimmed, p. 244, and cut in half*
  *lengthwise*
*½ teaspoon salt*
*4 tablespoons butter*
*½ cup finely chopped fresh mushrooms*
*Béchamel Sauce (see recipe) made with:*
  *1½ cups milk*
  *3 tablespoons butter*
  *3½ tablespoons flour*
  *¼ teaspoon salt*
*5 tablespoons freshly grated Parmesan*
*3 tablespoons bread crumbs*

Boil the fennel in salted water to cover for about 10 minutes. The bulbs should be tender but still resistant when pierced with a fork. Drain well, taking care to keep the fennel intact. Set aside to cool.

In a small frying pan, melt 2 tablespoons of butter, add the mushrooms, and sauté over a high heat for 2 to 3 minutes, until soft. Remove from the heat and set aside.

Preheat the oven to 375°F. and butter a baking dish large enough to hold the fennel in a single layer.

Make the béchamel in a saucepan and stir in 4 tablespoons of Parmesan and the sautéed mushrooms. Spread 3 tablespoons of sauce on the bottom of the baking dish. Place the fennel in the dish, cut side down. Pour the remaining sauce over the fennel, spreading it evenly. Combine the remaining Parmesan and the bread crumbs and sprinkle the mixture on top. Dot with the remaining 2 tablespoons of butter and bake in the preheated oven for 30 minutes or until a golden crust forms on top. Serve hot.

♦ ♦ ♦ ♦ ♦

## *Porri*
## *Gratinati*

Leeks have been cultivated since ancient times and were eaten in the past as much for their supposed healthful characteristics as for their flavor. We can't speak for the curative properties of leeks, but we certainly recommend them for their flavor.

LEEKS
AU
GRATIN

SERVES 6

6 *large leeks*
4 *cups Vegetable Broth (see recipe), more if necessary*
½ *cup freshly grated Parmesan*
⅓ *cup bread crumbs*
*freshly ground pepper to taste*
4 *tablespoons butter*
*salt, if necessary*

Remove most of the green top portion of the leeks and cut off and discard the first or second outer leaves if they seem tough. Trim the base, keeping the leaves attached to it. Cut the leeks in half lengthwise and rinse thoroughly, making sure that all sand and grit caught between the layers is washed away.

Pour the broth into a large, low-sided saucepan, bring to a boil, and add the leeks. It is best if the leeks fit in a single layer. Add more broth, if necessary, to cover the leeks. Place a lid on the saucepan, reduce the heat to low, and simmer for 5 to 10 minutes, until the leeks are cooked but still quite firm. Do not overcook—they will lose their flavor and texture. When cooked, remove the leeks carefully from the broth with tongs and place on a plate to cool.

Preheat the oven to 375°F.

Lightly butter a baking dish large enough to accommodate the leeks in a single layer. Place the leeks in the baking dish, overlapping the ends if necessary. Combine the Parmesan and bread crumbs in a mixing bowl and sprinkle the mixture over the leeks. Grind pepper over the leeks and dot with the butter. Add salt if necessary, but remember that the Parmesan is salty, as is the broth. Bake for 30 minutes in the preheated oven, until a golden crust forms on top. Serve hot in the baking dish.

◆ ◆ ◆ ◆ ◆

## *Lenticchie con Odori*

LENTILS
WITH
HERBS

SERVES 6

Lentils, a legume rich in protein and high in fiber, have been cultivated for millennia. They were eaten by the ancient Egyptians, by the Hebrews, Greeks, Romans, and practically every other ancient civilization. They are never eaten fresh, but instead are left on the plant to dry, then harvested and shelled. Lentils cooked with garlic and herbs as in this recipe make a tasty and satisfying vegetable accompaniment to a light main dish such as Eggs in Wine Sauce (see recipe).

FOR SOAKING THE LENTILS AND BOILING THEM:

1½ cups lentils
1 medium onion, quartered
2 medium carrots, cut in pieces
2 bay leaves
½ teaspoon salt

FOR THE SAUCE:

2 tablespoons olive oil
2 medium carrots, finely chopped
2 stalks celery, finely chopped
3 garlic cloves, finely chopped
3 tablespoons finely chopped parsley
¼ cup canned Italian plum tomatoes, drained and
    chopped
salt and freshly ground pepper

Soak the lentils for 8 hours or overnight in 4 cups of water. Drain and rinse the lentils and place them in a large enamel or stainless steel saucepan. Do not use aluminum, as it will cause the lentils to discolor. Add the onion, carrots, bay leaves, salt, and water to cover. Simmer, covered, over low heat until the lentils are tender, but not mushy, about 20 minutes. Drain, discard the bay leaves, and set the lentils aside. Reserve the liquid for soup.

To make the sauce, heat the olive oil in a frying pan, add the carrots and celery, and sauté over medium heat for 5 minutes. Add the garlic and parsley and sauté for another minute. Blend in the tomatoes and cook, stirring constantly, until the sauce is dense. Stir in the cooked lentils, about 3 to 3½ cups, and the pepper and salt to taste and simmer, stirring occasionally, over low heat until blended, about 5 minutes. Serve hot.

# MUSHROOMS

In the late summer and early fall, just before the leaves begin to color, our thoughts turn to mushrooms, for this is the peak of the wild mushroom season. If it is a good season, with a little rain and a lot of sun, the woods and fields will be teeming with wild mushrooms. Most mushrooms are not poisonous and only a few are deadly, but you should not collect them unless you are completely familiar with the species you are gathering. A small number of mushrooms are both edible and choice. These include the chanterelle, the parasol mushroom, the oyster mushroom, the honey mushroom, the field mushroom, the giant puffball, the morels (mushrooms that mature in the spring), and, best of all, the *porcini* or cêpes (*Boletus edulis*).

The visible part of the mushroom is actually the fruiting body of the plant that grows underground. The plant can live for years, but the life of the fruiting body is short—quite literally here today and gone tomorrow.

Only one kind of mushroom is widely cultivated in North America, a variant of the field mushroom called *Agaricus bisporus*. It is not a particularly flavorful species, but it is easy to grow. Recently, several varieties of cultivated mushrooms have appeared in specialty food shops, products of small growers. These include shiitake, oyster, and occasionally chanterelle mushrooms.

Mushrooms, fortunately, can be dried with fair success. Although nowhere near as good as fresh, for authentic Italian dishes, we recommend imported dried *porcini* (*Boletus edulis*). They are expensive, but it takes only a small amount to perk up a dish made with cultivated mushrooms.

## How to Prepare Mushrooms

To reconstitute dried mushrooms, soak them in warm water to cover for 20 minutes or until soft. Remove the mushrooms carefully from the water with a fork or slotted spoon without disturbing any sand or grit that has dropped to the bottom of the bowl. Rinse the mushrooms thoroughly under cold water to remove remaining grit and sand and use as directed. If the recipe calls for it, the water in which the mushrooms soaked can be used, but it must be filtered through a coffee filter, fine sieve, or piece of cheesecloth to trap the sand and grit.

When washing fresh mushrooms, do not immerse them in water but brush them lightly with a damp paper towel or special mushroom brush available in well-stocked kitchen supply stores to remove grit and earth. Then rinse them *very briefly* under running water. The object is to prevent the mushrooms from becoming waterlogged.

When sautéing mushrooms, no matter how they are cut, we recommend that they be cooked briefly over *high* heat, stirring constantly. This will seal in the liquid and keep them from stewing in their own juice. They will give up some of their juices, but the high heat will evaporate the liquid quickly.

To store fresh mushrooms, keep them in the refrigerator in a paper bag with holes cut in it. As an alternative, place loose in the vegetable bin in the refrigerator. Never keep them wrapped in plastic: they will rot.

♦ ♦ ♦ ♦ ♦

## Funghi al Funghetto

SAUTÉED
MUSHROOMS

SERVES 4 TO 6

This is the standard way of preparing mushrooms, so standard, in fact, that the Italian name, Funghi al Funghetto, translates as "mushrooms cooked mushroom style." Other vegetables, such as eggplant, can be prepared "mushroom style."

½ ounce dried wild mushrooms (Boletus edulis)
2 tablespoons olive oil
2 tablespoons butter
3 garlic cloves, thinly sliced
1½ pounds fresh mushrooms, washed, trimmed, and
    quartered
1 tablespoon chopped parsley
pinch of fresh or dried mint
½ teaspoon salt
freshly ground pepper to taste
1 tablespoon lemon juice
1 lemon, cut into wedges

Soak the dried mushrooms in 1 cup of warm water for 20 minutes and remove carefully from the water. Rinse thoroughly under cold water to remove grit and sand. Drain, chop, and set aside.

Heat the oil and butter in a large frying pan, add the garlic, and sauté over medium heat for 1 minute. Add the fresh and dried mushrooms and sauté over high heat for a few minutes, stirring constantly, until their juices evaporate. Then reduce the heat to low and simmer, stirring frequently, for 8 minutes, until the mushrooms brown.

When browned, blend in the parsley, mint, salt, and pepper. Transfer the mushrooms to a heated serving platter, stir in the lemon juice, and serve hot with lemon wedges on the side.

♦ ♦ ♦ ♦ ♦

## *Funghi al Vino*

### MUSHROOMS IN WINE SAUCE

SERVES 4

*½ ounce dried wild mushrooms (Boletus edulis)*
*3 tablespoons butter*
*1 medium onion, thinly sliced*
*2 garlic cloves, finely chopped*
*1 pound mushrooms, washed, trimmed, and thinly sliced*
*2 tablespoons chopped parsley*
*2 tablespoons capers, rinsed well and chopped*
*salt and freshly ground pepper to taste*
*1 tablespoon flour*
*⅔ cup dry white wine mixed with ⅓ cup Vegetable Broth (see recipe)*

Soak the dried mushrooms in 1 cup of warm water for 20 minutes and remove carefully from the water. Rinse thoroughly under cold water to remove grit and sand. Drain, chop, and set aside.

Heat 2 tablespoons of butter in a saucepan, add the onion, and sauté over low heat for 5 minutes. Add the garlic and sauté another minute. Raise the heat and add the mushrooms, fresh and dried, the parsley, capers, salt, and pepper. Cook until the water has evaporated, about 5 minutes, stirring frequently. Meanwhile, melt the remaining tablespoon of butter in a saucepan, add the flour, and combine to make a roux. Add the wine-broth mixture, and cook, stirring constantly, for 5 minutes. When the mushrooms are cooked, place them on a serving dish, cover with the wine sauce, and serve hot.

♦ ♦ ♦ ♦ ♦

## Funghi al Limone

MUSHROOMS
WITH LEMON
SAUCE

SERVES 4 TO 6

2 tablespoons butter
1½ pounds mushrooms, trimmed, washed, and
    quartered
2 tablespoons minced parsley
3 tablespoons flour
1½ cups Vegetable Broth (see recipe)
salt and freshly ground pepper to taste
2 tablespoons lemon juice
2 egg yolks

Heat the butter in a large frying pan, add the mushrooms, and sauté over high heat for a few minutes, stirring constantly, until the mushroom liquid evaporates. Reduce the heat to medium and cook another 8 minutes, until the mushrooms brown. Blend in the parsley and flour and cook for 1 or 2 minutes. Add the broth slowly in a thin stream, stirring constantly and, when it is all added, simmer for 2 minutes, until the sauce thickens. Taste and adjust for salt and pepper.

When ready to serve, combine the lemon juice and egg yolks in a small mixing bowl, pour over the hot mushrooms, and simmer for 1 minute, stirring constantly. Serve hot.

♦ ♦ ♦ ♦ ♦

## Funghi Gratinati alla Crema

BAKED
MUSHROOMS
WITH
CREAM

SERVES 4 TO 6

Mushrooms and cream seem made for each other, as you will discover when you try this recipe. It is rich and delicious. Serve with a light main course.

2 tablespoons butter
¾ cup finely chopped onions
2 garlic cloves, finely chopped
1½ pounds fresh mushrooms, trimmed, washed, and
    thinly sliced
2 tablespoons sherry
Béchamel Sauce (see recipe) made with:
  1 cup milk
  2 tablespoons butter
  2 tablespoons flour
  ½ cup thick cream
2 egg yolks
2 tablespoons freshly grated Parmesan

Preheat the oven to 350°F and lightly butter an 8-by-10-inch baking dish.

Heat 2 tablespoons of butter in a large frying pan, add the onions, and sauté over medium heat for 2 or 3 minutes, until translucent. Add the garlic, sauté another minute, then blend in the mushrooms and cook over a high heat for 5 minutes. Before removing the mushrooms, onions, and garlic from the pan with a slotted spoon, press down to squeeze any remaining juices into the pan. Then spread the mushroom mixture evenly in the buttered baking dish.

Transfer the mushroom juices from the frying pan into a saucepan suitable for making béchamel sauce. Place over medium heat, add the sherry, and reduce by half. Proceed with the béchamel sauce. Remove it from the heat, beat in the egg yolks, and pour the sauce over the mushrooms. Sprinkle the top with Parmesan and bake in the preheated oven for 30 minutes until a crust forms.

♦ ♦ ♦ ♦ ♦

*Funghi*

*Ripieni*

*Gratinati*

STUFFED
MUSHROOMS
AU
GRATIN

SERVES 4 TO 6

Mushrooms prepared this way are a perfect accompaniment for Stuffed Zucchini or the Basil-Parsley Flan (see recipes). They can be prepared ahead of time and baked just before serving.

*½ ounce dried wild mushrooms (Boletus edulis)*
*1½ pounds large fresh mushrooms*
*4 tablespoons butter*
*Béchamel Sauce (see recipe) made with:*
    *2½ cups milk*
    *5 tablespoons butter*
    *6 tablespoons flour*
    *½ teaspoon salt*
    *freshly ground pepper*
*pinch of nutmeg*
*2 egg yolks*
*½ cup heavy cream*
*⅓ cup freshly grated Parmesan*

Soak the dried mushrooms in 1 cup of warm water for 20 minutes, remove carefully from the water, and rinse thoroughly under cold water to remove grit and sand. Drain, chop, and set aside.

Clean the fresh mushrooms and carefully separate the stems from the caps, keeping the caps whole and intact. Set the caps aside. Chop the stems fine and combine them with the soaked dried mushrooms.

In a frying pan, melt 2 tablespoons of butter and, over high heat, brown the mushroom caps lightly, turning gently with a spatula. Remove from the pan and set aside. In the same pan, add the 2 remaining tablespoons of butter and sauté the chopped mushrooms over a high heat, stirring constantly, for 2 or 3 minutes. Remove from the heat and set aside.

Make a thick béchamel sauce, add the nutmeg, remove from the heat, and, when slightly cooled, blend in the egg yolks. Combine half of the béchamel sauce with the sautéed mushrooms.

Taste for seasoning and add salt and pepper as required.

Preheat the oven to 350°F.

Butter a baking dish large enough to hold the mushroom caps in a single layer. Spread 2 or 3 tablespoons of the béchamel-mushroom mixture on the bottom of the baking dish, fill the mushroom caps with some of the remaining mixture, and place them in the baking dish on top of the béchamel-mushroom mixture.

Blend the cream and Parmesan with the remaining béchamel sauce and pour it over the mushroom caps. Bake in the preheated oven for 20 minutes, until a golden crust is formed. Serve hot.

## ONIONS

Onions come in a variety of colors and flavors. The red Italian and large yellow Spanish are relatively mild and sweet; the cooking yellow and white are sharp and pungent. If you want to dull the sharpness of an onion, simply soak it in cold water for 15 to 30 minutes. In the recipes that follow, we recommend the use of red onions. If you substitute yellow or white ones, soak them or adjust quantities for the stronger flavor.

If onions have been dried properly by the grower, they can be stored in a cool, dry, dark place for months. The yellow cooking onions keep longest; the red generally have a shorter storage life. When choosing onions, buy firm ones with a well-dried outer skin. If your onions begin to sprout, try using the shoots as a substitute for chives.

♦ ♦ ♦ ♦ ♦

### *Stufato di Cipolle*

ONION
STEW

SERVES 4 TO 6

Onion stew may not sound like much of a dish, but it is, in fact, delicious, a wonderful blend of onions, herbs, and spices cooked in broth and wine. The stew can be served with slices of fried or toasted bread as an accompaniment to a cheese soufflé or a vegetable pudding.

3 tablespoons butter
1 tablespoon flour
1 cup Vegetable Broth (see recipe)

*½ cup dry white wine*

*½ teaspoon dried rosemary*

*½ teaspoon thyme*

*2 whole cloves*

*2 bay leaves*

*⅛ teaspoon cayenne pepper*

*salt to taste*

*3 large red onions*

*6 slices fried bread (see recipe for Croutons) or toast (optional)*

Melt the butter in a pan, add the flour, and cook over medium heat for 1 minute. Add the broth a little at a time, stirring constantly, making sure that the flour does not form lumps. Stir in the wine, herbs, and cayenne pepper. Taste and correct for salt. Simmer over a low heat for 1 or 2 minutes.

Peel the onions and cut them into eighths. Put them in the pan with the wine sauce and cook, covered, stirring occasionally, for 20 minutes, until cooked but still firm. If you prefer them softer, cook longer. Remove the lid for the last few minutes of cooking. The sauce should be thick. Serve surrounded by fried bread or toast.

♦ ♦ ♦ ♦ ♦

## Cipolle al Forno alla Virginia

SWEET-AND-SOUR BAKED ONIONS, VIRGINIA STYLE

SERVES 6

As we learned from Virginia, onions baked with rosemary and vinegar are a delicacy; they now rank as one of our favorite vegetables.

*6 medium red onions*

*1 tablespoon flour*

*2 tablespoons dried rosemary leaves*

*½ cup wine vinegar*

*¼ cup olive oil*

*¼ teaspoon salt*

*freshly ground pepper to taste*

Preheat oven to 350°F.

Remove the dry skin and 1 or 2 outer layers from the onions. Cut the onions in half horizontally across the grain. Place them face up in an oiled baking dish.

You may have to trim the bottoms to make them stand upright. Sprinkle the flour and the rosemary over each onion half.

In a small mixing bowl, combine the rest of the ingredients and blend together by beating with a whisk. Distribute half the mixture over the onions. Bake in the preheated oven for 45 minutes, basting frequently with the remaining mixture. It should all be absorbed when the onions are cooked.

Remove from the oven and serve directly from the baking dish or from a heated serving platter.

◆ ◆ ◆ ◆ ◆

## Cipolle Ripiene con Funghi

### ONIONS STUFFED WITH MUSHROOMS

SERVES 6

6 medium red onions
1½ cups finely chopped mushrooms
2 garlic cloves, finely chopped
4 tablespoons bread crumbs
3 tablespoons freshly grated Parmesan
2 tablespoons chopped parsley
¼ teaspoon salt
freshly ground pepper to taste
2 tablespoons olive oil

Remove the skin and 1 or 2 outer layers of the onions, leaving the tender inner part. Steam the onions whole until half cooked, about 20 to 30 minutes, depending on size. Test by inserting a fork or knife point. It should enter but meet with resistance. Drain the onions and let them cool until they can be handled.

Meanwhile, prepare the stuffing by combining the remaining ingredients in a small mixing bowl.

Preheat the oven to 350°F.

Cut the onions in half horizontally across the grain. Scoop out the pulp in the center, leaving a solid shell of 3 or 4 layers of onion and the bottom intact. Chop ½ cup of the pulp fine and add it to the stuffing mixture.

Fill the onion halves with the stuffing. Place them snugly side by side in an oiled baking dish. Bake for 30 minutes in the preheated oven. Serve warm or at room temperature.

♦ ♦ ♦ ♦ ♦

# *Piselli Stufati*

**BRAISED SWEET PEAS**

SERVES 6

This recipe is the classic way to cook sweet peas, a little more work perhaps than just boiling them but well worth the extra effort. Use very fresh garden peas or high-quality frozen ones.

*2 tablespoons butter*

*½ cup chopped onion*

*2 tablespoons chopped parsley*

*1 teaspoon flour*

*1 cup water or Vegetable Broth (see recipe) for fresh peas, ½ cup for frozen peas*

*1 teaspoon sugar*

*4 cups freshly shelled or frozen peas*

*2 or 3 lettuce leaves*

*salt and freshly ground pepper to taste*

Heat the butter in a saucepan, add the onion, and sauté over medium heat until translucent. Add the parsley, then stir in the flour and cook for 1 minute. Slowly add the water or the broth, stirring constantly to make a very thin roux. Add the sugar and the peas, reduce the heat, and simmer, stirring occasionally. When cooked halfway, stir in the whole lettuce leaves, salt, and pepper and continue cooking until the peas are done but still plump and firm. When cooked all the water should have evaporated. The lettuce leaves can be removed or eaten.

# PEPPERS

It is hard to imagine European cuisine without the pepper (*Capsicum*), and yet it was not until Columbus returned from the New World that peppers made their appearance in the Old.

Sweet peppers come in essentially two shapes, the square and boxlike bell pepper and the elongated and tapered frying pepper. The red bell pepper is a ripened, sweeter stage of the green. Another excellent variety is the large, thin-skinned yellow pepper, very popular in Italy and occasionally available here. It is always necessary to remove the seeds and inner membrane from mature bell peppers, but it is sometimes possible to obtain young and tender pale green frying peppers that can be cooked whole.

## *How to Choose and Prepare Peppers*

Choose sleek, glossy peppers with tight smooth skins and no blemishes. Rinse, core, and cut according to directions.

The skin of the pepper is sometimes tough and bitter, and its presence can detract from the flavor of a dish. We give three equally effective ways to peel peppers. We prefer the third method.

1. Place the peppers whole in a 475°F. oven until the skins blister, about 15 minutes. The peppers will be slightly cooked.
2. Place them whole or halved in a broiler directly below the heat. If they are whole, turn them frequently, allowing the skin to blister and char all around.
3. If you have a gas stove, spear peppers whole with a long fork and roast over the flame, turning frequently, until the skins blister and char. In this method each pepper must be treated individually.

Once the skins of the peppers are blistered, peel under cold water or in a bowl of cold water.

At this point, remove the stalk and seeds of the pepper according to directions in the recipe. The flesh of the pepper will be slightly cooked but tender and sweet.

♦ ♦ ♦ ♦ ♦

## Peperoni Stufati

BRAISED
BELL
PEPPERS

SERVES 6

2 tablespoons olive oil
6 bell peppers, seeded, cored, and thinly sliced
    lengthwise
2 large tomatoes, peeled, seeded, and coarsely chopped,
    approximately 1 cup, or 1 cup canned Italian
    plum tomatoes, drained and chopped
2 garlic cloves, chopped
1 tablespoon pine nuts
1 tablespoon capers, chopped
salt and freshly ground pepper to taste
1 tablespoon chopped parsley

Heat the oil, add the peppers, and cook over a medium heat without a lid, stirring frequently, for 10 minutes. Add the tomatoes and garlic and continue cooking for 10 more minutes. Add the pine nuts, capers, salt, pepper, and parsley, heat through, and serve.

♦ ♦ ♦ ♦ ♦

## Peperonata

PEPPER STEW

Our version of *peperonata*, a dish usually made with tomatoes, onions, and peppers, is a bit unorthodox because we add potatoes, but we find that the potatoes enrich the flavors of the dish and give it substance.

SERVES 6 TO 8

*¼ cup olive oil*

*2 large onions, thinly sliced*

*1½ cups peeled or unpeeled potatoes, cut into 1-inch*
*cubes*

*1 dried hot pepper, seeded and chopped*

*2 cups canned Italian plum tomatoes, drained*

*6 bell peppers, red or green or a combination, seeded*
*and thinly sliced lengthwise*

*2 garlic cloves, thinly sliced*

*½ teaspoon salt*

*½ teaspoon freshly ground pepper*

Heat the oil in a large, heavy saucepan, add the onions, and sauté until they are translucent. Do not allow them to brown. Add the potatoes and cook slowly, uncovered, for 5 minutes, stirring frequently. Add the hot pepper, cook for 1 minute, stir in the tomatoes, and simmer uncovered, stirring frequently, for 10 minutes.

Blend in the peppers and garlic, add the salt and pepper, and cook for 10 to 15 minutes, stirring frequently, until the peppers are tender. Serve hot or at room temperature.

♦ ♦ ♦ ♦ ♦

*Involtini di*

*Peperoni*

STUFFED
PEPPER
ROLLS

SERVES 6

These peppers, filled with capers, currants, pine nuts, onion, and herbs, are bursting with sunny Mediterranean flavors.

*6 green, yellow, or red bell peppers*

*½ cup bread crumbs*

*2 tablespoons capers, chopped*

*2 tablespoons pine nuts*

*4 tablespoons currants, soaked in water to cover for 30*
*minutes and drained*

*2 tablespoons chopped parsley*

*2 tablespoons chopped basil*

*¼ cup chopped celery*

*¼ cup chopped onion*

*¼ teaspoon seeded and chopped hot pepper (optional)*

*½ teaspoon salt*

*freshly ground pepper to taste*

*3 tablespoons Tomato Sauce I or II (see recipes) or*
*canned Italian plum tomatoes, drained and*
*chopped*

Preheat oven to 350°F.

Wash the peppers and peel, p. 257. Cut them in half lengthwise and remove the seeds and inner membrane.

In a mixing bowl combine the bread crumbs, capers, pine nuts, currants, parsley, basil, celery, onion, hot pepper (if desired), salt, and pepper. Mix well and place 2 or 3 tablespoons of this mixture into each of the bell pepper halves. Roll up the peppers from side to side. Place the peppers in a baking dish large enough to hold them tightly together in a single layer side by side. This will prevent the peppers from unrolling.

Mix the tomato sauce or the chopped tomatoes with 1 cup water and pour evenly over the peppers. Place in the preheated oven for 30 minutes, or until peppers are cooked but still firm. Transfer to a serving platter and serve hot or at room temperature.

♦ ♦ ♦ ♦ ♦

## Patate alla Fiesolana

POTATOES,
FIESOLE
STYLE

SERVES 6 TO 8

We often serve these potatoes as a main dish along with a salad and hearty soup. The dish is easy to prepare, tasty, and substantial.

2 pounds potatoes, peeled or unpeeled, washed and
    sliced in pieces ¼ inch thick
2 medium onions, thinly sliced
3 tablespoons Tomato Sauce I (see recipe), or ¼ cup
    canned Italian plum tomatoes, drained and
    chopped
¼ cup olive oil
1 teaspoon oregano
½ teaspoon salt
abundant freshly ground pepper
½ pound mozzarella or Gruyère
3 to 4 tablespoons bread crumbs

Preheat the oven to 400°F. Oil well a 10-inch square baking dish.

Place a layer of potatoes in the bottom of the dish and upright along the sides. Place a layer of onions over the potatoes in the bottom of the dish, cover with a thin layer of tomato sauce or chopped tomatoes, drizzle with oil, sprinkle with oregano, salt, and pepper, and top with a layer of cheese.

Repeat the process until all the ingredients are used, finishing with a layer of cheese. Sprinkle with bread crumbs, drizzle with the remaining oil, cover the dish with aluminum foil, and bake in the preheated oven for 30 minutes. Remove the foil and bake another 15 minutes.

Remove from the oven, and carefully drain off all the excess oil. Serve the potatoes hot from the baking dish.

♦ ♦ ♦ ♦ ♦

## *Patate Savoiarde*

POTATOES
SAVOY

SERVES 6 TO 8

These potatoes, parboiled then baked with a rich mixture of milk, cheese, and cream, are substantial enough to be a main course for a light meal. Serve with a soup such as Asparagus Soup (see recipe) and a hearty salad such as Mixed Winter Vegetables with Mozzarella (see recipe).

*2½ pounds potatoes*
*2 tablespoons butter*
*¼ teaspoon salt*
*1 teaspoon freshly ground pepper*
*4 tablespoons freshly grated Parmesan*
*½ pound Gruyère, thinly sliced*
*2 to 3 cups milk*
*¼ cup heavy cream*

Peel the potatoes and boil them in salted water until almost tender. They should be slightly undercooked. Drain and set aside.

Preheat the oven to 350°F.

Butter a 10-inch square baking dish. Slice the potatoes approximately ¼ inch thick. Place a layer of potatoes on the bottom of the baking dish and upright along the sides. Dot with 1 tablespoon of butter, sprinkle with ⅛ teaspoon of salt, ½ teaspoon of pepper, 2 tablespoons of Parmesan, and cover with half the slices of Gruyère. Repeat the process, using all the remaining ingredients. The last layer should be at least ½ inch below the top of the baking dish.

Pour in the milk. It should cover the potatoes entirely and just touch the top layer of cheese. Pour the cream on top of the cheese and place the dish in the oven. Bake for 1 hour, until a brown crust forms and the milk is absorbed. Serve the potatoes hot.

♦ ♦ ♦ ♦ ♦

## Sformato di Patate e Cipolle

POTATO
AND
ONION
PIE

SERVES 6

This pleasing, unpretentious dish achieves its delightful flavor through the combination of basic ingredients cooked in simple ways. It is perfect for family dinners.

4 tablespoons butter
1½ pounds red onions, thinly sliced
⅓ cup dry white wine
2 pounds potatoes
1 cup milk
¼ cup freshly grated Parmesan
2 eggs, beaten
½ teaspoon salt
freshly ground pepper to taste

Melt 2 tablespoons of butter in a medium-size saucepan, add the onions, and sauté over a medium heat until they begin to color. Reduce the heat to low, add ⅓ cup water and the wine, cover, and simmer gently for 40 minutes, stirring occasionally.

Meanwhile, peel the potatoes, cut in pieces if large, and boil gently, covered, until tender. Drain and transfer them to a mixing bowl. Add 2 tablespoons of butter and mash with a potato masher until smooth. Slowly add the milk, beating with a whisk or wooden spoon, until all the milk is incorporated and the mixture is smooth and homogeneous. Add the Parmesan, eggs, salt, and pepper. Combine and set aside.

Preheat the oven to 350°F.

Butter an 8-cup soufflé pan or the equivalent and sprinkle with bread crumbs. Drain the onions, if necessary, and combine half of them with the potato mixture. Spoon the mixture into the soufflé pan and bake in the preheated oven for 35 to 40 minutes, until the mixture is firm and beginning to color.

Remove from the oven and distribute the remaining onions over the top of the pie. Serve hot.

### VARIATION

If you wish, the pie can be unmolded. Allow it to rest for 15 minutes, then run a sharp knife between the pie and the pan. Place a serving dish over the pan, invert, and remove the soufflé pan. Distribute the onions over the unmolded pie and serve.

## Patate in Tegame

### PAN-FRIED POTATOES, ITALIAN STYLE

SERVES 6

♦ ♦ ♦ ♦ ♦

salt
2 pounds potatoes, washed and cut in half
1 tablespoon olive oil
1 tablespoon butter
1 large onion, finely sliced
2 teaspoons fresh rosemary, or 1 teaspoon dried
2 tablespoons chopped parsley
freshly ground pepper

Bring 4 cups of water with 1 teaspoon of salt to a boil, add the potatoes, peeled or unpeeled, and cook until tender but firm, about 15 minutes. The potatoes can also be steamed. When the potatoes are cooked, drain, cut into ¼-inch slices and set aside.

Heat the oil and butter in a large saucepan, add the onion, and sauté over medium heat until transparent. Add the rosemary, sauté for another minute, stir in the potatoes, add the parsley, salt, and pepper to taste, and continue to cook, stirring, until the potatoes brown and form a crust. Serve hot.

## Patate al Formaggio

### POTATOES AND CHEESE

SERVES 6 TO 8

♦ ♦ ♦ ♦ ♦

Potatoes mashed with carrots and onions are excellent on their own, but when combined with Gruyère or fontina and Parmesan and baked, they are spectacular. This dish is nourishing enough to serve as the main course for a light supper or luncheon.

2 pounds potatoes, peeled and cut into quarters
2 medium carrots, trimmed and cut into small pieces
1 large onion, cut into quarters
1 tablespoon butter
½ teaspoon salt
freshly ground pepper to taste
⅓ cup milk
2 tablespoons chopped parsley
½ pound Gruyère or fontina, thinly sliced
4 tablespoons freshly grated Parmesan

Place the potatoes, carrots, and onion in a saucepan, add water to cover, and simmer until tender, about 15 to 20 minutes. When cooked, drain, place in a large mixing bowl, add the butter, salt, and pepper, and mash with a potato masher. Add the milk, a little at a time, stirring constantly with a wooden spoon, until the potato mixture is smooth and homogeneous.

Preheat the oven to 400°F.

Butter a 6-by-10-by-2-inch baking dish. Spread half the potato mixture on the bottom of the dish, sprinkle all the parsley on top, then cover with half the Gruyère or fontina and half the Parmesan. Repeat the process, omitting the parsley, ending with the layer of cheeses. Bake in the preheated oven for 30 minutes, until the cheese begins to brown. Remove from the oven, allow to cool for 5 minutes, then serve.

♦ ♦ ♦ ♦ ♦

## *Patate Stufate allo Sherry*

BRAISED
POTATOES
WITH
SHERRY

SERVES 6

Use new potatoes for this dish, if possible small ones that can be cooked whole.

2 tablespoons olive oil
2 pounds new potatoes, washed, left whole or cut into
    walnut-size pieces
2 garlic cloves, sliced
1 medium onion, thinly sliced
1 teaspoon crushed sage
¾ cup sherry
½ teaspoon salt
freshly ground pepper to taste

Heat the olive oil in a saucepan, add the potatoes, garlic, onion, and sage, and cook covered over a low heat for 7 minutes, stirring frequently. Remove the cover, add the sherry, salt, and pepper, and continue cooking, stirring frequently, until the potatoes are tender. Serve hot.

♦ ♦ ♦ ♦ ♦

*Spinaci con*

*Salsa al*

*Formaggio*

SPINACH
WITH
CREAMY
CHEESE
SAUCE

SERVES 6

A sauce made with cheeses and cream adds zest to sautéed fresh spinach.

2 pounds fresh spinach
2 tablespoons butter
pinch of nutmeg
⅔ cup heavy cream
½ cup fontina or Gruyère, diced
⅓ cup grated Parmesan
salt and freshly ground pepper
2 hard-boiled eggs, sliced (optional)

Trim, wash very well, drain, and roughly chop the spinach. Heat the butter in a saucepan, add the spinach and nutmeg, and sauté until the water has evaporated and the spinach is cooked. Meanwhile, heat the cream in a saucepan over low heat, add the cheeses, and continue cooking until the cheeses melt. Place the spinach on a serving platter, add salt and pepper to taste, pour the cheese sauce over the spinach, and serve immediately. Slices of hard-boiled eggs can be used to decorate the spinach.

♦ ♦ ♦ ♦ ♦

*Polpettone di*

*Spinaci*

SPINACH
LOAF
WITH
BÉCHAMEL

SERVES 6

This is a truly inspired way to prepare spinach—simple, attractive, and delicious. The spinach is cooked, finely chopped, shaped into a loaf, and served covered with a thick béchamel sauce.

2 pounds spinach, washed very well and drained
Béchamel Sauce (see recipe) made with:
    2 cups milk
    4 tablespoons butter
    5 tablespoons flour
    ½ teaspoon salt
2 extra-large eggs, beaten
¼ cup freshly grated Parmesan
⅔ cup heavy cream
2 tablespoons butter
salt and freshly ground pepper

Preheat the oven to 350°F. and generously butter an 8- or 9-inch loaf pan.

Cook the spinach and drain by squeezing it with your hands or by pressing it against the sides of a colander. Chop it fine, place it in a saucepan over medium heat, stirring constantly, for 3 minutes. Transfer it to a mixing bowl and set aside.

Make béchamel sauce. Add 1 cup of the sauce to the spinach, mix well, then add the eggs and the Parmesan.

Pour the mixture into the buttered loaf pan and bake for 30 minutes. Meanwhile, place the remaining béchamel sauce in a small saucepan and add the cream and butter. Stir, warm through, season to taste, and set aside. Keep warm.

When the spinach is ready, remove it from the oven and allow it to cool for 5 minutes, then unmold onto a heated serving dish. Spread the warm béchamel-cream sauce over the top and sides of the loaf with a spatula. Serve warm.

### VARIATION

Make a Hollandaise Sauce (see recipe) and spread it on top of the loaf as an alternative to the béchamel-cream sauce. Béchamel sauce is still combined with the spinach and baked.

♦ ♦ ♦ ♦ ♦

## Zucca
## Rifatta

SAUTÉED
SQUASH

SERVES 4 TO 6

A very dependable vegetable dish to serve during the winter months. The herbs and garlic bring out the rich, sweet flavor of squash. We have found that the best substitutes for Italian pumpkin are butternut, Queen Anne, or Hubbard squash.

¼ cup olive oil
4 garlic cloves, chopped
1 teaspoon rosemary
2 pounds butternut, Queen Anne, or Hubbard squash, peeled, seeded, and cut into 1-inch squares
2 tablespoons chopped parsley
1 tablespoon chopped basil
¼ teaspoon salt
freshly ground pepper

Heat the oil in a large frying pan, add the garlic and rosemary, and cook over a medium heat for 30 seconds. Blend in the squash and continue cooking for a few minutes, stirring and scraping frequently with a wooden spoon or spatula to prevent the squash from sticking. Lower the heat and cook, stirring frequently, for 10 minutes. Add the parsley, basil, salt, and pepper, and cook for another 5 minutes, until the squash is done but still firm in the center. Serve hot.

◆ ◆ ◆ ◆ ◆

*Fagiolini*
*Stufati*

BRAISED
STRING
BEANS
IN
SPICY
TOMATO
SAUCE

SERVES 4 TO 6

3 tablespoons olive oil
1 carrot, finely chopped
1 stalk celery, finely chopped
3 to 4 garlic cloves, sliced
1 to 2 hot peppers, seeded and chopped
1 pound ripe fresh tomatoes, peeled, seeded, and
    chopped, or 1½ cups canned Italian plum
    tomatoes, drained and chopped
1½ pounds string beans, washed, trimmed, and cut
    into 1½-inch pieces
1 tablespoon capers, chopped
salt to taste
½ teaspoon freshly ground pepper
2 tablespoons chopped parsley

Heat the olive oil in a saucepan, add the carrot and celery, and sauté over a medium heat until they begin to color. Stir in the garlic and hot pepper and sauté another minute. Add the tomatoes, reduce the heat, and simmer for 15 to 20 minutes, until the sauce begins to thicken. Add the string beans, capers, salt, and pepper and cook, partly covered, stirring occasionally, until the string beans are tender, about 15 minutes. Add water if necessary, but only enough to prevent the beans from sticking to the pan. When cooked, blend in the parsley, and serve the string beans hot.

◆ ◆ ◆ ◆ ◆

*Fagiolini al*
*Vino*

STRING
BEANS
IN
WINE

SERVES 4

In this recipe, string beans are simmered with tomatoes and herbs in wine. Serve as *contorno* to a savory soufflé or Ricotta and Herbs Crêpes (see recipe).

1½ pounds fresh string beans
2 tablespoons olive oil
½ cup fresh tomatoes, peeled, seeded, and chopped, or
    ½ cup canned Italian plum tomatoes, drained and
    chopped
2 garlic cloves, chopped
1 tablespoon chopped parsley
1 tablespoon chopped basil
½ cup full-bodied red wine
salt and freshly ground pepper to taste

Place the string beans in the bottom of a large, low-sided saucepan. Pour the olive oil, tomatoes, garlic, and herbs over them and bring to a brisk simmer, stirring with a wooden spoon for 3 or 4 minutes. Pour in the wine, sprinkle with salt and pepper, and simmer, covered, for 10 minutes, until the string beans are cooked but still firm. Serve hot.

# ZUCCHINI

Zucchini are members of the *Cucurbitaceae* family, which includes the squash, gourds, melons, and cucumber. As we know from the Bible, the species has been cultivated for a very long time. In Italy, the flower of the zucchini is also eaten, dipped in batter and fried, or cut up and sautéed as a sauce for pasta.

## How to Choose and Prepare Zucchini

Choose zucchini that are firm, with tight glossy skins. Except for stuffing, they should be small and pale green. For stuffing, use larger, more mature squash. Zucchini quickly lose their flavor, so do not keep them for more than a day or two.

It is not necessary to peel zucchini, since the skin is tender, but they should be washed well and scrubbed lightly with a vegetable scrubber to loosen dirt and remove the fuzz on the skin. Trim both ends with a sharp knife and proceed according to directions in the recipe.

♦ ♦ ♦ ♦ ♦

## Zucchini alla Studentesca

ZUCCHINI
WITH
GARLIC
AND
TOMATO

SERVES 4 TO 6

The secret of this dish is to cook the zucchini quickly and only for a short time. It should be served a little undercooked.

3 tablespoons olive oil

1½ pounds zucchini, washed, trimmed, and sliced in
    ½-inch rounds

3 or 4 garlic cloves, finely chopped

1 large tomato, peeled, seeded, and chopped, or ½ cup
    canned Italian plum tomatoes, drained and
    chopped

½ teaspoon salt

freshly ground pepper to taste

2 tablespoons chopped parsley

Heat the oil in a large frying pan, add the zucchini and the garlic, and sauté over a medium heat, stirring and turning the zucchini so that they color on both sides, for 4 to 5 minutes. Add the tomatoes, salt, and pepper and cook for 5 more minutes, stirring occasionally. Turn off the heat and add the parsley. The zucchini should still be quite firm and almost crunchy. Serve warm.

♦ ♦ ♦ ♦ ♦

## *Zucchini al Forno*

BAKED
ZUCCHINI
IN
TOMATO
SAUCE

SERVES 4 TO 6

*1½ pounds zucchini, washed and cut in half lengthwise*
*2 tablespoons olive oil*
*½ teaspoon salt*
*freshly ground pepper to taste*
*½ cup Tomato Sauce I or II (see recipes)*
*2 garlic cloves, finely sliced*
*1 tablespoon chopped parsley*

Preheat the oven to 350°F. Oil a baking dish large enough to hold the zucchini in two layers.

Steam the zucchini for 5 or 6 minutes. Drain them briefly and place them in the baking dish, cut side down. Make two layers with the zucchini all pointing in the same direction. Sprinkle with salt and pepper. Mix the tomato sauce with the garlic and pour it over the zucchini. Bake in the preheated oven for 20 to 30 minutes, until the zucchini are cooked but still firm.

Sprinkle with parsley and serve.

♦ ♦ ♦ ♦ ♦

## *Fiori di Zucca Fritti*

FRIED
ZUCCHINI
FLOWERS

If you are lucky enough to obtain zucchini flowers, try this dish. It will be a delightful surprise for guests. We always have a large number of zucchini plants on our farm near Fiesole, and in midsummer, when the plants are in full bloom, we eat the flowers almost every day. If you grow your own plants, pick the flowers early in the morning when they are wide open and fresh with dew.

SERVES 4

1 egg, *separated*
1 tablespoon olive oil
1 tablespoon lemon juice
1¼ cups of unbleached all-purpose flour
salt
12 large zucchini flowers
½ cup seed oil
1 lemon, cut in wedges

First make the batter. Beat the egg yolk in a mixing bowl until lemon colored. Beat in the olive oil, 1 cup of water, and the lemon juice. Slowly add the flour, beating constantly with a whisk, to form a light batter the thickness of heavy cream. Add a pinch of salt, combine, and set aside to rest for 2 hours. When ready to use, beat the egg white until very stiff and fold into the batter.

Carefully rinse the zucchini flowers. Drain and dry them on a dish towel. Remove the pistils from the inside of the petals and the small leaves of the calyx at the base of each flower where it joins the stem.

Heat the seed oil in a frying pan until moderately hot. Grasp a flower by its stem and dip it into the batter. Hold it over the bowl and allow any excess batter to drip off, then deep-fry the flower until golden brown on all sides. The flowers can be fried a few at a time. When golden, remove from the pan with a slotted spoon and drain on a paper towel. When ready to serve, sprinkle with salt and arrange on a serving platter with a doily to absorb excess oil, garnish with lemon wedges, and serve hot.

## VARIATION

We sometimes vary the dish by placing a thin slice of mozzarella in each flower before dipping it into the batter and frying it. Hold flower by the open end, dip into batter, then proceed as in master recipe. Prepared in this way, fried zucchini flowers become much more substantial and can serve as a main dish.

♦ ♦ ♦ ♦ ♦

*Verdure*

*Miste alla*

*Romana*

MIXED
VEGETABLES,
ROMAN
STYLE

SERVES 6 TO 8

The vegetables are cooked separately in this recipe and combined just before serving. Drain the vegetables well, and cook them in as little oil and butter as possible. This will result in a light, digestible dish. The vegetables can be sautéed ahead of time and assembled before serving.

2 tablespoons olive oil
2 tablespoons butter
2 small onions, finely chopped
2 garlic cloves, finely chopped
¼ teaspoon cayenne pepper (optional)
1 pound fresh tomatoes, seeded, drained, and chopped, or 1½ cups canned Italian plum tomatoes, drained and chopped
3 large bell peppers, peeled, seeded (p. 257), and cut into 1-inch squares
3 medium zucchini, washed and cut into ¼-inch-thick strips
3 small eggplants, peeled and cut into ¾-inch cubes
¼ cup dry white wine
1 tablespoon chopped basil
1 tablespoon chopped parsley

In a large saucepan heat ½ tablespoon of oil and ½ tablespoon of butter. Add the onions and sauté over a medium heat until translucent. Add the garlic and continue to sauté until the onions and garlic begin to color. Remove the pan from the heat and stir in the cayenne pepper and the tomatoes. Return to the heat and cook for 10 to 15 minutes until the sauce thickens. Remove the pan from the heat and set aside.

In a frying pan, heat ½ tablespoon of butter and ½ tablespoon of oil. Add the bell peppers and sauté over medium heat until cooked but still firm. Remove from the pan with a slotted spoon and drain on paper towels. Set aside.

In the same oil-and-butter mixture (add more if necessary) sauté the zucchini over medium to high heat, until brown on all sides. They should be cooked but firm. Remove, drain on paper towels, and set aside. Sauté the eggplants in the same pan, adding more oil and butter, over medium to high heat until cooked but not mushy. Remove from the pan, drain on paper towels, and set aside.

When ready to assemble, return the large saucepan with the tomatoes to medium heat and add the wine. Allow to evaporate for a few minutes. Add the peppers, zucchini, and eggplants and heat through. Sprinkle with basil and parsley, stir, and serve hot or at room temperature.

♦ ♦ ♦ ♦ ♦

*Verdure*

*Invernali*

*alla Toscana*

The mixture of lightly cooked vegetables bound together by a tasty tomato sauce can, of course, be varied according to the whim of the cook and the availability of good fresh vegetables. We include here our favorite combination, a delicious mixture of fresh winter vegetables. The flavor improves with age.

WINTER
VEGETABLES,
TUSCAN
STYLE

SERVES 8

3 artichokes

3 tablespoons olive oil

1 small onion, sliced

1 large or 2 small leeks, cleaned and sliced, green parts included, into 1-inch segments

1 celery stalk, cut into 1-inch segments

1 large fennel or 2 small ones, cut into wedges 1 inch thick

4 cups cauliflower, cut into flowerets

2 cups canned Italian plum tomatoes, with juice, chopped

3 garlic cloves, minced

1 tablespoon sugar

4 tablespoons vinegar

4 tablespoons chopped parsley

4 tablespoons chopped basil

3 tablespoons capers

½ teaspoon salt

freshly ground pepper to taste

Clean, trim, quarter, and remove the chokes from the artichokes as explained on p. 216. Place them in water acidulated by the juice of 1 lemon until ready to use.

Put enough water in a saucepan to cover the artichokes and bring the water to a boil. Drain the artichokes and place them in the boiling water. Cook for 5 to 10 minutes, until half done. Make sure they are still very firm, as they will be cooked later for at least 15 minutes. Drain and set aside.

In a large, low-sided saucepan, heat the oil and sauté the onion, leeks, and celery over high heat for 5 minutes, stirring constantly. Add the fennel, cauliflower, tomatoes, garlic, artichokes, and sugar. Stir to combine, reduce heat to low, and simmer, covered, for 10 minutes.

Add the remaining ingredients, combine well, and simmer, uncovered, until the vegetables are cooked but still firm. Serve hot.

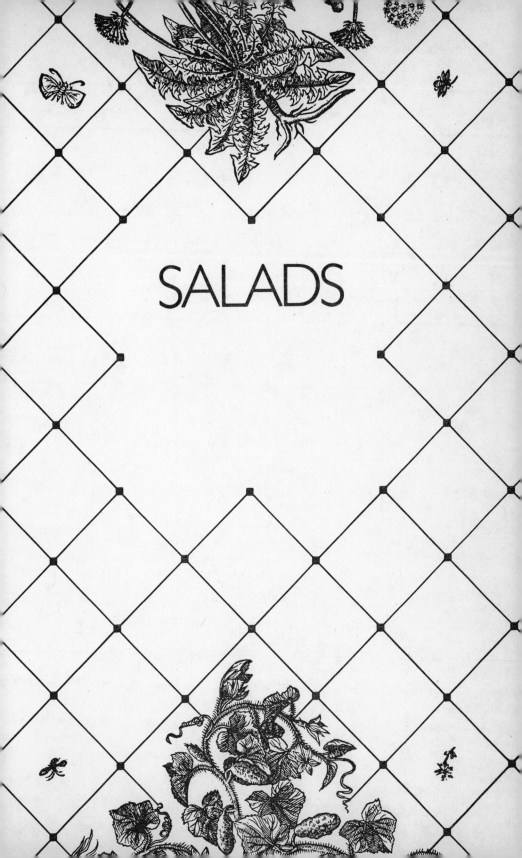

# SALADS

Italians eat salad at the end of the meal, just before the fruit, cheese, or dessert. Standard salads, especially in restaurants or trattorie, are either green or mixed, the former usually lettuce alone or in combination with some wild salad greens, the latter lettuce mixed with wild greens, tomatoes, carrots, and whatever else is available. The dressing is invariably oil and vinegar, or less common but still popular, oil and lemon, with a little salt and pepper. The ingredients in salads, as in other vegetable dishes, vary with the seasons—chicories are prominent in winter, tomatoes and lettuce in the summer.

There are a large number of cold cooked or marinated vegetables, rice, bean, and pasta dishes that in Italy are served as antipasti, or as vegetable courses that we in North America would classify as salads. Most of the raw vegetable salads and some marinated ones work well as salads, while others, especially the rice, bean, and pasta salads, are ideal as part of a buffet or as a first course in the summer. And in some cases, for example salads with mozzarella, they may even serve as a main dish for a light luncheon.

## Ingredients

Some salad ingredients deserve special attention. The first and most common of all is lettuce. Italian lettuce is either loose leaf or head, similar to Boston, Bibb, and sometimes romaine. Italians often add wild greens such as arugula, purslane, chicory, garden burnet, and dandelions to their salads to enliven the flavor. Some of these greens are cultivated in the United States and are available in markets. If you are unable to obtain them, however, watercress makes an acceptable substitute.

Some salad vegetables are standard in Italy but often difficult to find here. These include, in particular, the chicories, red chicory (*radicchio rosso*) and common (Catalonia) green chicory. They make excellent salads on their own or in combination with lettuce. We urge you to search them out and try them.

## Condiments

In making salads, use the best olive oil you can afford. The finest and most expensive is *olio extra vergine* from Lucca. It is dark green, richly flavored, and worth every penny.

It is hard to believe how good vinegar can be until you've tried high-quality, unpasteurized wine vinegar. It is possible to find excellent vinegars in specialty food shops, and if you are able to obtain a vinegar starter (the "mother"), you can make your own at home with a bottle of dry red or white wine. It's simple: just add the starter and let it stand until the vinegar is formed. The vinegar can be used to start the next batch. Wine left open will not become vinegar unless by some remote chance the correct bacteria wanders into your wine.

For some salads, mayonnaise is needed. There is no comparison between commercial and homemade mayonnaise, and we urge you to make your own, a relatively easy and quick process with a blender, food processor, or electric beater as explained on p. 16.

## *Preparation*

All salads, of course, can be made ahead of time and some, such as the marinated ones, improve with age. However, do not add dressing to a plain green or mixed salad made with raw vegetables until the last minute. Salt and vinegar will cause the greens to wilt.

We attempt in these recipes to give an idea of the amount of olive oil, vinegar, and salt necessary to make a dressing for a given quantity of vegetables. However, so much depends on the quality of the olive oil, the strength of the vinegar, and the preferences of the cook that the amounts must be taken as rough approximations. We recommend that you make the dressing, pour some of it over the salad, taste it, and then decide whether you need more oil or vinegar or both. After a while, you will know the way you like it and you won't have to measure at all.

♦ ♦ ♦ ♦ ♦

## *Puntarelle*

### CHICORY
### SALAD

SERVES 4 TO 6

*Puntarelle* is a salad made with the long, green, serrated leaves of the common (Catalonia) chicory. It is often available throughout the late fall and winter in North America and is a marvelous salad green, mildly bitter with a slight peppery tang. We discovered it in Rome, where it is eaten in the spring, many years ago and have never lost our fondness for it. It is always served swimming in oil, vinegar, and garlic (in Rome anchovies are included). Eat this earthy salad with good Italian bread, preferably homemade.

*1 large head of chicory*
*2 garlic cloves, finely chopped*
*⅓ to ½ cup olive oil*

> 4 tablespoons wine vinegar
> salt and pepper to taste
> 1 tablespoon capers, chopped (optional)

Wash the chicory well to eliminate all soil and grit and discard the tough outer leaves. Drain well. In Rome, they often cut the tougher leaves lengthwise down the middle. This is time-consuming and, we find, unnecessary. The leaves should, however, be left fairly long, about 3 inches in length.

Place the chicory in a large salad bowl. Combine the garlic, oil, vinegar, salt, and pepper and use it to dress the salad. If desired, add capers. Unlike other green salads, *puntarelle* should sit with the dressing at least 30 minutes before serving. You may want to adjust the quantity of dressing or the proportion of ingredients to suit your taste.

♦ ♦ ♦ ♦ ♦

## Insalata Mista alla Siciliana

SICILIAN
MIXED
SALAD

SERVES 6 TO 8

> 1 large head of romaine or Boston lettuce, washed and
>   drained
> 2 medium, ripe tomatoes, cut in wedges
> 1 cup peeled and thinly sliced cucumber
> ½ cup Italian black olives, pitted, rinsed under cold
>   water if salty, and roughly chopped
> juice of 1 lemon
> ⅓ cup olive oil
> 2 tablespoons coarsely chopped fresh mint, or 1
>   tablespoon crushed dried mint
> 2 tablespoons coarsely chopped parsley
> 1 garlic clove, finely chopped
> salt and freshly ground pepper to taste
> 1 medium red or white onion, thinly sliced, and soaked
>   in cold water for 30 minutes

Arrange half the whole lettuce leaves around the rim of a salad bowl. Tear the remaining leaves into small pieces and place them in the salad bowl. Distribute the tomatoes, cucumber slices, and olives over the torn lettuce and set the vegetables aside.

Place in a mixing bowl the lemon juice, olive oil, mint, parsley, garlic, salt, and pepper and combine well, stirring until the salt dissolves.

When ready to serve, distribute the onions over the vegetables, pour the dressing evenly over all, and serve without tossing. The dressing and salad ingredients will combine as the salad is served.

♦ ♦ ♦ ♦ ♦

## Insalata Arlecchino

### HARLEQUIN SALAD

SERVES 4 TO 6

In this recipe, layers of overlapping slices of to-matoes, cucumbers, mozzarella, and hard-boiled eggs are spread with a pesto-mayonnaise sauce and served on a bed of watercress with a lemon-mustard dressing. Serve as a main dish for a luncheon or as an antipasto, in place of the pasta course. We find it too rich to serve as a salad after the main course.

¼ cup Pesto (see recipe)
¼ cup Mayonnaise (see recipe)
3 medium, firm tomatoes, sliced and seeded
1 pound mozzarella, sliced
3 hard-boiled eggs, sliced
1 small cucumber, peeled and sliced
¼ cup olive oil
2 tablespoons lemon juice
¼ teaspoon prepared mustard
¼ teaspoon salt
2 tablespoons capers
5 or 6 basil leaves, roughly chopped
watercress sprigs

Combine the pesto with the mayonnaise in a small mixing bowl. On one end of an oval or round serving dish, place one slice of tomato. Spread 1 teaspoon of the pesto-mayonnaise sauce on it. On top of that, overlapping the tomato but not covering it completely, place a slice of mozzarella; on top of the mozzarella, without covering it completely, place 1 egg slice, and do the same with the cucumber. Repeat in an attractive pattern, starting with the tomato slice until all the ingredients are used.

Make the dressing by combining in a mixing bowl the olive oil, lemon juice, mustard, and salt. Mix until the salt is dissolved. Add the capers and basil and combine.

When ready to serve, garnish the plate with watercress, placing some in the center if you are using a round serving platter. Drizzle the dressing over the salad and serve.

♦ ♦ ♦ ♦ ♦

*Insalata di*

*Finocchio*

FENNEL
SALAD

SERVES 4 TO 6

The clean, fresh flavor of raw fennel, enhanced by the faint hint of anise, is perfect at the end of a meal. It is particularly welcome after a hearty main course.

4 medium fennel
1 tablespoon chopped parsley
pinch of dried oregano
¼ teaspoon salt
freshly ground pepper
¼ to ⅓ cup olive oil
2 to 3 tablespoons wine vinegar

Cut off and discard the tops of the fennel and trim the base. Discard tough outer layers. Rinse well under cold water.

Cut the fennel horizontally into slices ⅛ to ¼ inch thick and place them in a salad bowl. Combine the remaining ingredients in a mixing bowl, and stir until the salt dissolves. Pour over the fennel, toss, and serve.

NOTE: A delightful way to eat fresh fennel is *al pinzimonio*, that is, dipped into a dressing of oil and vinegar or lemon seasoned with salt and pepper. Clean, trim, and quarter a fennel bulb. Prepare the dressing in a small bowl. The fennel is eaten by breaking off a layer and dipping it in the dressing.

♦ ♦ ♦ ♦ ♦

*Insalata di*

*Sedano*

CELERY
SALAD

SERVES 4 TO 6

3 celery hearts, cut into 1-inch segments
½ cup crumbled Gorgonzola
1 tablespoon brandy or Cognac
⅓ cup olive oil
3 tablespoons wine vinegar
salt and freshly ground pepper to taste
1 hard-boiled egg, sliced
¼ cup black Italian olives, pitted, rinsed in cold water
     if salty, and roughly chopped
a few sprigs of celery leaves

Place the celery pieces in a salad bowl.

Place the Gorgonzola in a small mixing bowl and mash with a fork to form a smooth paste. Slowly add the brandy or Cognac, oil, and vinegar, stirring the cheese constantly. Blend well to obtain a homogeneous creamy dressing. Add salt and pepper to taste.

Just before serving, combine the dressing with the celery and toss to coat. Garnish with the hard-boiled egg slices, olives, and celery leaves. Serve at room temperature.

♦ ♦ ♦ ♦ ♦

## Radice di Sedano

CELERY ROOT
SALAD

SERVES 6

1 large celery root or 2 small ones
1 lemon
1 teaspoon salt
⅔ cup Mayonnaise (see recipe)
⅛ teaspoon powdered mustard
2 tablespoons chopped chives or scallions
1 tablespoon chopped parsley
salt and freshly ground pepper to taste

Peel the external layer of the celery root, exposing the tender white flesh. Grate it fine and place it in a mixing bowl. Toss with the juice of ½ lemon and the teaspoon of salt. Set it aside to expel some of its water for 30 minutes to 1 hour. Drain thoroughly by squeezing the pulp in your hands or by pressing it against the sides of a colander. Place in a serving bowl.

Make a dressing by combining in a small mixing bowl the mayonnaise, mustard, chives or scallions, parsley, and the juice of the remaining ½ lemon. The dressing should have the consistency of heavy cream. If it is too thick, thin it with olive oil. If it is too thin, add more mayonnaise. Pour the dressing over the celery root, a little at a time, tossing to combine. Taste and correct for salt and pepper. Allow to marinate for 1 hour. Serve at room temperature.

♦ ♦ ♦ ♦ ♦

## Insalata di Carote

GRATED
CARROT
SALAD

SERVES 6

There is almost no salad simpler to make than this one, but few are as welcome at the end of a meal. The sweet taste of carrots is highlighted and enhanced by the tart lemon dressing. We occasionally add currants or raisins to intensify the sweet-sour contrast. Choose tender carrots with a strong orange color.

7 to 8 medium carrots
2 tablespoons currants or raisins (optional)
2 tablespoons lemon juice

¼ teaspoon salt
¼ cup olive oil
6 large leaves Boston lettuce
1 tablespoon chopped parsley

Peel the carrots and cut off and discard the ends. Grate carrots and place them in a mixing bowl. Add currants or raisins, if desired. In a separate bowl, make a dressing with lemon juice, salt, and olive oil. Mix until the salt dissolves, pour it over the carrots, and toss to coat. Refrigerate until ready to serve.

When ready, distribute the lettuce leaves on a serving platter, place the grated carrots on the leaves, decorate with the parsley, and serve.

◆ ◆ ◆ ◆ ◆

## Insalata di Funghi Crudi

MUSHROOM
SALAD

SERVES 6

This may be the original raw mushroom salad and, perhaps, the best. We make it with Bel Paese cheese, but fontina or Gruyère is perfectly adequate. Do not marinate for more than 1 hour. The mushrooms lose their texture and flavor and the salad loses its character.

1½ pounds very fresh mushrooms
lemon juice
½ pound Bel Paese
⅓ cup olive oil
2 garlic cloves, finely chopped
2 tablespoons finely chopped parsley
salt and freshly ground pepper to taste
6 large leaves Boston lettuce

Wash the mushrooms and rub the caps with lemon juice. Slice them thin and place in a mixing bowl. Cut cheese into 1-inch squares roughly ⅛ inch thick. Place the cheese in the mixing bowl with the mushrooms.

In a small mixing bowl, combine the olive oil, 3 tablespoons of lemon juice, garlic, and parsley. Blend well and pour over the mushrooms and cheese. Mix gently and refrigerate for 45 minutes.

When ready, add salt and pepper, combine, and serve on lettuce leaves on individual plates or a serving platter.

♦ ♦ ♦ ♦ ♦

## *Panzanella*

TUSCAN
BREAD
SALAD

SERVES 6 TO 8

Here is a perfect opportunity to use stale home-made Tuscan bread. This dish can be served as a conventional salad, as an antipasto, or as a first course.

4 cups diced stale whole wheat or Italian bread,
    preferably homemade
1 head romaine, Boston, or leaf lettuce, torn into small
    pieces
1 cup chopped carrots
1 cup peeled, seeded, and chopped cucumbers
1 cup Sott'aceti (see recipe), chopped
3 tablespoons capers
1 small red onion, thinly sliced, soaked in cold water for
    30 minutes, drained, and patted dry
5 scallions, chopped
½ cup chopped radishes
1 to 2 garlic cloves, finely chopped
2 tablespoons chopped fresh basil
¼ to ⅓ cup olive oil
3 tablespoons vinegar
salt and freshly ground pepper to taste

Soak the bread in water to cover for 30 minutes.

While the bread soaks, combine all the vegetables, including garlic and basil, in a large salad bowl. When ready, drain the bread cubes and squeeze all the water out of them, using your hands, Tuscan style, or pressing the pieces against the side of a colander. Crumble the bread over the salad and mix well.

In a small bowl, combine the oil, vinegar, salt, and pepper and stir until the salt dissolves. When ready to serve, pour the dressing over the salad and toss to combine.

♦ ♦ ♦ ♦ ♦

## *Insalata di Giglio*

GIGLIO'S
FRUIT
SALAD

We are forever grateful to a friend for this unique and delicious fruit salad, a daring blend of fresh summer fruit, cream, hot pepper, and champagne or sparkling wine. We first tasted it on a warm summer evening on a terrace under the pine trees of Forte dei Marmi. The setting could bring out the best in any dish, but we've since tried it elsewhere and it is always outstanding. Serve as a regular salad.

SERVES 6 TO 8

*8 plums, pitted and sliced*

*6 peaches, peeled, pitted, and sliced*

*1 banana, thinly sliced and mixed with 1 tablespoon
    lemon juice*

*½ cup grapes, seedless if available*

*½ hot pepper, seeded and cut in half*

*½ cup heavy cream*

*½ cup champagne, dry sparkling wine, or a good dry
    red wine*

*salt and freshly ground pepper*

*1 small head Boston or leaf lettuce, torn into small
    pieces*

Place the plums, peaches, banana, and grapes in a mixing bowl, toss to combine, drain off the liquid, and reserve it.

Place the hot pepper, the cream, the juices from the fruit, and the champagne or wine in a small saucepan. Bring to a boil and remove immediately from the heat. Cool slightly, discard the hot pepper, and add salt and pepper to taste.

Just before serving, combine the fruit and lettuce in a salad bowl, add the warm dressing, and toss to combine.

◆ ◆ ◆ ◆ ◆

## *Radicchio Rosso con Fagioli*

RED
CHICORY
SALAD
WITH
BEANS

SERVES 4

Red chicory (*radicchio rosso*), crisp, juicy, bittersweet, may be the best of all salad "greens." As an added bonus, it is as beautiful—deep burgundy red leaves streaked with white—as it is goodtasting. Belgian endive (witloof chicory) can be used as a substitute for red chicory in this salad. However, we urge you to search the Italian markets for red chicory and try it. It is also excellent on its own or in combination with lettuce.

*1 pound red chicory or Belgian endive, thinly sliced*

*1½ cups cooked white kidney beans or chick-peas*

*⅓ cup olive oil*

*3 to 4 tablespoons wine vinegar*

*salt and freshly ground pepper to taste*

Place the red chicory or Belgian endive in a salad bowl, add the beans or chick-peas, and combine. Mix together the oil, vinegar, salt, and pepper and pour over the salad. Toss well and serve.

♦ ♦ ♦ ♦ ♦

*Pomodori*

*Ripieni alla*

*Fantasia*

STUFFED
TOMATOES
WITH
RAW
VEGETABLES
AND
PICKLES

SERVES 6

You can vary the ingredients used to stuff the tomatoes to suit your taste and the supply of vegetables. But the Italian pickles are essential—they give the dish its zesty character and must be included. Although this dish requires many ingredients, it is very simple to prepare and delicious. It is ideal as a first course or as an antipasto in the summer.

6 large ripe tomatoes
salt
½ cup peeled and chopped cucumbers
½ cup seeded and chopped red or green bell peppers
½ cup drained and chopped marinated artichoke hearts
½ cup Sott'aceti (see recipe), chopped
2 tablespoons capers
⅓ cup Mayonnaise (see recipe) combined with ½ teaspoon prepared mustard
romaine or Boston lettuce leaves
12 Italian black olives, pitted
24 marinated mushrooms, preferably homemade (see recipe)
2 cups steamed string beans or cooked peas
1 tablespoon olive oil

Wash the tomatoes, slice 1 inch off the top of each, and discard the cap. Scoop the pulp out of each tomato with a spoon. The pulp will not be used in this recipe, but you can reserve it for use in tomato sauce. Proceed with care—the tomatoes must remain intact. Sprinkle the inside of the tomatoes lightly with salt and turn upside down on a plate to drain for 30 minutes.

Combine the raw vegetables and the pickles in a mixing bowl with the mustard-flavored mayonnaise. Set aside until ready to assemble.

When ready, place the tomatoes on individual serving plates or on a single large platter on a bed of lettuce leaves. Stuff the tomatoes with the mayonnaise mixture. Decorate the top of each tomato with the black olives and distribute the marinated mushrooms and cooked string beans or peas around the base of the tomatoes. Drizzle the olive oil onto the cooked vegetables and serve at room temperature.

♦ ♦ ♦ ♦ ♦

## Insalata di Patate e Carciofi

POTATO
AND
ARTICHOKE
SALAD

SERVES 8

Fresh artichokes are preferable, but canned may be used, if necessary. Homemade mayonnaise is essential.

*10 artichokes or 2 cups canned artichoke hearts, drained*
*1½ pounds new potatoes*
*¼ cup black Italian olives, pitted, rinsed in cold water*
*if very salty, and sliced*
*2 tablespoons chopped scallions*
*½ cup Mayonnaise (see recipe)*
*juice of ½ lemon*
*salt and freshly ground pepper to taste*

Prepare the fresh artichokes for cooking, p. 215, and cut each artichoke into 8 wedges. Cook them in salted water to cover for 15 minutes or steam them until cooked but still firm. Drain well and set aside.

Boil the potatoes, peeled or unpeeled, in water to cover or steam them until cooked but still quite firm. Drain and cut into pieces roughly the size of the artichoke wedges.

Combine the potatoes, artichokes, black olives, and scallions in a salad bowl. Mix the mayonnaise and lemon juice in a separate bowl, pour over the vegetables, toss gently, and correct for salt and pepper. Serve chilled or at room temperature.

♦ ♦ ♦ ♦ ♦

## Insalata di Riso

RICE
SALAD

SERVES 6

Although it may come as a surprise to some, cooked rice is excellent in salads. It complements raw vegetables and responds well to a good vinaigrette dressing. The ingredients are very much a matter of taste. We like it spicy and always include hot marinated peppers. You can substitute sweet peppers if you prefer them or other pickled vegetables. Serve this salad in the summer in place of pasta or, garnished with hard-boiled eggs, as the main dish for a luncheon or light dinner. It is too substantial to serve as a conventional salad or vegetable dish.

FOR THE SALAD:

1½ cups Italian or long-grain rice
¼ to ⅓ cup olive oil
3 tablespoons vinegar
1 garlic clove, minced
3 scallions, chopped
1 tablespoon chopped parsley
1 tablespoon chopped basil
⅓ cup diced bell pepper, red or green
⅓ cup diced celery
⅓ cup peeled and diced cucumber
2 large firm tomatoes, seeded and diced
¼ cup chopped Italian hot marinated peppers
2 tablespoons capers
¼ cup Italian black olives, pitted, rinsed if salty, and
    chopped
salt and freshly ground pepper to taste

FOR THE GARNISH:

1 large firm tomato, seeded and cut into wedges
black or green olives
a few parsley sprigs
3 hard-boiled eggs (optional)

Bring 4 cups of salted water to a boil, add the rice, reduce the heat, and simmer for 15 minutes, until the rice is cooked al dente. Drain and place the rice in a mixing bowl. Add the olive oil, vinegar, garlic, and scallions. Combine well and set aside to cool.

When cooled, add the remaining salad ingredients, toss to mix thoroughly, and adjust for salt and pepper. Mound the salad on a serving platter, and garnish with tomato wedges, olives, parsley, and hard-boiled eggs (if desired). Serve at room temperature.

♦ ♦ ♦ ♦ ♦

## Insalata "da Spiaggia"

PASTA SALAD

When our children were young, we spent a few summers at Fregene, a small seaside resort near Rome. It was often difficult to tear ourselves away from the sun, sand, and sea at lunchtime, and we were quite prepared to forgo the traditional Italian lunch in favor of sandwiches on the beach. Our cook, Virginia, however, was of the opinion that

SERVES 6 TO 8

lunch without pasta was no lunch at all. Since hot pasta had to be eaten immediately, we needed a compromise that would satisfy everyone. The delicious solution was a cold pasta salad. The vegetables in this recipe are plentiful in midsummer. You can substitute spring vegetables, such as asparagus, peas, and artichokes or, in the fall, cauliflower and broccoli.

*1 pound short, stout pasta, such as elbow macaroni, rigatoni, or shells*
*⅓ cup plus 1 tablespoon olive oil*
*½ pound fresh tender string beans, washed and trimmed*
*3 small tender zucchini, scrubbed and thinly sliced*
*3 small tender carrots, peeled and thinly sliced*
*3 medium tomatoes, seeded and cut into wedges*
*⅓ cup Italian black olives pitted, rinsed in cold water if salty, and sliced*
*½ cup diced green or red bell pepper*
*3 tablespoons wine vinegar*
*2 tablespoons chopped scallions*
*1 tablespoon chopped basil*
*pinch of oregano*
*salt and freshly ground pepper to taste*

Bring 4 quarts of salted water to a rapid boil, add the pasta, and cook, stirring occasionally, until al dente. Drain, rinse the pasta with cold water, place in a salad bowl, combine with 1 tablespoon olive oil, and set aside to cool.

Meanwhile, cut the string beans into 1½-inch pieces and steam them until just cooked, but still very firm, about 5 to 10 minutes. Drain and add to the pasta. Blanch the zucchini in boiling water or steam them for a few seconds, drain, and place in the bowl with the pasta. Add the carrots, tomatoes, olives, and bell pepper and combine well.

Combine ⅓ cup olive oil, vinegar, scallions, basil, oregano, salt, and pepper in a small mixing bowl, stirring until the salt dissolves. Pour the dressing over the pasta and vegetables, toss to coat, and serve at room temperature.

VARIATION

The pasta salad can also be served with ½ cup of Tomato Sauce I (see recipe) and 1 tablespoon of olive oil instead of the vinaigrette dressing.

◆ ◆ ◆ ◆ ◆

## Insalata Primaverile

SPRING
SALAD

SERVES 6 TO 8

This salad consists of nothing more than cooked spring vegetables, arranged attractively on a bed of lettuce and served with a simple oil and vinegar dressing. And yet it is a superb dish, a treat for the palate and a delight to the eye.

2 medium artichokes, prepared for cooking (p. 215), each cut into 8 wedges

1 large fennel, prepared for cooking (p. 244), cut into thin wedges

1 pound asparagus, prepared for cooking (p. 222)

3 carrots, peeled and sliced lengthwise

1 head romaine, leaf, or Boston lettuce

1 large or 2 small Belgian endives

6 to 8 medium radishes

2 hard-boiled eggs

1 teaspoon prepared mustard

⅓ to ½ cup olive oil

¼ cup wine vinegar

1 teaspoon salt

freshly ground pepper to taste

1 tablespoon capers

Steam or boil the artichokes, fennel, asparagus, and carrots separately until all are cooked but still firm. Do not overcook. Drain well and set aside.

Shred the lettuce with a sharp knife and arrange it to cover the surface of a large circular serving platter. Slice the endive and radishes and distribute them on top of the lettuce along the rim of the platter.

Now arrange the cooked vegetables on the lettuce. Place the asparagus on the bed of lettuce with the tips facing outward from the center in a configuration that resembles the spokes of a wheel. Distribute the remaining vegetables in an attractive pattern on top of the asparagus.

Separate the egg whites and the yolks of the hard-boiled eggs, dice the whites fine, and sprinkle them over the vegetables. Place the yolks in a small mixing bowl, crush them with a fork, beat in the mustard, oil, vinegar, salt, and pepper, and pour evenly over the vegetables. Sprinkle on the capers and serve chilled or at room temperature.

♦ ♦ ♦ ♦ ♦

*Insalata Mista con Mozzarella*

MIXED
WINTER
SALAD
WITH
MOZZARELLA

SERVES 6

This salad can be served as an antipasto or the main dish for a light lunch or dinner. You can, if you wish, add a pound of boiled potatoes to give it even more substance.

1 celery heart, cut into thin 2-inch-long sticks
1 large fennel, trimmed and thinly sliced, p. 244
2 carrots, peeled and cut into thin 2-inch-long sticks
6-ounce jar marinated artichoke hearts
¾ cup homemade Marinated Mushrooms (see recipe),
    or a 6-ounce jar
2 tablespoons capers
½ pound mozzarella, cut into thin 2-inch-long sticks
¼ cup olive oil
3 tablespoons wine vinegar
½ teaspoon salt
freshly ground pepper to taste
2 hard-boiled eggs, cut into wedges

Place the celery, fennel, and carrots in a salad bowl. Slice the artichokes and mushrooms and add them to the bowl, along with the capers and mozzarella.

Combine the oil, vinegar, salt, and pepper in a small mixing bowl and pour over the vegetables. Toss, garnish with the hard-boiled eggs, and serve.

♦ ♦ ♦ ♦ ♦

*Melanzane alla Virginia*

VIRGINIA'S
MARINATED
EGGPLANT

SERVES 4 TO 6

Fried eggplant seasoned with garlic and parsley makes a delicious addition to a buffet. We sometimes sprinkle the eggplant slices with hot pepper and serve as an antipasto or as a vegetable with yogurt on the side.

3 medium eggplants, approximately 2½ pounds
1 tablespoon salt
¼ cup seed oil
3 garlic cloves, finely chopped
2 tablespoons finely chopped parsley
freshly ground pepper to taste

Peel the eggplants, slice them lengthwise in ¼-inch slices, sprinkle with salt, and set to drain in a colander for 30 minutes. Rinse and pat dry between paper towels.

Heat the oil in a frying pan, add the eggplant slices, and fry, a few at a time, turning until lightly browned on both sides. Remove from the pan when cooked, drain on paper towels, and place on a serving platter. Combine the garlic and parsley and sprinkle over the eggplant slices. Sprinkle with pepper, add salt if necessary, and set aside for at least 1 hour. Serve at room temperature.

◆ ◆ ◆ ◆ ◆

## *Zucchini Marinati*

MARINATED
ZUCCHINI
SALAD

SERVES 4 TO 6

*¼ to ⅓ cup olive oil*
*2 to 3 tablespoons lemon juice*
*3 garlic cloves, minced*
*1 tablespoon minced parsley*
*⅓ teaspoon minced fresh mint or dried mint, crushed*
*salt and freshly ground pepper to taste*
*2 pounds fresh, small zucchini scrubbed, trimmed, and cut lengthwise into ¼-inch-thick strips*
*1 large firm tomato, seeded and cut into wedges*

Combine in a small mixing bowl the olive oil, lemon juice, garlic, parsley, mint, salt, and pepper. Set aside.

Steam the zucchini for 4 to 5 minutes, until barely tender. Do not overcook; they must be firm. While still hot, drain quickly and transfer them to a salad bowl and combine with the dressing.

Allow the zucchini to cool slowly at room temperature, tossing occasionally to coat the zucchini with the marinade. Garnish with the tomato wedges and serve.

◆ ◆ ◆ ◆ ◆

## *Zucca Marinata*

MARINATED
SQUASH

SERVES 4 TO 6

This is a marvelous marinated salad. If possible, make it a day ahead of time so that the herbs and spices have ample time to permeate the squash. In Italy, this is made with a kind of pumpkin not available here, but golden Hubbard or butternut squash makes a good substitute.

*2 pounds golden Hubbard or butternut squash*
*½ cup chopped bell pepper, red or green*
*2 garlic cloves, finely chopped*
*1 tablespoon finely chopped basil*
*2 scallions, chopped*

¼ cup olive oil
3 tablespoons vinegar
pinch of oregano
few drops of Tabasco sauce

Preheat the oven to 375°F.

Cut the squash in half, remove the seeds, place on a cookie sheet or jelly roll pan, and bake in the preheated oven until cooked, but still very firm, about 30 to 45 minutes. Remove and set aside to cool.

When cool enough to handle, peel the squash, cut into ½-inch cubes, and combine with the bell pepper.

In a small mixing bowl, make a dressing with the remaining ingredients, pour it over the squash, and mix well. Cover and place in the refrigerator for at least 1 hour. Serve at room temperature.

♦ ♦ ♦ ♦ ♦

*Insalata di Rinforzo*

CAULIFLOWER
SALAD

SERVES 8

Other cooked vegetables such as broccoli, zucchini, and green beans can be added to this salad. It will keep for several days in the refrigerator.

1 large or 2 small cauliflowers, trimmed and left whole
5 or 6 medium carrots, peeled, trimmed, and left whole
4 or 5 celery stalks, washed and cut in half
¼ cup capers
½ cup Italian black olives, pitted, rinsed in cold water
        if salty, and roughly chopped
¼ cup Sott'aceti (see recipe), roughly chopped
¼ to ⅓ cup olive oil
3 to 4 tablespoons wine vinegar
¼ teaspoon salt
¼ teaspoon freshly ground pepper
1 tablespoon chopped basil

Steam or boil in separate saucepans the cauliflower, carrots, and celery until cooked but still firm. Drain well and set aside until cool enough to handle.

Divide the cauliflower into flowerets and cut the carrots and celery into 1-inch-long pieces. Place the vegetables in a large serving bowl and combine with the capers, olives, and pickles.

Combine the olive oil, vinegar, salt, pepper, and basil in a small mixing bowl and mix well until the salt dissolves. Pour the dressing over the vegetables and toss gently. Marinate for an hour or two and serve at room temperature.

♦ ♦ ♦ ♦ ♦

## Insalata di Lenticchie

LENTIL
SALAD

SERVES 6

If you are not already a fan of lentils, this salad is almost guaranteed to make you one. It is also simple to prepare.

1 cup dried lentils
1 carrot, peeled and cut in small pieces
1 onion, cut in half
1 bay leaf
½ teaspoon salt
freshly ground pepper
½ cup olive oil
3 tablespoons lemon juice
2 tablespoons chopped parsley

Soak the lentils for 8 hours or overnight in 3 cups of water. Drain and rinse the lentils; place them in an enameled or stainless steel saucepan with the carrot, onion, bay leaf, and 3 cups of water. Bring to a boil and simmer covered for 20 to 25 minutes, until the lentils are cooked but still firm and intact. Remove and discard the onion and bay leaf. Drain, reserving the liquid for use in soup, and place the lentils and carrot in a small salad bowl.

Combine the salt, pepper, oil, and lemon juice in a small mixing bowl and pour it over the lentils while they are still warm. Add the parsley, combine well, and refrigerate for a couple of hours. Serve cold or at room temperature.

♦ ♦ ♦ ♦ ♦

## Ceci e Carciofi Marinati

MARINATED
CHICK-PEAS
AND
ARTICHOKE
SALAD

SERVES 8

Canned chick-peas are perfectly adequate for this dish, and canned artichokes, while a poor substitute for fresh, can be used. The garlic flavor will intensify as the vegetables marinate, so adjust to suit your taste.

1 cup dried chick-peas or 2 cups canned, drained
1 tablespoon flour if using dried chick-peas
12 medium artichokes, or 2 cups canned artichoke hearts, drained
2 scallions, all the white and some green, roughly chopped
1 green or red bell pepper, diced
2 tablespoons chopped parsley
¼ teaspoon oregano
¼ teaspoon paprika

2 garlic cloves, minced
⅓ cup olive oil
¼ cup wine vinegar
½ teaspoon salt
freshly ground pepper to taste

Soak the dried chick-peas in 3 cups of water with 1 tablespoon of flour for 8 hours or overnight. The flour softens the skins of the chick-peas. Drain, rinse, and cook in 4 cups of water for 1 to 1½ hours, until tender. As an alternative, cook in a pressure cooker for 30 minutes. Drain, reserving the liquid for soup, and set the chick-peas aside.

Prepare the artichokes, p. 215. Cut each into 8 wedges and cook in salted water to cover for 15 minutes, until cooked but still firm. Drain well. If using canned artichoke hearts, drain them and cut in half.

Combine in a salad bowl the chick-peas, artichokes, scallions, and bell pepper. Mix the remaining ingredients in a small bowl and pour over the vegetables. Toss well to combine and place in the refrigerator for at least 3 to 4 hours, preferably overnight, to marinate. Serve chilled or at room temperature.

# DESSERTS

An Italian meal usually ends not with a rich dessert but with a big bowl of fresh seasonal fruit. This does not mean that Italians have rejected the fine art of dessert making—quite the contrary. It is just that they tend to eat their sweets in the late morning with coffee, in the late afternoon with tea, and, most important of all, in connection with religious festivals.

Desserts more than other foods reflect the historical and geographical differences among the regions of the country. The stately desserts of the Piedmont display close affinity with those of France, the rich nut cakes of the Trentino recall the Austro-German connection, while the rich, sweet, honey-flavored sweets of the south commemorate ties with the Near and Middle East. Practically every municipality in the country, and there are a great many, has its own dessert specialty; Prato has its *biscottini*, Siena its *panforte*, Genoa its own special sponge cake, Milan the illustrious *panettone*, Florence *zuccotto* and *zuppa inglese*. The list could be extended for pages.

This dazzling array of desserts presented us with a problem. How were we to decide which to include in the book and which to leave out? After much searching, testing, and discussion we arrived at a list that, not surprisingly, reflects our own personal preferences. Italians make marvelous desserts with fruit, and we are partial to them. We have thus included a number of fruit desserts and tarts. Italians are justly famous for their ices and ice creams, and we adore them. Our first stop when we return each year to Florence is at our favorite ice cream bar. You will be surprised at the ease with which you can reproduce these excellent sweets at home. In addition, we have chosen what we consider some of the best cakes, puddings, and custards. We tend to prefer relatively simple, easy-to-prepare, and not excessively rich desserts, and this bias too is reflected in our choices.

◆ ◆ ◆ ◆ ◆

## Pasta Frolla

SHORT
SWEET
DOUGH
I

This is the dough used most often for tarts and flans (*crostate*) in Italy. It is light, crumbly, delicious, and, because of the high sugar content, difficult to handle. It must be worked quickly with a light touch. The dough should rest in the refrigerator at least 1 hour before rolling out.

The proportion of ingredients for *pasta frolla* can be varied to suit one's palate and requirements. The recipe we give below makes a shell large enough for a 10-inch tart pan.

2 cups unbleached all-purpose or pastry flour
8 tablespoons butter
3 egg yolks
zest of 1 lemon
1 teaspoon vanilla extract or Cognac
½ cup superfine sugar

Place the flour in a large mixing bowl, add the butter and mix in with a pastry knife or your fingers until the butter is the size of small peas. Add the egg yolks, lemon zest, vanilla or Cognac, and sugar and combine thoroughly with a wooden spoon.

Turn the dough out onto a floured work surface and knead briefly, using the heel of your hand, until the ingredients are thoroughly blended. The dough should be soft but not wet. Wrap in wax paper and refrigerate for 1 hour.

Butter well a tart pan. Roll the dough out on a floured work surface, reserving some of the dough to decorate the surface of the tart if the recipe calls for it, place the dough carefully in the pan, fitting it snugly along the bottom and sides, and proceed according to instructions in the specific recipe.

A few hints on preparing the dough:

1. When rolling out, roll from the center to the edge and turn the dough a quarter turn after each roll. Check constantly to make sure the work surface has enough flour.
2. When the dough is rolled out, the easiest way to transfer it to the pan is to roll it up on the rolling pin and unroll it over the pan. As an alternative, fold it into quarters and unfold it over the pan.
3. If the dough is extremely fragile, roll it between two sheets of wax paper and transfer on the wax paper to the pan.

♦ ♦ ♦ ♦ ♦

## Pasta Brisée

SHORT
SWEET
DOUGH II

This is a modified version of *pasta frolla*. It is made with less sugar than *pasta frolla* and no eggs and is therefore easier to handle and less rich (but also less flavorful). We often use it instead of *pasta frolla* for fresh fruit tarts made with Crema Pasticcera (see recipe). The quantities in this recipe make enough dough for a 10-inch tart pan.

     *2 cups unbleached all-purpose or pastry flour*
     *8 tablespoons butter*
     *2 tablespoons sugar*
     *pinch of salt*
     *5 tablespoons cold water*

Place the flour in a large mixing bowl and mix the butter into it with a pastry knife or your fingers until the butter is the size of small peas. Add the sugar, salt, and water and shape the dough into a ball.

Place the dough on a lightly floured work surface and knead with the heel of your hand briefly and quickly to form a homogeneous mixture. Wrap the dough in wax paper and refrigerate for at least 1 hour.

Roll the dough out on a lightly floured work surface to the size of the tart pan, rolling from the center and turning the dough a quarter turn after each roll. Butter the tart pan, carefully place the dough in it, and proceed according to instructions in the specific recipe.

♦ ♦ ♦ ♦ ♦

## Crema Pasticcera

There are many types of pastry cream and many different ways to make them. We find the one described here highly satisfactory and easy to prepare. It can be kept for a week in the refrigerator. It is used as an ingredient in a number of desserts.

PASTRY
CREAM

MAKES 1½ CUPS

*3 egg yolks*
*½ cup sugar*
*⅓ cup sifted unbleached all-purpose flour*
*1½ cups milk*
*1 teaspoon butter, melted*
*zest of ½ lemon*
*1 teaspoon vanilla extract or Cognac*

Beat the egg yolks and sugar in a mixing bowl with a wire whisk or electric beater until the mixture is creamy, pale yellow, and smooth, about 5 minutes. Add the flour and continue beating until thoroughly combined.

Bring the milk to a boil and pour it into the egg-flour mixture, beating constantly, until all the milk is added.

Place in a saucepan over moderate heat and cook for 3 minutes, stirring constantly with a whisk until the mixture is thick and smooth. Remove from the heat, stir in the butter, the lemon zest, and the vanilla or Cognac and let cool.

If you do not intend to use immediately, spread 1 teaspoon of melted butter over the surface of the cream to prevent a skin from forming.

◆ ◆ ◆ ◆ ◆

## Arance Affettate

SLICED ORANGES

SERVES 6

Fresh sliced oranges marinated in Cointreau, spices, and sugar are refreshing after a rich and filling meal.

8 seedless eating oranges
¼ cup lemon juice
⅓ cup sugar
¼ cup Cointreau
½ teaspoon powdered cinnamon

Peel 7 oranges over a plate with a sharp paring knife, making sure that all the white part is removed. Cut the oranges in thin horizontal slices and place them in a serving bowl, preferably glass.

Carefully cut the skin off the remaining orange, taking care not to include any of the white part. Cut the skin in very thin slivers no more than ⅛ inch wide. Squeeze the peeled orange and combine the juice in a mixing bowl with the lemon juice, sugar, liqueur, and slivers of orange skin. Pour the marinade over the sliced oranges and mix. Allow them to marinate in the refrigerator for 2 or 3 hours. Remove 30 minutes prior to serving. To serve, sprinkle with cinnamon.

◆ ◆ ◆ ◆ ◆

## Pesche al Vino

PEACHES IN WINE

SERVES 6 TO 8

The mellow flavor of peaches in wine has no rival on a hot midsummer evening.

8 to 10 ripe peaches, peeled, pitted, and sliced
1 cup dry red wine
2 tablespoons sugar or to taste
1-inch piece of cinnamon
2 cloves
zest of 1 lemon

Combine the ingredients in a mixing bowl. Allow to marinate for 1 hour. Remove the cinnamon and cloves. Serve cooled, but not chilled, with Amaretti, Biscottini di Prato, or pieces of Sbrisolona alla Lombarda (see recipes).

♦ ♦ ♦ ♦ ♦

## Pere al Forno

PEARS
BAKED
WITH WINE

SERVES 6

This is a particularly tasty version of a simple but superb fruit dessert.

*6 ripe but firm Bosc pears*
*2 cups full-bodied dry red wine*
*½ cup sugar*
*zest of 1 lemon*
*1-inch stick of cinnamon*
*2 cloves*

Preheat oven to 350°F.

Place the pears standing upright in a baking dish with sides at least 2 inches high, just large enough to hold the pears. Pour the wine over them, sprinkle with sugar, add the lemon zest, cinnamon, and cloves, and bake, basting periodically, until tender, about 40 minutes.

Remove the pears from the oven and place them on a serving platter. Pour the wine sauce into a small saucepan and reduce over medium heat, stirring frequently, until the consistency resembles syrup. Coat the pears with the syrup and serve warm or at room temperature. The pears will keep nicely for a few hours, especially if placed in the refrigerator. In that case, pour the sauce over the pears when ready to serve.

♦ ♦ ♦ ♦ ♦

## Cigliege al Vino Rosso

CHERRIES
STEWED
IN RED
WINE

SERVES 4

This is a fabulous fruit dessert. Use large, juicy, and ripe sweet cherries.

*1 pound dark sweet cherries*
*½ cup sugar*
*1 cup full-bodied dry red wine*
*¼ cup black currant or black cherry jam*
*1-inch stick of cinnamon*
*zest of 1 lemon*
*½ cup heavy cream*

Wash the cherries and pit them, leaving them whole. Combine them in a saucepan with the sugar, wine, jam, cinnamon, and lemon zest. Bring to a boil, reduce the heat, and simmer covered for 20 minutes. Remove from the heat, discard the cinnamon, place the cherries together with their juice in individual serving bowls, and chill.

Just before serving, whip the cream and place a dollop on top of the cherries in each bowl. Serve cold.

◆ ◆ ◆ ◆ ◆

## Mele con Crema Pasticcera

APPLES
WITH
PASTRY
CREAM

SERVES 6

Although the baked apples described in this recipe take more time to prepare than conventional methods, the extra effort is worthwhile. As the apples bake, the cream and the apple pulp amalgamate to form a rich combination.

6 medium cooking apples
juice of ½ lemon
⅓ cup sugar
Crema Pasticcera (see recipe)
¾ cup almonds, peeled, lightly toasted in a medium
    oven, and roughly chopped
1 cup currants
1 tablespoon Cognac
6 tablespoons butter
3 tablespoons sherry or Marsala

Carefully cut off the tops (stem part) of the apples, ½ inch down. Reserve. Core the apples, making sure that you do not cut through to the bottom. Using a serrated spoon or a melon scoop, remove roughly half the pulp from inside each apple. Drizzle the cavities with lemon juice, sprinkle each with 1 teaspoon of the sugar, and set aside.

Preheat the oven to 375°F.

Make the Crema Pasticcera and set aside.

Combine the almonds, currants, and Cognac in a mixing bowl. Add the crema and mix thoroughly.

Butter a baking dish large enough to hold the apples. Prick the skin of each apple in a few places with a fork and place them in the baking dish. Fill the cavities three-fourths full with the crema mixture and cap each apple with the reserved tops. Sprinkle the outside of the apples with sugar, approximately 1 tablespoon for all the apples. Dot each with a teaspoon of butter. Combine the remaining sugar, approximately 2 tablespoons, with the sherry or Marsala and ½ cup water. Pour in the bottom of the baking dish and bake for approximately 40 minutes, basting occasionally, until the apples begin to color. Serve warm.

♦ ♦ ♦ ♦ ♦

## Pesche Ripiene

STUFFED PEACHES

SERVES 6

A close friend of ours who lives in Florence insisted that we include this recipe. His family comes from the Piedmont, and this is the way they have prepared this regional specialty for generations. Bitter almonds can often be found in specialty food stores or in Greek, Italian, or Hungarian groceries. If unavailable, use regular almonds.

*6 large ripe freestone peaches*
*3 bitter almonds*
*6 to 7 Amaretti (see recipe)*
*2 teaspoons Kirsch*
*2 egg yolks*
*2 tablespoons bread crumbs*
*2 tablespoons butter*

Preheat oven to 375°F.

Cut the peaches in half and remove the pits. Also remove some of the pulp from each cavity, taking care not to break the skin. Place the pulp in a mixing bowl and crush with a fork.

Put the peach halves close together in a buttered 8-by-12-inch baking dish.

Blanch and peel the bitter almonds. Crush them in a mortar or process them in a food processor until powdered and add them to the pulp mixture. Pulverize the Amaretti in a food processor or blender and add to the peach pulp. Add the Kirsch and egg yolks. Combine thoroughly and fill each peach half with the mixture. Sprinkle the bread crumbs on top of each peach half and dot with butter.

Bake for 20 to 25 minutes. The peaches should be tender but still firm. Serve at room temperature or chilled.

♦ ♦ ♦ ♦ ♦

## Gelato di Fragole

STRAWBERRY ICE

SERVES 6 TO 8

This recipe is suitable for any type of berry. It is simple, absolutely foolproof, and excellent. Berry ices are best made at least 12 hours in advance.

*1 to 1½ cups sugar, depending on the sweetness of the*
*    berries*
*2 cups water*
*4 cups fresh, ripe, flavorful strawberries, stems removed*
*juice of ½ lemon*

Combine the sugar and 2 cups of water in a saucepan and simmer for 10 minutes. Remove from the heat and allow to cool.

Purée the strawberries in a food processor, blender, or food mill. Add the lemon juice.

Blend in two-thirds of the sugar water and taste. Add more, if necessary. Place the mixture in a glass or metal container and freeze for 2 hours, until the mixture begins to harden. Remove from the freezer and beat with an electric mixer or process in a food processor until smooth and creamy. Return to the freezer and freeze until hard. Remove from the freezer 30 minutes before serving to allow the ice to soften and mellow in the refrigerator.

As an alternative, freeze in a hand-cranked or electric ice cream maker according to the manufacturer's instructions.

◆ ◆ ◆ ◆ ◆

## Gelato di Pesche

PEACH
ICE

SERVES 6 TO 8

Bitter almonds are often available in specialty food shops or in Greek, Italian, or Hungarian groceries. If unavailable, use regular almonds. Peach ice is best if made 12 hours in advance.

6 to 7 ripe freestone peaches
3 bitter almonds, blanched and peeled
¾ cup sugar
1 cup water
juice of 1½ lemons

Place the peaches in boiling water for 30 seconds to blanch. Peel, cut in half, and remove the pits.

Purée peaches together with the bitter almonds in a blender, food processor, or food mill and set aside.

Combine the sugar and 1 cup water in a saucepan and simmer for 10 minutes. Remove from the heat and let cool.

Blend the lemon juice and the sugared water with the peach purée and freeze in a glass or metal container for 2 hours, until mixture begins to harden. Remove from the freezer and beat with an electric mixer or process in a food processor until creamy and smooth. Return to the freezer and freeze until hard. Remove from the freezer 30 minutes before serving to allow the ice to soften and mellow in the refrigerator.

As an alternative, freeze in a hand-cranked or electric ice cream maker according to the manufacturer's instructions.

♦ ♦ ♦ ♦ ♦          This is a delightfully fresh-tasting ice.

*Gelato di*

*Arance*

ORANGE ICE

SERVES 6

1 cup water
1 cup sugar
juice of 4 large juicy oranges
juice of 1½ lemons
zest of 1 whole orange and 1 whole lemon
1 tablespoon Cognac or rum

Boil together in a small saucepan for 2 minutes 1 cup of water and the sugar, until the sugar is completely dissolved. Remove from the heat. Add the juice, zest, and Cognac or rum. Allow the mixture to sit, covered, for 15 minutes.

Pour into a glass or metal container and place in the freezer for approximately 2 hours. Remove, blend in a blender or food processor to break up the ice crystals, return to the freezer, and freeze until hard. Remove 30 minutes prior to serving to allow the ice to soften in the refrigerator. Freeze in a hand-cranked or electric ice cream maker according to the manufacturer's instructions.

♦ ♦ ♦ ♦ ♦          This can be made as an ice, with water, or as an ice
                    cream, with cream. It is excellent both ways.

*Gelato di*

*Banana*

BANANA
ICE CREAM

SERVES 6

5 very ripe bananas
juice of ½ lemon
½ cup milk
¾ cup sugar
1½ cups whipping cream

Cream the bananas in a food processor, blender, or with a fork and add the lemon juice. Heat the milk in a saucepan, add the sugar, and simmer until the sugar melts. Allow to cool, combine with the bananas, and set aside.

Whip the cream until thick but not too stiff. Combine thoroughly with the bananas and freeze in a glass or metal container for 2 hours until the mixture begins to harden. Remove from the freezer and beat with an electric beater or process in a food processor until smooth and creamy. Return to the freezer until hard. Remove from the freezer 30 minutes before serving to allow the ice cream to soften and mellow in the refrigerator.

As an alternative, freeze in a hand-cranked or electric ice cream maker according to the manufacturer's instructions.

### VARIATION

To make banana ice, substitute 2 cups of water for the milk and eliminate the cream. Serve with whipped cream.

♦ ♦ ♦ ♦ ♦

## *Granita di Caffe con Panna*

COFFEE
ICE
WITH
WHIPPED
CREAM

SERVES 6

*Granite*, or semisoft ices, are among the delights of summer in Italy. Every bar serves them, and nothing is quite so refreshing on a hot day. They have been popular in Italy and other Mediterranean countries for many centuries. In the past they were the confection of the rich, made with snow brought down from the high mountains and stored through the summer in salt.

*Granite* are made in various flavors, especially of citrus fruits, but our favorite is coffee.

*¾ cup plus 1 tablespoon sugar*

*2 cups water*

*½ cup strong Italian espresso*

*1 cup whipping cream*

Combine ¾ cup of sugar and 2 cups of water in a saucepan, bring to a boil, and simmer until the sugar dissolves. Remove from the heat and add the espresso. Cool for 10 minutes, transfer it to a glass or metal container, and place in the freezer until almost firm, about 2 hours. Remove and blend in a blender or food processor to break up the ice crystals. Return to the freezer for at least 2 hours.

Thirty minutes before serving, transfer the ice to the refrigerator to allow it to mellow. Just prior to serving, whip the cream until firm with 1 tablespoon of sugar.

Serve in individual parfait dishes or glass dessert bowls, putting in first whipped cream, then the coffee ice, then covering with more whipped cream.

# Gelato di Zabaione

♦ ♦ ♦ ♦ ♦

ZABAIONE
ICE
CREAM

SERVES 6 TO 8

Although Zabaione Ice Cream can be made as described below, it is much creamier and lighter if made in a hand-cranked or electric ice cream maker. If you have one, by all means use it.

*Zabaione (see recipe) made with:*
*5 egg yolks*
*¾ cup sugar*
*½ cup Marsala*
*zest of 1 lemon*
*1½ cups heavy cream*

Make the *zabaione* and allow it to cool. Meanwhile, whip the cream until it begins to thicken and has a consistency resembling thick sour cream. You will need about 2½ cups of the semiwhipped cream. Combine with the *zabaione*, place in a metal or glass container, cover, and place in the freezer for 2 hours, until the mixture begins to harden. Remove from the freezer and beat with an electric beater or process in a food processor until smooth and creamy. Return to the freezer until firm. Remove from the freezer 30 minutes before serving and store in the refrigerator. This will permit the ice cream to soften and mellow.

# Crema allo Zabaione

♦ ♦ ♦ ♦ ♦

ZABAIONE

SERVES 6 TO 8

No description can do justice to *zabaione*. It must be tasted and savored to be fully appreciated. It is the best of all custards, a marvelously rich concoction of egg yolks, sugar, Marsala, and lemon zest. Although a little goes a long way, one can never make too much.

*6 egg yolks*
*½ cup sugar*
*1 tablespoon cold water*
*¾ cup Marsala*
*zest of 1 lemon*
*¼ teaspoon vanilla extract*
*1 cup whipping cream*

Place the yolks and sugar in the top half of a double boiler, add 1 tablespoon cold water, and cook slowly over a low heat, beating constantly with a wire whisk, until the sugar dissolves and the mixture is pale yellow, creamy, and smooth, about 5 minutes. Add the Marsala a little at a time, beating constantly. Finally, blend in the lemon zest and vanilla. Continue to cook, beating constantly, until the *zabaione* thickens and has doubled in size. This will take about 10 to 15 minutes.

Remove from the heat and allow to cool completely.

When cool, whip the cream until firm, without adding sugar, combine thoroughly with the *zabaione*, and chill in individual attractive glass bowls. Serve chilled with Savoiardi (see recipe) or other light cookies.

NOTE: *Zabaione* can also be cooked directly over low heat, but you must beat the yolks continuously, making sure that you cover the entire bottom of the pan. The results are the same, but it takes less than half the time.

♦ ♦ ♦ ♦ ♦

## Budino di Semolino

SEMOLINA
PUDDING

SERVES 6 TO 8

Puddings are very popular in Italy and are standard items in the dessert repertoire. Semolino makes a light, mild, and easily digested pudding. Serve hot or cold.

*3 cups milk*
*½ cup sugar*
*¼ teaspoon vanilla extract*
*pinch of salt*
*1 cup Italian semolino or semolina*
*1 tablespoon butter*
*4 extra-large eggs, beaten*
*½ cup currants soaked in 2 tablespoons Cognac or rum*
*3 tablespoons candied fruit*
*3 tablespoons fine bread crumbs*
*⅓ to ½ cup tart jam, preferably plum or black currant*

Preheat the oven to 350°F.

Combine the milk, sugar, vanilla, and salt in a heavy saucepan, bring to a boil, and add the semolino slowly in a thin stream, stirring constantly. Reduce heat to low and continue cooking, stirring constantly, for 5 minutes, until the mixture is very dense. Remove from the heat, add the butter, and combine. Allow to cool a few minutes, then blend in the eggs, mixing thoroughly. Finally, add the currants along with the Cognac or rum in which they were soaked, and the candied fruit.

Butter and sprinkle with bread crumbs a 6-cup pudding mold. Add the pudding mixture and bake for 20 to 25 minutes in the preheated oven, until the pudding is firm and begins to color. Remove, unmold, and spread with a very thin coating of jam. Serve warm.

♦ ♦ ♦ ♦ ♦

## Budino di Riso

RICE
PUDDING

SERVES 6 TO 8

The Italian *budino* can be roughly translated by the word "pudding" but does not have much in common with that dessert. A *budino* is firm and can be sliced in wedges, a little like a cake without a crust. Our favorite combines the full-bodied flavor of pistachios, walnuts, candied fruits, currants, and rice enlivened by rum.

*½ cup Arborio or long-grain rice*
*3 cups milk*
*⅔ cup sugar*
*3 tablespoons currants*
*½ teaspoon vanilla extract*
*4 extra-large eggs, beaten*
*4 tablespoons butter*
*1 tablespoon chopped walnuts*
*1 tablespoon chopped pistachios*
*¼ cup rum*
*zest of 1 lemon*
*3 tablespoons candied fruit*
*3 tablespoons fine bread crumbs*
*2 tablespoons powdered sugar*

Combine the rice and milk in a saucepan and simmer gently, uncovered, for 10 minutes. Add the sugar, currants, and vanilla and continue to simmer, stirring occasionally, for another 10 minutes, until the rice is cooked and the milk absorbed.

Remove from the heat, let cool for a few minutes, then blend in thoroughly the beaten eggs, 2½ tablespoons of butter, the nuts, the rum, the lemon zest, and the candied fruit.

Preheat the oven to 350°F.

Butter a 6-cup pudding mold and sprinkle with bread crumbs to coat. Discard excess bread crumbs, spoon the pudding mixture into the mold, and bake in the preheated oven for 20 minutes until firm.

Remove from the oven and let cool for 20 minutes. Unmold the pudding onto a serving dish. Sprinkle with powdered sugar passed through a fine sieve. Serve hot or cold.

♦ ♦ ♦ ♦ ♦

*Monte*

*Bianco*

CHESTNUT
PURÉE
WITH
WHIPPED
CREAM

SERVES 6 TO 8

Monte Bianco is sheer ecstasy for those with a special fondness for chestnuts. The dessert is named after and shaped to resemble Mont Blanc, the highest mountain in Europe and the one that separates Italy and France. The puréed chestnuts are piled high and covered with whipped cream.

The secret of this dessert is to build up the mountain of puréed chestnuts as lightly as possible. The chestnuts can be cooked and mashed ahead of time, but it is best to pass them through a ricer or food mill not too long before serving, as they tend to compress as they sit.

*2 pounds chestnuts*
*3 cups milk*
*¼ teaspoon vanilla extract*
*½ cup plus 2 tablespoons sugar*
*2 cups whipping cream*

Make crosswise cuts in the flat sides of the chestnuts with a sharp paring knife. Place them in a saucepan with water to cover and boil for 30 minutes. Drain and when cooled off sufficiently to handle, but still hot, peel off the outer shell and inner skin. Return the chestnuts to the saucepan, add the milk and vanilla, and simmer over a low heat for 30 minutes more until the chestnuts are tender and the milk has evaporated or been absorbed.

With a potato masher, mash the chestnuts to a pulp, add ½ cup of sugar, and stir over low heat for a few minutes to amalgamate with the sugar. Set aside to cool.

Whip the cream until stiff, adding 2 tablespoons of sugar.

Pass the purée through a food mill or a potato ricer, allowing the fine strands of purée to drop onto a large platter. Try to give the pile of strands a conical shape.

Without pressing the mound, lightly spread the whipped cream over the cone with a cake spatula to create the effect of a snow-capped mountain. Serve chilled or at room temperature.

♦ ♦ ♦ ♦ ♦

## Torta di Ricotta

RICOTTA
CAKE

SERVES 8

This classic Italian cheesecake is lighter, more flavorful, and less sweet than North American ones.

*Short Sweet Dough I (see recipe)*
*¾ cup sugar*
*3 tablespoons almonds, blanched, peeled, toasted, and*
  *roughly chopped*
*zest of ½ lemon*
*zest of ½ orange*
*¼ teaspoon vanilla extract*
*2 extra-large eggs plus 2 yolks, beaten*
*1 pound fresh ricotta, drained if very moist*
*¼ cup raisins soaked in 2 tablespoons rum*
*1 egg, beaten*

Make the short sweet dough and divide it into two parts, one roughly two-thirds of the total, the other one-third. Roll out the larger part ⅛ to ¼ inch thick and use it to line the bottom and sides of a 10-inch tart pan with a removable rim. If the dough is difficult to handle, roll it between sheets of wax paper and use the paper to help you transfer it to the flan pan. Remove any excess dough.

Preheat the oven to 350°F.

Combine all remaining ingredients (except 1 beaten egg) for the filling in a large mixing bowl, then spread it evenly over the dough.

Roll out the remaining third of the dough roughly ⅛ inch thick and, using a pastry wheel, cut the dough into thin strips. Use the strips to form a lattice or any other pattern that you prefer over the surface of the cake. Wet the ends of the strips with water to facilitate attaching them to the crust.

Paint the lattice and all exposed parts of the crust with the beaten egg. Bake in the preheated oven for 30 minutes, until the filling is firm to the touch. Remove and let cool for 15 minutes before removing the rim. Place the pan on top of a 1-quart Mason jar and slide off the rim, leaving the cake on the bottom of pan.

♦ ♦ ♦ ♦ ♦

## Torta al Brandy

MARIA'S
BRANDY
PIE

A success every time, this dessert is a special treat for those who like *zabaione*, since the pie filling is a delightful variation on the traditional Italian custard. Keep chilled until ready to serve.

FOR THE CRUST:

*2 cups Italian Ladyfinger crumbs, approximately 7*
  *ounces (see recipe)*
*½ cup melted butter*

SERVES 8

**FOR THE FILLING AND TOPPING:**

*5 egg yolks*
*½ cup sugar*
*½ cup brandy or Cognac*
*2 teaspoons grated lemon zest*
*1 tablespoon lemon juice*
*1½ cups heavy cream*
*2 tablespoons grated or shaved bittersweet chocolate*

Preheat the oven to 350°F. Make the ladyfingers and put aside until ready to use.

To make crumbs of the ladyfingers, process them in a food processor or a blender. Combine the crumbs with the melted butter in a mixing bowl. When thoroughly blended, line the bottom and 1½ inches up the sides of an 8-inch springform pan. Press the crumbs with a rubber cake spatula against the bottom and sides to form a uniform crust. Place in the oven and bake for 10 to 15 minutes. Remove and set aside.

Place the egg yolks in the top half of a double boiler and, over a low heat, beat them with a wire whisk for 2 to 3 minutes. Add the sugar slowly, beating constantly. Continue beating until the sugar dissolves and the mixture is creamy, smooth, and pale yellow, about 5 minutes. Add the brandy or Cognac, a little at a time, beating constantly. Beat in the lemon zest and lemon juice. Continue to cook the mixture over a low heat, beating with the whisk, until thickened and doubled in size, about 10 to 15 minutes. Remove from the heat and let cool.

Whip 1 cup of cream until firm and fold gently into the custard with a rubber spatula. Pour into the crust, smooth the top, and chill in the refrigerator for at least 2 hours.

When ready to serve, remove from the springform and place on a serving platter. Whip the remaining ½ cup of cream until firm, place it in a pastry bag, and, using a fluted tip, decorate the surface of the pie. Sprinkle with the grated or shaved chocolate and serve.

◆ ◆ ◆ ◆ ◆

## Torta di Mandorle

### ALMOND CAKE

*⅔ cup butter, at room temperature*
*1 cup plus 1 tablespoon sugar*
*3 extra-large eggs, separated*
*1½ cups unbleached all-purpose flour*
*¼ cup potato starch*
*juice of 1 lemon*
*1 cup almonds, blanched and peeled*
*3 bitter almonds, blanched and peeled, if available, or*
  *8 regular almonds*

SERVES 6 TO 8

*¼ teaspoon cream of tartar (optional)*
*pinch of salt*
*¼ cup slivered almonds*

Cream the butter and 1 cup sugar together in a mixing bowl, until the mixture is creamy, smooth, and thoroughly blended. Incorporate the egg yolks, flour, potato starch, and lemon juice into the sugar-butter mixture.

Preheat the oven to 350°F. and butter and flour an 8-inch springform pan.

Grind the 1 cup of almonds and bitter almonds, if available, in a blender, food processor, or mortar until a relatively smooth paste is obtained. Add the almonds to the cake batter and mix well.

Beat the egg whites in an unlined copper bowl or in a mixing bowl with the cream of tartar. When the egg whites begin to form soft peaks, add the salt and the 1 tablespoon of sugar and continue beating until they form stiff peaks. Fold the egg whites carefully into the cake batter.

Transfer the batter to the springform pan and bake in the preheated oven, about 40 minutes. It is cooked when a toothpick plunged into the center of the cake comes out clean and dry.

Allow to cool for 10 minutes, then remove from the pan. Decorate the top with slivered almonds lightly toasted for 5 minutes in the preheated oven.


◆ ◆ ◆ ◆ ◆

*Sbrisolona*
*alla*
*Lombarda*

CORNMEAL
"SHORTBREAD"
CAKE

SERVES 8

This cake has a marvelous texture and an outstanding flavor. It can be served on its own or as an accompaniment for fruit salad, peaches and wine, or fruit compote. It will stay fresh for a week or so if wrapped in aluminum foil and kept cool.

*1 cup almonds, peeled and ground fine*
*1½ cups unbleached all-purpose flour*
*1½ cups finely ground cornmeal*
*¾ cup sugar*
*zest of 1 lemon*
*pinch of salt*
*1 egg plus 1 yolk, beaten*
*¼ teaspoon vanilla extract*
*8 tablespoons butter*
*6 tablespoons vegetable shortening*

Preheat oven to 400°F.

Combine well in a large mixing bowl all the dry ingredients—the almonds, flour, cornmeal, sugar, lemon zest, and salt. Add the beaten egg and yolk and vanilla and stir vigorously. Cut the butter and shortening into ½-inch cubes and using your fingers or a pastry cutter combine the butter and shortening with the other ingredients, working the dough as little as possible. Knead the dough on a floured working surface, using the heel of your hand, just enough to combine the fat with the dry ingredients. Wrap in a dish towel and place in the refrigerator for 20 minutes.

Meanwhile, butter and sprinkle with 1 tablespoon of fine cornmeal a 12-inch round baking dish with low straight sides—a layer cake pan is suitable.

Remove the dough from the dish towel, place it in the baking dish, and spread it evenly in the pan with your fingers. Do not overwork the dough—it should be crumbly. Place in the oven and bake until golden, about 40 minutes. If the edges of the cake begin to burn, cover with aluminum foil.

Remove from the oven when cooked, let cool, then transfer from the baking dish to a serving platter. Serve at room temperature.

♦ ♦ ♦ ♦ ♦

## Zuppa Inglese alla Fiesolana

TRIFLE,
FIESOLE
STYLE

SERVES 8

This recipe looks more complicated than it is. There are essentially two parts: first, making a sponge cake; and second, combining it with the liqueur, jam, and whipping cream.

FOR THE SPONGE CAKE:

zest of ½ lemon
¾ cup sugar
4 eggs, separated
¼ cup cold water
1 tablespoon lemon juice
a few drops of vanilla extract
1 cup unbleached all-purpose flour
1½ teaspoons baking powder
½ teaspoon cream of tartar (optional)

FOR THE TRIFLE:

¼ cup Cointreau, Drambuie, or another liqueur
¾ cup tart jam or marmalade
2 cups whipping cream
2 tablespoons sugar

FOR THE GARNISH:

3 tablespoons slivered almonds
½ cup sliced fresh fruit

Make the sponge cake first.

Preheat the oven to 325°F. Butter and lightly flour a 9-inch tube pan and set it aside.

Combine in a small mixing bowl the lemon zest and sugar. Beat together in a large mixing bowl with a wire whisk the 4 egg yolks and ¼ cup of cold water until light and pale yellow. Gradually beat in the sugar mixture until thoroughly combined. Blend in the lemon juice and vanilla and set aside.

Sift together the flour and baking powder, and add it slowly to the egg-yolk-and-sugar mixture. Beat until well blended.

Whip until stiff the 4 egg whites. If you do not whip them in an unlined copper bowl, add cream of tartar when the whites begin to foam.

Mix a fourth of the egg whites with the batter, then fold in the remaining egg whites gently. Pour the mixture carefully into the tube pan and bake in the preheated oven until cooked, about 50 minutes. Remove from the oven and place on a cake rack to cool.

When cooled, slip a sharp knife along the sides between the cake and the pan. Remove the cake from the pan.

Cut the cake into ¾-inch-thick pieces. Line the bottom of an attractive glass serving bowl approximately 9 inches in diameter by 8 inches deep with the slices of sponge cake. Sprinkle liqueur on the slices, spread evenly over them ¼ cup jam or marmalade, and set aside.

Whip the cream with the 2 tablespoons of sugar until firm. Spread a 1-inch layer of the whipped cream over the jam. Then repeat the layering process, ending with a layer of whipped cream. Keep chilled until ready to serve.

Decorate the top with slivered almonds toasted for 5 minutes in a 350°F. oven or with thin slices of fresh fruit or both.

♦ ♦ ♦ ♦ ♦

## Schiacciata con Zibibbo

SWEET
SCHIACCIATA
WITH
RAISINS

SERVES 8

One of the great treats of my childhood was sweet *schiacciata*, a flat, sweet bread dotted with raisins and, surprisingly, flavored with rosemary. Every once in a while on a bread-baking day the cook would make one of these. I could smell it all over the house and could hardly wait for it to be done. This *schiacciata* is wonderful as a midmorning snack or served with tea in the afternoon. Try to obtain large raisins made from Muscat grapes available in Italian or Greek food stores that stock dried fruits. Raisins made from Thompson grapes are adequate, but are simply not as flavorful as the imported variety.

> ½ cup plus 1 tablespoon sugar
> 1½ tablespoons (1½ packages) dry active yeast
> 3 cups unbleached all-purpose flour
> ¾ cup raisins (see above)
> 1 egg, beaten
> 2 tablespoons plus 1 teaspoon fresh or dried rosemary
> 3 tablespoons olive oil
> 1 tablespoon vegetable shortening
> pinch of salt

Combine ½ cup warm water with 1 tablespoon sugar. Add the yeast and set aside for a few minutes to activate.

Place 1 cup of flour in a mixing bowl, add the yeast and water, combine thoroughly, cover with a dry dish towel, and set aside in a warm spot until doubled in bulk, about 1½ hours.

Meanwhile, soak the raisins in warm water to cover for 20 minutes. Drain, pat dry, and set aside.

When the dough has risen, add the egg, raisins, ½ cup sugar, 1 teaspoon of rosemary, 1 tablespoon of olive oil, 1 tablespoon of vegetable shortening, and a pinch of salt; combine thoroughly. Add the remaining 2 cups of flour to the mixture and blend.

Turn the dough out onto a floured working surface and knead for 10 minutes, until smooth and elastic.

Oil a jelly roll pan approximately 10 by 15 inches and set aside. Roll out the dough with a heavy rolling pin until roughly the size of the jelly roll pan. Transfer the dough to the pan and spread it with your fingers until it fills the pan. Sprinkle the remaining rosemary and olive oil evenly over the surface of the *schiacciata*, cover with a dish towel, and place in a warm spot for 1½ hours, until the *schiacciata* has risen. Twenty minutes before you wish to bake the *schiacciata*, preheat the oven to 375°F.

Bake the *schiacciata* in the preheated oven for 20 minutes, until the crust is golden and the dough is cooked. Serve warm or at room temperature.

♦ ♦ ♦ ♦ ♦

### Crostata di Marmellata

JAM TART

This is the quintessential dessert tart of Florence. And it has all the features that appeal to Florentines. It relies on plain ingredients, is uncomplicated to prepare, and is refined in appearance and taste. One word of advice: since the flavor of the tart depends on the jam or marmalade, use a high-quality commercial variety or make your own.

SERVES 8

This tart tends to improve with age. If possible, make 24 hours before you need it and store in a cool dry place.

*Short Sweet Dough I (see recipe)*
*1 cup tart jam or marmalade*
*1 egg, beaten*

Preheat oven to 350 °F.

Butter and flour lightly a 10- to 12-inch round pizza pan or the equivalent.

Prepare dough, divide it into two parts, one part roughly two-thirds of the total, the other a third of the total. Roll out the larger part ¼ inch thick. If difficult to handle, roll out between sheets of wax paper. Transfer the dough to the round pan. Spread the jam or marmalade evenly over the dough, leaving a ½-inch border around the edge.

Roll out the remaining dough approximately ⅛ to ¼ inch thick and cut into thin strips with a scalloped pastry wheel. Use some of the strips to decorate the top of the tart. It is customary to lay them out in a crisscross pattern. Use the remaining strips to form a border around the edge of the tart. If you wet the dough with a little water, it sticks easily.

Brush the strips and edge of the tart with the beaten egg and bake in the preheated oven for 25 to 30 minutes, until the dough is golden. Remove from the oven, let cool, then transfer to a serving platter.

♦ ♦ ♦ ♦ ♦

## *Crostata di Pesche*

FRESH
PEACH
TART

SERVES 8

This uncomplicated tart of fresh fruit glazed with jam is a typical dessert of northern Italy. The recipe is given for peach tart, but other fruits such as apples or apricots can be used, or any combination of them. If a combination is used, it is important to place them attractively on the tart, alternating rows with different fruits.

*Short Sweet Dough I (see recipe)*
*6 to 8 ripe peaches, peeled and sliced into thin wedges*
*1 cup peach jam*
*3 tablespoons slivered almonds*

Preheat the oven to 375°F. Butter and lightly flour a 10-inch tart pan.

Roll out the dough ¼ inch thick and fit it snugly into a tart pan with a removable bottom. If difficult to handle, roll the dough out between sheets of wax paper.

Drape excess dough over the edge of the pan and remove by passing a rolling pin over the rim of the pan. Prick the dough in several places with a fork.

Place the peaches on top of the dough in a decorative pattern and bake in the preheated oven for 30 minutes, until the dough is firm. Remove from the oven. When cool, place the tart pan over a 1-quart Mason jar and remove the pan rim. You can, if you wish, leave the tart on the pan bottom.

Brush the jam over the peaches. If the jam is too dense, dilute it with some water. Sprinkle with the slivered almonds and return to the oven for 10 minutes. Allow to cool, then serve.

NOTE: If you use apples, dip the wedges into ¼ cup of lemon juice as soon as they are peeled and sliced; this will prevent discoloration. If you use a fruit other than peaches, use an apricot glaze made with apricot jam diluted with a little water.

♦ ♦ ♦ ♦ ♦

## Crostata di Fichi e Pinoli

FIG
AND
PINE
NUT
TART

SERVES 8

This is a fabulous combination: fresh figs, pine nuts, and custard in a tart shell. We make it whenever fresh figs are available.

Short Sweet Dough II *(see recipe)*
3 tablespoons pine nuts
Crema Pasticcera *(see recipe)*
9 medium figs, washed, stems removed, thinly sliced
    horizontally with the peel

Preheat the oven to 375°F.

Butter and flour lightly a 10-inch tart pan with a removable rim.

Make the dough. Roll it out ¼ inch thick, then snugly line the bottom and sides of the tart pan draping excess dough over the edges and removing it by running a rolling pin over the rim of the pan. Prick the bottom of the dough in several places with a fork, line the bottom and sides with buttered aluminum foil, fill with dried beans or baking weights, and bake in the preheated oven for 10 minutes. Remove the foil and the weights, return to the oven, and bake for 10 more minutes until the crust is golden. Remove and set aside to cool.

Toast the pine nuts in the oven for 5 minutes and set aside.

Make the Crema Pasticcera and allow it to cool. When the crema and the crust are both cool, spread a layer of the crema about ⅜ inch thick on the dough and lay the figs and pine nuts evenly on top. Remove the rim of the pan. You can, if you wish, leave the tart on the bottom of the pan.

◆ ◆ ◆ ◆ ◆

*Crostata*

*d'Uva*

GRAPE
TART

SERVES 8

Grapes are particularly attractive and tasty for fresh fruit tarts. Strawberries, raspberries, pears, and persimmons are also suitable fruits to use in a tart of this sort.

*Short Sweet Dough I (see recipe)*
*Crema Pasticcera (see recipe)*
*1 pound seedless grapes*
*1 cup apricot jam mixed with 1 tablespoon Cognac,*
*Cointreau, or Maraschino*

Preheat oven to 375°F. Butter well and flour lightly a 10-inch tart pan with a removable rim.

Make the dough and roll it out ¼ inch thick. If difficult to handle, roll out between sheets of wax paper. Snugly line the inside and sides of the tart pan with the dough, draping any extra over the edges of the pan. Cut away the excess by passing the rolling pin along the rim of the tart pan. Prick the dough in several places with a fork, cover the bottom and sides of the dough with buttered aluminum foil, fill it with dried beans or special baking weights, and bake for 10 minutes in the preheated oven. Remove the foil and weights and return to the oven for another 10 minutes, until the crust is golden. Remove and set aside.

Make the crema and allow to cool. When the crust and the crema have cooled, spread a layer of the crema approximately ⅜ inch thick over the crust. Wash and dry the grapes and place them snugly and evenly over the tart. Brush the grapes and the border of the tart with the jam. If too thick, dilute the jam with a little water. Remove the rim of the pan. Leave the tart on the bottom of the pan, if you wish.

♦ ♦ ♦ ♦ ♦

# *Nepitelle*

CALABRIAN
MINCE
PIES

SERVES 10 OR MORE

These pastries from southern Italy, made with a *pasta frolla* dough and stuffed with a delectable mixture of figs, almonds, pine nuts, spices, and Marsala, are ideal for a Christmas buffet or afternoon tea.

FOR THE DOUGH:

*4 cups unbleached all-purpose flour*
*⅔ cup sugar*
*½ cup butter, at room temperature*
*4 tablespoons vegetable shortening*
*zest of 1 lemon*
*3 extra-large eggs, beaten*

FOR THE FILLING:

*½ pound dried figs*
*¾ cup raisins, soaked in water to cover for 15 minutes and drained*
*⅓ cup almonds, blanched, peeled, and chopped*
*1 tablespoon pine nuts*
*½ teaspoon ground cinnamon*
*¼ teaspoon ground cloves*
*zest of ½ orange*
*2 tablespoons Marsala*
*freshly ground black pepper*
*pinch of salt*
*1 tablespoon powdered sugar*

Combine the flour and sugar in a large mixing bowl. Add the butter and shortening and cut into the flour with a pastry cutter or mix with your fingers until the mixture resembles coarse oatmeal. Add the lemon zest and eggs and combine well with your fingertips or a fork. Add up to 2 tablespoons of cold water, 1 teaspoon at a time, to make a manageable but firm dough. Turn the dough onto a work surface and knead with the heel of your hand only long enough to combine the ingredients. Wrap in wax paper and chill for 30 minutes in the refrigerator.

Meanwhile, place the figs in a saucepan, cover with water, and simmer until tender, about 15 minutes. Drain, pat dry, chop, and place in a mixing bowl. Chop the raisins and blend them with the figs. Add the almonds, pine nuts, cinnamon, cloves, orange zest, Marsala, pepper, and salt and combine thoroughly. Set aside.

Preheat the oven to 400°F. Butter a cookie sheet or jelly roll pan.

Remove the dough from the refrigerator and roll to a thickness of ⅛ inch. Cut the dough with a cookie cutter into rounds 3 inches in diameter. Reserve the scraps. Place a tablespoon of the filling in the center of one of the rounds, leaving a ¼-inch border free from filling. Wet this border with water, wet the border of another round, and cover the first with the second. Seal well. Use the tines of a fork to make holes in the top of the pastry and place on the buttered cookie sheet or jelly roll pan. Repeat with the remaining rounds.

Combine the scraps of dough, roll, and repeat the operation. Reserve the extra filling.

Bake in the preheated oven for 20 minutes, until the pastries begin to brown. Remove and let cool on a wire rack. Before serving place a dollop of the leftover filling on the top of each pastry and sprinkle lightly with powdered sugar.

### VARIATION

The dried-fruit-and-nut mixture is also delicious used as the filling in Jam Tart (see recipe). Spread a thick layer of the mixture before adding the strips to the top.

♦ ♦ ♦ ♦ ♦

## *Biscottini di Prato*

COOKIES
FROM
PRATO

MAKES APPROXIMATELY 60
COOKIES

These cookies are dry, hard, and crunchy, not too sweet, with a wonderful nutty flavor. In Tuscany, they are usually served after dinner along with Vin Santo, a well-aged and much prized dessert wine. They are dipped into the wine to soften, then eaten.

The staler the cookies get, the better they are. They should be made at least 2 or 3 days ahead. Store in a cool dry place in a cookie tin or paper bag. Do not store in a plastic bag. Serve these *biscottini* with a tawny port or madeira, if Vin Santo is unavailable.

¼ cup whole almonds, blanched and peeled
4¼ cups unbleached all-purpose flour
2 tablespoons butter
5 extra-large eggs
1¼ cups of sugar
pinch of salt
½ teaspoon powdered anise
¾ cup unpeeled whole almonds

Dry the blanched almonds in a warm oven for 5 minutes. Do not brown. Chop very finely 2 tablespoons of the blanched almonds and set aside.

Mound the flour on a working surface and make a well in the center. Place the butter, 4 beaten eggs, sugar, salt, the 2 tablespoons of chopped almonds, and anise in the well and combine with the flour, drawing the flour from the inside of the well. When mixed, knead the dough for 5 minutes, adding flour to the work surface if the dough sticks.

Preheat the oven to 375°F. Chop the unpeeled almonds very roughly into 3 or 4 pieces and add them to the dough. Knead for another 5 minutes.

Butter and lightly flour two cookie sheets or jelly roll pans approximately 15 inches in length. Divide the dough into 6 parts and roll out each part into rolls approximately 1¼ inches in diameter the length of the cookie sheets and place 3 rolls on each of the prepared sheets. Brush the top of each roll with a beaten egg and cook in the preheated oven for 15 minutes.

Remove from the oven and reduce the temperature to 275°F. Cut the cookie rolls with a sharp knife diagonally across the roll into approximately ¾-inch segments. Return to the oven for 40 minutes, until the cookies are hard and dry. Remove and set aside to cool.

♦ ♦ ♦ ♦ ♦

## Amaretti

ITALIAN
MACAROONS

MAKES APPROXIMATELY 50
MACAROONS

Although amaretti imported from Italy are readily available in most Italian groceries, homemade ones are much better and worth the extra effort involved.

¾ cup almonds, blanched and peeled
¼ cup bitter almonds, blanched and peeled (if available), or regular almonds
1¼ cups granulated sugar
2 egg whites
2 tablespoons powdered sugar

Preheat the oven to 325°F.

Dry the almonds in the preheated oven for a few minutes. Remove and grind in a mortar, blender, or food processor with the granulated sugar. Blend the egg whites into the ground almonds, adding the egg whites a little at a time. The batter should have the consistency of soft dough.

Cover a large cookie sheet with aluminum foil. Butter and flour it lightly and set aside. Place the batter in a pastry bag and squeeze onto the foil in rounds approximately the size of small walnuts. Leave 1 inch of space between the amaretti, since they expand as they cook. Sprinkle with powdered sugar and bake in the preheated oven for 20 minutes, until golden. Remove and let cool. Store in airtight jars or tins.

♦ ♦ ♦ ♦ ♦

## *Savoiardi*

### ITALIAN
### LADYFINGERS

MAKES 50 TO 60
LADYFINGERS

*4 eggs, separated*
*¾ cup plus 1½ tablespoons sugar*
*few drops of lemon juice*
*¾ cup potato starch*

Preheat the oven to 350°F. Line 2 or 3 jelly roll pans or cookie sheets with aluminum foil, butter well, sprinkle with flour, and set aside.

Combine the egg yolks, ¾ cup of sugar, and lemon juice in a mixing bowl, and beat with a whisk or electric mixer until the yolks are pale yellow, creamy, and form long ribbons when the beater is lifted. Slowly add the potato starch, beating the mixture constantly.

Beat the egg whites until stiff and firm. Mix a fourth of the whites with the yolk batter to make it lighter, then fold the batter into the egg whites, working quickly and with a light touch.

Place the mixture in a pastry tube with a small round tip and squeeze it onto the baking sheets, making each ladyfinger ½ inch wide by 4 inches long, spacing them 1 inch apart. Sprinkle the top of the ladyfingers with the remaining 1½ tablespoons of sugar, allow to rest for a few minutes, then bake in the preheated oven for 10 minutes, until the cookies are golden on top and just brown on the edges. When cooled slightly, remove from the baking dish and set aside to cool completely.

# SAMPLE
# MENUS

The menu selections in this section are divided into three groups: dinner parties, family dinners, and luncheons and light suppers. The first are elaborate five-course meals that take time to prepare but are elegant and impressive. Family dinners are less elaborate and much less time-consuming to prepare, appropriate for daily fare or less formal dinner parties. Luncheons and light suppers are two- or three-course meals, ideal for a light but elegant midday or evening repast.

The menus are intended to give you an idea of what we consider good combinations of recipes and also how to incorporate into a meal some of the more unusual dishes in the book. They are mere suggestions, and we urge you to alter them or draw up your own to suit your tastes and requirements. We find that meals without meat lend themselves especially well to creative mixing and matching. For example, a hearty salad or vegetable dish or even a soup can often serve as a main course. For that matter, you need have no main course at all but instead an imaginative blend of vegetables, pasta, salad, and dessert. In planning a menu, however, it is useful to keep in mind some of the considerations that went into drawing up those included here.

Look for contrasts in color, texture, and taste when combining recipes but, at the same time, take care not to overwhelm a delicately flavored dish with a strongly flavored one. Try to balance vegetable sources of protein and go easy on rich dishes. Legumes and grains, for example, are good but partial proteins on their own but in combination are complete ones. Cheeses and eggs are nourishing but are also high in saturated fats—it takes only a little to keep you healthy and well fed. Let the seasons influence your menus. This makes sense economically and also pays off in flavor and quality. Finally, be considerate of yourself. Do not combine in one meal a number of elaborate dishes and try to avoid more than one that requires last-minute preparation.

## *Dinner Parties*

Asparagus with Mayonnaise (p. 37)

Panzerotti with Cheese (p. 64)

Three-Vegetable Pudding (p. 175)

Fried Artichokes (p. 222)

Tossed Green Salad

Jam Tart (p. 316)

Eggplant Salad (p. 44)
Spaghetti with Gorgonzola (p. 79)
Artichoke Torte (p. 187)
Marinated Carrots (p. 232)
Zabaione Ice Cream (p. 307)

Neapolitan Pizza (p. 58)
Stuffed Zucchini (p. 159)
Chick-Peas, Roman Style (p. 239)
Celery Salad (p. 279)
Cherries Stewed in Red Wine (p. 301)

Eggplant, Calabrian Style (p. 43)
Rigatoni with Raw Tomato Sauce (p. 87)
Baked Omelet with Ricotta and Mushrooms (p. 12)
Artichokes, Roman Style (p. 221)
Tossed Green Salad
Chestnut Purée with Whipped Cream (p. 310)

Celery Root Salad (p. 280)
Fusilli with Capers (p. 83)
Tomatoes Stuffed with Cheese (p. 162)
Braised Sweet Peas (p. 257)
Giglio's Fruit Salad (p. 282)
Peach Ice (p. 304)

Tortellini with Herbs (p. 96)
Peppers Stuffed with Lentils (p. 160)
Sautéed Mushrooms (p. 250)
Tossed Green Salad
Banana Ice Cream (p. 305)

Tomatoes with Herbed Mayonnaise (p. 38)
Cream of Mushroom Soup (p. 138)
Ricotta and Saffron Flan (p. 185)

Leeks au Gratin (p. 247)
Red Chicory Salad with Beans (p. 283)
Semolina Pudding (p. 308)

Mixed Antipasto
Baked Penne (p. 86)
Artichoke Soufflé (p. 166)
Sautéed Celery (p. 238)
Tossed Green Salad with Tomatoes
Pears Baked with Wine (p. 301)

Cannelloni with Bell Peppers (p. 100)
Cheese Soufflé (p. 165)
Artichokes with Mushrooms (p. 217)
Sicilian Mixed Salad (p. 277)
Zabaione Ice Cream (p. 307)

Rigatoni with Artichokes (p. 89)
Eggs in Cream Sauce (p. 202)
Fried Fennel (p. 245)
Marinated Lentil Salad (p. 292)
Cornmeal "Shortbread" Cake (p. 313)

Sweet-and-Sour Baked Onions, Virginia Style (p. 255)
Virginia's Shells with Fresh Vegetables (p. 85)
Puffed Crêpes with Cheese Soufflé (p. 172)
Mushrooms with Lemon Sauce (p. 252)
Tossed Green Salad
Almond Cake (p. 312)

Asparagus Soup (p. 133)
Cornmeal Molds (p. 179)
Stuffed Pepper Rolls (p. 259)
Grated Carrot Salad (p. 280)
Sliced Oranges (p. 300)

Tomatoes Stuffed with Rice, Virginia Style (p. 111)
Deviled Eggs "Il Poggio" (p. 203)
Eggplant Sautéed with Garlic (p. 242)
Mushroom Salad (p. 281)
Peaches in Wine (p. 300)

Zucchini, Virginia Style (p. 41)
Cream of Chestnut Soup (p. 140)
Mushroom Crêpes (p. 169)
Braised Endive (p. 242)
Celery Root Salad (p. 280)
Ricotta Cake (p. 311)

Rice with Eggs (p. 109)
Sardinian Artichoke Pie (p. 180)
Cauliflower Mimosa (p. 285)
Tuscan Bread Salad (p. 282)
Coffee Ice with Whipped Cream (p. 306)

Risotto with Artichokes and Mushrooms (p. 106)
Ricotta and Herbs Crêpes (p. 170)
Steamed Broccoli with Hollandaise Sauce (p. 17)
Tossed Green Salad with Tomatoes
Orange Ice (p. 305)

Paola's Crostini (p. 34)
Cold Cream of Cucumber Soup (p. 136)
Easter Torte (p. 190)
Spring Salad (p. 288)
Maria's Brandy Pie (p. 311)

Mushrooms with Parmesan (p. 38)
Crêpes in Broth (p. 146)
Swiss Chard Torte (p. 186)
Cauliflower Salad (p. 291)
Strawberry Ice (p. 303)

Ravioli with Spinach and Ricotta (p. 94)
Omelet Flan (p. 209)
Spring Salad (p. 288)
Trifle, Fiesole Style (p. 314)

## *Family Dinners*

Sliced Hard-Boiled Eggs with Parsley Sauce with Walnuts (p. 23)
Potatoes, Fiesole Style (p. 260)
Spring Salad (p. 288)
Fresh Fruit

Tomatoes with Herbed Mayonnaise (p. 38)
Cream of Mushroom Soup (p. 138)
Basil-Parsley Flan (p. 185)
Tossed Green Salad
Fresh Fruit

Cream of Tomato Soup (p. 137)
Eggs in Pie Shell (p. 207)
Red Chicory Salad with Beans (p. 283)
Banana Ice Cream (p. 305)

Cold Cream of Cucumber Soup (p. 136)
Poached Eggs in Salad (p. 206)
Tuscan Bread Salad (p. 282)
Fresh Peach Tart (p. 317)

Cold Spicy Spinach Soup (p. 133)
Spring Salad (p. 288)
Schiacciata with Cheeses (p. 61)
Zabaione Ice Cream (p. 307)

Capers on Toast (p. 36)
Cauliflower Pudding with Onion Sauce (pp. 174, 25)
Baked Beans in a Flask (p. 228)
Fresh Fruit

Agnolotti with Three Cheeses (p. 95)
Eggplant Croquettes (p. 153)
Steamed Carrots with Mushroom Sauce (p. 24)
Rice Pudding (p. 309)

Vegetable Soup with Pesto (p. 129)
Cheese-Filled Onions (p. 162)
Pan-Fried Potatoes, Italian Style (p. 263)
Sliced Oranges (p. 300)

Risotto with Tomatoes (p. 107)
Crêpes with Fondue (p. 171)
Mushrooms with Lemon Sauce (p. 252)
Tossed Green Salad
Peach Ice (p. 304)

Cornmeal with Mushrooms and Peppers (p. 122)
Cauliflower Soufflé (p. 167)
Sautéed Celery (p. 238)
Fresh Fruit

Spaghetti with Tomato Sauce I or II (p. 77, 19, 20)
Mozzarella in a Carriage (p. 156)
Steamed String Beans with Olive and Caper Sauce (p. 29)
Peaches with Wine (p. 300)

Tuscan Vegetable Soup (p. 126)
Onion Flan (p. 184)
Steamed Zucchini with Pungent Green Sauce (p. 26)
Stuffed Peaches (p. 303)

Cooked Water (p. 135)
Fondue from the Val d'Aosta (p. 173)
Tossed Green Salad
Semolina Pudding (p. 308)

Neapolitan Pizza (p. 58)
Artichokes au Gratin (p. 178)
Celery Salad (p. 279)
Banana Ice Cream (p. 305)


Spaghetti with Garlic, Oil, and Hot Pepper (p. 77)
Alberto's Eggplant Parmesan (p. 179)
Beans with Tomato Sauce (p. 226)
Tossed Green Salad
Fresh Fruit


Stuffed Mushroom Caps (p. 39)
Baked Eggplant and Pasta (p. 194)
Mixed Winter Salad with Mozzarella (p. 289)
Cookies from Prato (p. 321) with Fresh Fruit


Sliced Hard-Boiled Eggs with Mayonnaise (p. 16)
Baked Risotto with Cheese (p. 199)
Sicilian Mixed Salad (p. 277)
Fresh Fruit


Cornmeal with Fontina (p. 123)
Eggs Poached in Tomato Sauce (p. 205)
Cauliflower Salad (p. 291)
Fresh Fruit


Penne with Spicy Tomato Sauce (p. 86)
Eggs in Wine Sauce (p. 205)
Mixed Vegetables, Roman Style (p. 271)
Jam Tart (p. 316)


Florentine Dumplings (p. 121)
Fried Eggplant Sandwiches (p. 158)
Asparagus with Mushroom Sauce (p. 225)
Orange Ice (p. 305)

Virginia's Pasta and Bean Soup (p. 142)
Artichoke Omelet (p. 208)
Grated Carrot Salad (p. 280)
Fresh Fruit


Tuscan Bread Salad (p. 282)
Potatoes and Cheese (p. 263)
Broccoli Smothered in Wine (p. 229)
Peach Ice (p. 304)

Fried Vegetables (p. 45)
Lasagne, Fiesole Style (p. 102)
Giglio's Fruit Salad (p. 282)

Artichokes with Egg Sauce (p. 37)
Pasta Mold with Spinach and Mozzarella (p. 196)
Tossed Green Salad
Fresh Fruit

Marinated Chick-Peas and Artichoke Salad (p. 292)
Lasagne with Eggplant (p. 103)
Tossed Green Salad
Strawberry Ice (p. 303)

## Luncheon and Light Supper

Schiacciata Sandwiches (p. 60)
Harlequin Salad (p. 278)
Ricotta Cake (p. 311)

Cannelloni, Neapolitan Style (p. 98)
Tossed Green Salad
Zabaione Ice Cream (p. 307)

Milanese Vegetable Soup (p. 128)
Mushroom Salad (p. 281)
Almond Cake (p. 312)

Cream of Tomato Soup (p. 137)
Pasta Roll Stuffed with Spinach and Ricotta (p. 197)
Tossed Green Salad
Fresh Fruit

Asparagus Soup (p. 133)
Spaghettini Baked in a Mold (p. 192)
Grape Tart (p. 319)

Baked Semolina Dumplings (p. 117)
Steamed String Beans with Tomato Sauce with Vinegar (p. 28)
Trifle, Fiesole Style (p. 314)

Rice and Pea Soup (p. 131)
Marinated Zucchini Salad (p. 290)
Maria's Brandy Pie (p. 311)

Stuffed Eggs (p. 46)
Pasta Salad (p. 286)
Peach Ice (p. 304)

Cold Cream of Cucumber Soup (p. 136)
Rice Salad (p. 285)
Strawberry Ice (p. 303)

Capricious Pizza (p. 59)
Sicilian Mixed Salad (p. 277)
Fresh Fruit

Calzone with Mozzarella and Tomato Sauce (p. 62)
Giglio's Fruit Salad (p. 282)
Banana Ice Cream (p. 305)

Bread and Cheese Strands in Broth (p. 147)
Tomato, Cheese, and Olive Flan (p. 66)
Tossed Green Salad
Fresh Fruit

Omelet, Fiesole Style (p. 207)
Simmered Cabbage on Garlic Toast (p.231)
Sliced Oranges (p. 300)


Grilled Peppers (p. 40)
Rice Croquettes (p. 152)
Cherries Stewed in Red Wine (p. 301)


Asparagus Rolled in Crêpes (p. 224)
Mixed Winter Salad with Mozzarella (p. 239)
Pears Baked with Wine (p. 301)

# Index